CHARITIES
~TRADING~
AND
THE LAW

by Stephen Lloyd

Charities Advisory Trust
in association with the
Directory of Social Change

CHARITIES, TRADING AND THE LAW

by Stephen Lloyd

Published by The Charities Advisory Trust,
Radius Works, Back Lane, London NW3 1HL
in association with
The Directory of Social Change.

Designed and Typset by Diarmuid Burke
and Kate Bass

Printed and bound by W M Print Limited, Walsall

British Library Cataloguing in Publication Data
A catalogue record for this book is available from
the British Library

ISBN 1 873860 76 5

Contents

Introduction

This book is the product of two strands in my life. For the last ten years I have been partner with Bates Wells & Braithwaite, solicitors, where I specialise in advising charities and commercial organisations on both charity and commercial law. For much of that period as well I have obtained practical knowledge of the problems charities face in relation to trading through giving lectures. Those lectures have made me aware of the amazing variety of activities that charities undertake in the form of primary purposes and for-profit trading. At the end of one such lecture, about two years ago, in a moment of weakness, I suggested to Hilary Blume of the Charities Advisory Trust that I would like to write a book on the subject of charities and trading and which the Charities Advisory Trust might be interested in publishing. Much to my initial pleasure and subsequent consternation, Hilary accepted with alacrity as did her husband, Michael Norton of the Directory of Social Change and the two have been urging me on to complete this book ever since.

I have written it to help people who work in and for charities - it is not written as an academic or legal tome and is therefore not exhaustive. I have tried to highlight the key points with which charities or their associated trading companies will need to be familiar and my comments are, necessarily, generalised and may well not be sufficiently detailed to cover the particular circumstances which a charity and/or its trading company could confront. Accordingly, readers will need to take appropriate professional advice on particular questions.

Now this book is completed my thanks are due to Hilary and Michael for their support; to Michael for his extremely thorough and constructive editing; to my partner (legal!) Fiona Middleton for reading the draft and putting me right in various places; to Rosamund Smith and Judith Schrut also colleagues from Bates Wells & Braithwaite, for researching various tricky points and finally to my secretary Janis Turner for typing and re-typing the many drafts.

The law is stated as at 1st December 1994.

Stephen Lloyd
Autumn 1994

Chapter I
TRADING AND THE POWER TO TRADE

This book considers the range of trading activities which charities undertake. It is written from the perspective of English law. In certain areas Scottish law is different and this book does not cover Scottish law.

1.1. A changing world

There is a popular misconception that charities cannot trade, that they are debarred by law from trading. This is wrong. In certain defined circumstances, charities are able to carry on a trade. These circumstances are defined by what is deemed to be a proper charitable activity, but also by the powers given to the charity in its constitution.

Charities are raising the money they need in all sorts of imaginative and ingenious ways. Some of these involve the carrying on of a trade. Reflect on the many ways in which charities (including their associated trading companies) actually do sell goods or supply services: organising coffee mornings; selling new and donated goods in "charity shops"; the sale of tickets by the Royal Opera House or a fringe theatre group; the provision of education by public schools; the provision of health care by clinics and hospitals; selling educational books; running conferences; licensing charity logos to "affinity" credit card companies; running a children's home under contract to a local authority or a residential home under contract to a health authority. This is just a sample of the very many ways in which charities do trade. The range of trading activity is huge and growing.

The radical changes in the roles of central and local government and other statutory agencies during the 1980's and 1990's have resulted in a considerable growth in the demand for services supplied by charities. Charities are being elevated into a third force, to stand alongside government and the private sector as a deliverer of health, welfare, housing and caring services.

In the field of housing for example, housing associations (many of which are charities) have taken over the function of supplying social housing for rent previously discharged by local authorities. Housing associations carry on a *trade* of acquiring or constructing buildings and renting out accommodation.

As a consequence of the changes introduced by *The National Health Service and Community Care Act, 1990* many charities which formerly received grant aid from local authorities are now providing a similar service but under a contract. This new form of arrangement between the voluntary sector 'providers' and the statutory sector 'purchasers' has been termed the "Contract Culture".

The change from receiving grant aid to supplying services under contract may not seem very significant, but in legal terms the charity will now be deemed to be carrying on a trade, which has important legal consequences.

1.2. Constitutional Issues

Charities do not just face the usual problems associated with trading: problems of obtaining finance, problems of risk, problems of management, problems of profitability and cash flow (although of course they may encounter all of these). Charities wishing to trade encounter a number of particular issues which stem from the nature and structure of their charitable status.

If a charity is to carry on a trade itself it must have the necessary constitutional capacity - what lawyers (ever dependent on Latin terminology) call "vires". This will be set out in the *'objects'* clause in the charity's constitution.

A typical *object* to carry out a form of primary purpose trading would read:

"to advance the education of the public"

In addition its constitution should give the charity the *power* to:

"run schools, lectures and educational programmes and to charge fees at such levels as the trustees shall from time to time think appropriate."

If a charity wishes to carry on a primary purpose trade (i.e. a trade which fulfils the charity's object) and does not have a necessary power in its constitution, e.g. to charge for services rendered, it will need to amend its constitution. If the charity is a company, this is done by passing a Special Resolution, i.e. one passed with the consent of 75% of the members present at a meeting for which 21 days notice has been given. If the charity is *not* a company, the provisions for amending its constitution should be set out in a clause in the constitution. If there is no such clause (and some constitutions do regrettably lack one) the charity will have to obtain the consent of the Charity Commission to amend its constitution by a scheme.

Hence the constitution of a charitable school will include the *object* of educating the public and a *power* to sell educational services by charging school fees. The constitution of a university will contain the *object* of educating the public and a power to carry out research for public purposes, but there will not be a power to carry out private "bespoke" research (where the results of the research are known only to the person commissioning the research), as such an activity has no public benefit and is not charitable. Equally the school's constitution will not have the *power* to run a full time bar open to the general public, seven days a week.

Such an activity of running a bar would be ultra vires; i.e. beyond the scope of the school's objects. As Cohen L.J put it in *Tennant Plays Limited v. IRC* (1948) 1A11ER506 at p.510:

"I feel some doubt whether a company can be said to be established 'for charitable purposes only' if it carried on a substantial non-charitable purpose, for instance, if it took power permanently to run a public house in order to produce funds for its charitable purpose".

The consequences for the trustees of carrying on an ultra vires activity are serious. Win or lose they are at risk! If the charity suffers any loss as a result of the activity the trustees will potentially be personally liable to repay that loss to the charity out of their own pockets. The position is the same whether the charity is a limited liability company, incorporated by Royal Charter, a trust or an unincorporated association.

On the other hand if the charity makes a profit from the ultra vires activity the profits will be taxable. As will be seen later, a charity is exempt from taxation on profits derived from carrying out one of its primary purposes. But a *commercial* trading activity cannot be the primary purpose of the charity. Hence the profits will be taxable. Yet if the bar had been run through a separate, non-charitable trading company, the activity would have been properly separated off from the charity, which would cause no problem with charitable status. In addition, by paying over the profits of the trading company to the charity in a tax-effective way, the profits could have been received by the charity free of tax (see *Chapter 10*). In paragraph 44 of their 1988 Report, the Charity Commissioners commented:-

"Trustees have a duty to consider the tax effectiveness of the arrangements between them and any associated trading company, and they may be personally liable to account for taxation liabilities which are unnecessarily incurred directly or indirectly as a result of the inefficient administration of the charity".

Hence the trustees could be made personally liable to pay out of their own pockets, to the charity, a sum equal to the tax that could have been avoided if the trade of running the commercial bar had been set up in a different way!

1.3.   The complexities of the situation

Charities are exempt from income and/or corporation tax on the profits from primary purposes trading. Charities can also structure their trading so that the profits of for-profit, non-primary purposes trading are received tax-free from the charity's trading company. But charities enjoy no similar exemption from VAT. There are a few VAT concessions for charities (see *Chapter 4*), but these are not great. In addition, the different taxes apply in different circumstances and many a charity has adopted a practice to avoid, say, an income tax problem only to find that this has created a VAT problem.

For example, sales of donated goods by a trading company are zero rated for VAT provided the trading company covenants all its profits to the parent charity. The trading company may decide to retain some of its profits so as to provide working capital and to reduce its dependence on loans from the parent charity. That may well be very sensible as regards charity law. But it would have serious VAT effects. Because not all the profits of the trading company are covenanted to the charity the trading company will lose its advantageous zero rated status and would have to charge VAT on sales (if supplies exceed £45,000 for 1994/95), thus affecting either the prices it charges or its profit margins or both!

As this book seeks to show, the field of charities and trading is littered with traps for the unwary. Many of these traps spring from the need to separate for-profit, non-primary purposes trading activities and to put them into a trading company. This then throws up problems, such as: how to finance the trading company; inter-company charges; VAT (for example whether the charity and the trading company can be part of the same VAT group); profit shedding to create a tax-free income for the charity and rate relief on the premises occupied by the trading company.

If for-profit trading activities undertaken by a charity could be treated as either incidental trading or fund-raising, then all these problems would drop away and there would be little need for this book! Charities would be liberated from the need to create complex and costly structures. But it is unlikely that the government will reform the law by exempting from tax the profits made by a charity from any for-profit trading activity, for if it were to do so there is a strong possibility that such a move would cause considerable public outcry from commercial competitors and could also be seen by the European Commission as an impediment to the free market. Such a concession to the charity sector might well be seen as a bump on the much-sought-after "level playing field" of the common market and could be held to be illegal under European Competition Law.

Chapter 2
FUND-RAISING OR TRADING

This chapter defines what is fund-raising and what is trading. It shows the distinction between fund-raising and trading and concludes that fund-raising and trading are two different activities which require separate legal analysis.

2.1. What is fund-raising?

When considering charities and trading it is important to appreciate the distinction between fund-raising and trading.

To many people, very understandably, fund-raising means raising money for a charity *by whatever means*. This could cover collecting money in a can on a street corner, collecting money whilst carol singing, holding a sponsored walk, selling donated and new goods in a charity shop or selling Christmas cards. Despite the popular perception that all income-generating activity is fund-raising, the law draws a distinction between generating income through fund-raising and through trading.

Because fund-raising and trading are two quite separate activities, we can define fund-raising as raising money for a charity in a manner which does not amount to trading. Trading is defined in *Chapter 2.2*.

Fund-raising, then, covers such activities as: public appeals for donations (whether of money or goods) such as the Poppy Day appeal; television appeals, such as the Telethon; sponsored walks; soliciting covenants, legacies and donations.

But people's altruism is limited. Getting people to give something for nothing is not the only way of getting support. Charities also raise funds by *giving something in return* to their supporters. Hence the proliferation of jumble sales, carnivals, balls, quiz nights, shops selling donated goods, etc.

A vivid illustration of the subtle borderline that divides fund-raising from trading is the creation of databases for charities. The use of a database comprising the names and addresses of potential or actual donors is a vital part of modern fund-raising. It allows a charity to send fund-raising material by post or to telephone potential donors in order to solicit donations. For many charities income derived from such fund-raising activities constitutes a major part of their total revenue.

But in order to create such a database, a charity may have to expend very considerable amounts of money, on renting lists of names of potential donors, or by paying a fund-raising agency to compile such a list by telephoning potential donors. This initial expenditure will be categorised by the *fund-raiser* as an "investment". Indeed the charity may well lose money on the initial fund-raising if the expenditure is contrasted with the immediate income generated. The sums involved can be very considerable, but this is not an investment in the commercial sense. A charity could spend many thousands of pounds in building a database, but as the charity is not carrying on a trade of creating and selling databases - although it would be doing just this if it hired out its own list on a commercial basis – the creation of the database is not a trading activity, but rather an expense of fund-raising.

Similarly, charities may spend much money on a one-off fund-raising event (such as a ball), in order to generate revenue. Is this trading? Again this is not, because a one-off fund-raising event does not comply with the "badges of trade" (see *Chapters 2.2* and *2.3*).

The position was very clearly stated in *IRC -v- The Yorkshire Agricultural Society* (1927) 13 TC 58 at 82:

"It is a common thing for a charitable institution to offer all kinds of privileges and benefits which are in no sense charitable in order to obtain funds for the purpose of carrying out its objects. As an instance I might mention the giving of dinners, dances and theatrical entertainments, all of which entail an expenditure of money on non-charitable objects incurred for the purpose of obtaining funds to be applied for the charitable objects of the institution ... None of the operations of this kind results in making the purposes of the institution non-charitable".

Hence one-off fund-raising, even though it involves expenditure by the charity on non-charitable activities, does not amount to trading.

2.2. What is trading?

Section 832(1) of the *Income and Corporation Taxes Act 1988* defines "trade" as follows:

"'Trade' includes every *trade*, manufacture, adventure or concern in the nature of *trade"*

This is a wonderfully circular definition and a statement of the obvious. The term "trade" is used twice in the definition. "Trade" = "trade" = "trade!". Trade is said to include trade, but other activities may be caught as well. Hence, the Taxes Act 1988 does not assist much in arriving at a definition.

The Courts have considered this question on many occasions over the last century since the definition quoted first became law and have worked out certain hallmarks or 'badges' which indicate the type of transactions that constitute a trade. It is necessary to apply these tests to the income-generating activities undertaken by a charity to determine whether or not the activities are 'fund-raising' or whether they amount to trading.

To be considered a trading activity, the following points need to be considered:

(a) **There must be repetition**. A one-off transaction (e.g. a ball), is unlikely to amount to trading. In contrast, it was established in *British Legion Peterhead Branch Remembrance and Welcome Home Fund v. IRC* (1953) 3STC 84 that running dances regularly on Saturday nights *did* amount to trading. But the position is not always so simple. Lack of repetition by itself does not rule out the possibility of a trading activity. In another case, an individual who ran a cinema purchased and sold a quantity of toilet paper in a single job lot, thereby making a profit. He was taxed on the profits of the sale - because there was a profit motive and because of the nature of the goods involved.

(b) **There should be a profit motive**. This is one of the key 'badges' of trade. Charities will enter into many different arrangements to make a profit (e.g., the sale of Christmas cards). The fact that a charity will have other motives (e.g. applying the profits to charitable purposes) is irrelevant. A case involving Oxfam and rate relief illustrates the fact that applying the profits to charitable purposes does not rule out a profit motive. In *Oxfam v. City of Birmingham District Council (1979) AC126,* the Court of Appeal held that the occupation by Oxfam of premises for the sale of donated goods was not occupation of the property for charitable purposes. This decision subsequently led to a change in the law to give rating relief to charity shops. But the case illustrates the principle that the Courts and the Inland Revenue distinguish between the *purposes* of the charity and the *means* by which monies are raised in order to carry out those purposes (e.g. sale of mugs, tee-shirts, holding of pop concerts etc.). Trading for profit is a separate step in the carrying out of the purposes of a charity.

But beware. A trade may be carried on even though there is *no intention* of making a profit. If a trade is being carried out and a profit is made even though this was not intended, the Inland Revenue can seek to tax any profit arising. In a case involving the Council for Law Reporting for England and Wales and whether it was carrying on a trade or business, Lord Coleridge C.J., said (1888) 22 QBD 279;293:

"I should have thought it capable of strong argument that they carried on a trade, because it is not essential to the carrying on of a trade that the persons engaged in it should make, or desire to make, a profit from it".

(c) **The existence of a selling organisation**. The existence of a mechanism for selling (such as a shop or a catalogue) will point to a trade being carried out. But if a charity shop only sells donated goods, this will not amount to trading, as this particular activity is seen as a form of fund-raising (the translation of a donation made by a supporter into cash). This is covered in *Chapter 3*.

(d) **The acquisition of items for the purpose of being re-sold**. The sale of items (such as Christmas cards and tee-shirts) which are acquired to be sold will point to a trading activity. The sale of milk from a cow on a city farm would *not* be trading, unless the cow was being kept for the purpose of producing milk. It would simply be the disposal of an item produced as a consequence of having the cow on the farm!

For a trade to be carried out it is not necessary for a particular activity to display all the four 'badges' of trade. If one or more is present, then that may be sufficient to establish that there is a trade. The cinema owner with his job lot of toilet paper did not repeat the exercise and did not have a selling organisation: the presence of the profit motive and the nature of the goods bought and re-sold were sufficient in that case to allow the Inland Revenue to establish that there was a trading activity.

2.3. Fund-raising versus trading

A charity must be able to decide if particular income-generating activities are merely fund-raising, or whether they amount to trading. The following list illustrates how the 'badges of trade' tests can be applied to particular activities:

(i) **Sale of tickets to an annual ball**

- Although the ball is run annually, that amount of repetition will not constitute trading
- There is a profit motive
- There is no formal selling organisation

This is fund-raising. But if the ball is run regularly, i.e. more than three times a year in the locality, the Inland Revenue will regard this as trading. (See *Chapter 5*)

(ii) **Sale of Christmas cards**

- Unlike an annual ball (which takes place on one night of the year), the sale of cards is repeated over a period of weeks or months
- There is a profit motive
- The goods are purchased with the intention that they be sold
- There is a selling organisation - through shops, or in halls, or to retailers, or through a network of supporters

This is trading.

(iii) **Sale of tickets by the Royal Shakespeare Company**
(which is a charity)

- There is repetition
- There is probably a profit motive (even if the RSC is also supported by grants or sponsorship) but the absence is not fatal to the argument that there is trading. (See *Chapter 2.2(b)*)
- The nature of the service (spending money on putting on plays and recouping such money through ticket sales) is of a commercial nature
- There is a selling organisation

This is trading.

(iv) **Sale of educational books by the Oxford University Press**
(which is a charity)

- There is repetition
- There is probably a profit motive (see the point above concerning the RSC)
- The nature of the service (selling books) is clearly of a commercial nature
- There is a selling organisation

This is trading.

(v) **The provision by a charity under contract to a Health Authority of services to help alcohol and drug abusers**

- The service is supplied continuously for the period of the contract, hence there is repetition
- The charity structures its prices to make a surplus, i.e. it has a profit motive. The nature of the service is not of the type that is typically commercial, although there is nothing to prevent a business organisation providing such a service

- There is no selling organisation such as a shop

This is trading.

(vi) **A charitable school running occasional quiz nights to raise money for the building fund**

- There is no regular repetition
- There is a profit motive
- The nature of the service is not of a commercial nature
- There is no selling organisation

This is fund-raising, because the quiz nights are only being run occasionally - if they are held more than three times a year this will constitute a "regular" trading activity and therefore will no longer be treated as fund-raising (see *Chapter 5*).

2.4. The VAT position on income generated by fund-raising events

A supply of goods or services is exempt from VAT if:

(a) The supply is made in connection with a fund-raising event organised for charitable purposes; and

(b) The event is organised:

  (i) by a charity; or

  (ii) by a body corporate which is wholly owned by a charity and whose profits from whatever source - are payable to a charity by virtue of a deed of covenant or otherwise; or

  (iii) jointly by two or more such charities or bodies corporate.

What is a fund-raising event?
This is defined as a fete, ball, bazaar, gala show, performance or similar event which is separate from and does not form part of a series or regular series of like or similar events. The VAT exemption, therefore only applies to one-off events.

What is or is not considered to be a "one-off event"?
Inevitably the distinction between regular and one-off events and their different tax treatment raises questions of definition. The case of *Northern Ireland Council for Voluntary Action -v- C&E Commissioners* quoted in *De Voil, Value Added Tax at 33,5451* illustrates the difficulties. Northern Ireland Council for Voluntary Action is a charity. It organised a week of fund-raising events including a run of seven performances of a play. Customs and Excise sought to recover VAT which it claimed should have been charged on the tickets to the play. The charity argued that the seven performances constituted a single fund-raising event and were hence exempt from VAT. But the tribunal

upheld Customs' view that the UK government was entitled under European law to limit the scope of the exemption by excluding an activity which was one of a series of like or similar events from the definition of "fund-raising events". Hence the seven performances were not a one-off event, but seven separate performances constituting a regular event. The restriction of the exemption solely to one-off events had been a necessary measure to prevent distortion of competition. The charity was ordered to account for VAT on the sale of tickets.

2.5. Conclusion

Fund-raising is different from trading - although sometimes the distinction is hard to make.

If a charity carries on trading it must consider the issues set out in *Chapters 3* to *5*.

A charity will need to have the necessary constitutional capacity to undertake the particular activity. The consequences of a charity undertaking ultra vires activities were considered in *Chapter 1*.

Chapter 3
THE SALE OF DONATED GOODS

This chapter covers the following topics: whether the sale of donated goods is considered trading; the availability of rate relief for 'thrift shops'; and whether a trading company needs to be used for the sale of donated goods.

3.1. Background

Many charities seek to raise money by encouraging their supporters and the general public to donate surplus clothes or other items for resale. This has proved to be a method which both generates income for charities and attracts public interest in their work. Hence Oxfam is in the "Top Six" in terms of numbers of retail outlets in the United Kingdom (although clearly in terms of turnover or retail square footage Oxfam ranks far behind such retail titans as Sainsbury's and Marks and Spencer!) Shops selling donated goods are often called "thrift shops".

For many charities, their thrift shops are more than a means of attracting and selling donated goods. The presence of a shop bearing the charity's name and logo in a high street can be a valuable source of publicity, reminding the public of the charity's existence. This can (and does) lead many individuals not only to purchase goods at charity shops but also to make a donation at the same time - or even to leave a legacy in their Will.

3.2. Does the sale of donated goods constitute trading?

If the badges of trade (see *Chapter 2.2*) are applied to the sale of donated goods by a charity, it is clear that the charity is carrying on a trade:

(a) There is repetition; it is not a "one off" transaction;

(b) There is a profit motive; the charity receives the goods and re-sells them so as to raise money;

(c) The nature of the goods acquired (second-hand clothes, etc.) are not generally acquired commercially, although there are a number of commercial shops which buy and sell certain types of second hand clothes or which sell on an agency basis, taking a commission on each sale made;

(d) There is a selling organisation - a shop or indeed a chain of shops.

Notwithstanding that the sale of donated goods falls within the scope of a number of the badges of trade, the Inland Revenue has accepted that this activity does *not* constitute a trade. Instead the Revenue regard it simply as a case of the charity converting a donation it has received in kind into cash. Hence the Revenue will not seek to tax the profits derived from the sale of donated goods.

The Charity Commissioners adopt the same view. In paragraph 8 of their 1980 Report they stated:

"There can be no objection to transitory and incidental trading by charities, for example, by jumble sales, or *by the running of shops to sell articles given by charitably minded people" (Author*'s italics).

Thus the Charity Commissioners accept that the sale of donated goods by a charity is a form of "incidental" trading which does *not* constitute for-profit trading. It is an activity that can be carried out by a charity itself and need not be carried out through a separate trading company (see *Chapter 7*).

3.3. Rate Relief

Where a ratepayer is a charity and occupies property which is wholly or mainly used for charitable purposes (whether by one or more charities), the charity is entitled to 80% relief from Uniform Business Rate by virtue of Section 43(5) of the *Local Government Finance Act 1988*. This is known as *mandatory relief*. By Section 47 of the same Act, a local authority may, in its discretion, award up to a further 20% *discretionary relief*. It is made expressly clear by Section 64(10) that a property:

"shall be treated as wholly or mainly used for charitable purposes at any time if at the time it is wholly or mainly used for the sale of goods donated to a charity and the proceeds of sale of the goods (after any deduction of expenses) are applied for the purposes of the charity".

In other words a charity shop which is occupied by a charity for the purpose of selling donated goods is entitled to the mandatory 80% relief and is eligible for the further maximum 20% discretionary relief. If the shop is run by a trading company and not by the charity, the trading company is not eligible for rate relief. Occupation by a trading company, even if wholly owned by a charity, is not occupation *by a charity* for the purposes of rating law.

3.4. Should a trading company be used for the sale of donated goods?

Some charities operate the sale of donated goods through a separate, non-charitable trading company. This is not necessary so far as the Charity Commissioners, the Inland Revenue or the local rating authority are concerned (see *Chapters 3.2 and 3.3*). However, a charity may nonetheless establish a separate trading company to sell donated goods for the very understandable reason that by doing so it will insulate the charity from the potential risks attached to selling goods. At first glance such risks may seem negligible but on closer analysis it is clear that establishing a network of charity shops selling donated goods can constitute a risk for the charity.

The risks include:

(a) **Losses**

The operation may make a loss. If the activity is conducted directly by the charity, the charity will have to finance it. If it is run through a separate trading company, any losses will be incurred by the trading company and not by the charity. But, even where the activity is run through a separate trading company, in all probability the charity will have to bear any loss, since the trading company will almost certainly have been financed by the charity (see *Chapter 7*). Establishing a separate trading company to sell donated goods will not in itself insulate the charity from the attendant risk of loss. Moreover if the charity lends money to the trading company which it cannot recover, it will have to write off the loan. It may be prudent to seek the consent of the Charity Commissioners prior to writing off the loan, as they may otherwise pick up the point from the charity's accounts. Having to write off a loan may give rise to questions as to whether the trustees acted prudently in making the loan to the trading company in the first place.

(b) **Leases**

The property market is more flexible at the time of writing (1994) than it has been for decades. This means that many tenants have been able to negotiate more favourable terms in respect of repairing obligations, limits on service charge payments, length of leases, and "break" clauses (whereby the tenant can terminate the lease, say after 3 or 5 years on giving an agreed amount of notice) than previously But this happy state of affairs has only recently developed and may disappear if the property market recovers. For years landlords have forced harsh terms on would-be tenants, and in particular have often sought long leases with onerous repairing obligations, regular upwards-only rent reviews and no break clauses. Due to a strange quirk of English law a tenant remains liable to fulfil the obligations under a lease until the lease has expired, even if the tenant has transferred the lease to another occupier. If the transferee goes out of business or is otherwise unable to meet the obligations under the lease the landlord can claim any outstanding rent and/or service charge and/or the continuing liabilities under the lease from the original tenant and any subsequent transferee. This can mean that a tenant has ongoing contingent liabilities under a lease which might materialise years after it has been transferred. Clearly, if the lease is in the name of a separate trading company then claims made under that lease will not be made against the charity which controls the trading company, unless the charity has guaranteed the obligations of the trading company under the lease. If a charity is asked to give such a guarantee, this should be strenuously resisted by the charity on the basis that it does not have the constitutional capacity to guarantee the obligations of a commercial entity, albeit one which it owns (see *7.10 for further details*). If the charity does give a guarantee, and if the charity is unincorporated, the liability under the guarantee should be limited to the charity's assets and it should provide that the trustees shall not incur any personal liability under the guarantee.

It might, therefore, be prudent for a charity to establish a separate company to take on leases and protect the charity from any risks arising. This company could simply be a property holding company, which would then sub-let the premises to the charity on a short-term basis with much less onerous conditions attached to the sub-lease. A potential flaw in this apparently attractive arrangement is that landlords usually insist that any sub-tenant covenants directly with the landlord to honour all the tenant's covenants in the lease. If so, the charity will end up in a direct contractual relationship with the landlord. Nonetheless, a merit of this scheme is that it might reduce the period of the charity's exposure under the lease to the length of the sub-lease (if that is shorter than the lease itself). But it is worth remembering that landlords may be extremely reluctant to grant a lease to a company with no assets.

(c) **Trading risks/ product liability**
The seller of donated goods is under a duty to the buyer under the Sale of Goods Act 1979, that the goods supplied will be of "satisfactory quality", i.e. they must be reasonably fit for their normal expected use. A lower standard is expected for second-hand goods than for new goods. If the seller breaks this duty and sells second-hand goods which are not of satisfactory quality, he can be sued for breach of contract by the buyer (for example, where the goods sold cause personal injury).

In addition, the seller will owe a duty to third parties who may be injured or whose property may be damaged by the defective goods sold by the seller. Such liability arises under what lawyers call "tort". It is more complicated and difficult to establish that the seller has committed a tort rather than broken a contract, but nonetheless in both cases the seller runs a risk of incurring liability. Despite the lower standard of care expected of the seller by the courts in the case of second-hand goods, the seller runs risks in selling such products. A charity may, perfectly reasonably, decide that the sale of such goods is too risky for the charity, and may therefore wish to isolate the risk in a separate trading company.

Whether the donated goods are sold by a charity or a trading company, the seller should arrange suitable insurance cover (Product Liability Insurance) (see *Chapter 11*). With effect from 29th June 1994, the law is affected by the General Product Safety Directive (EC Directive No. 92/59 of 29th June 1992). This Directive applies to any product intended for consumers or likely to be used by consumers, whether new, used or reconditioned. The principal effect of this Directive is the requirement imposed on producers to place only safe products on the market. It applies only if the sale "is in the course of a commercial activity". The sale of donated goods for these purposes is assumed to be "in the course of a commercial activity", so the Directive *does* apply to the sale of donated goods. Hence if a charity or a trading company breaches this requirement, it will be *strictly* liable for any damage caused by the product without the necessity for the injured person to prove negligence. This is similar to the position under the Consumer Protection Act 1987 (which does not apply to second-hand goods) - see *Chapter 11* for further details.

3.5. The donation of goods by the charity to its trading company

The goods donated to a charity are part of the charity's assets. They are given to the charity for *it* to sell and apply the proceeds to the charity's purposes. The charity cannot give away its property to a trading company, even though it owns the company, as to do so would be a breach of the duties of the trustees of the charity to exploit the charity's assets so as to obtain a proper return. Thus the charity should charge a reasonable price to its trading company if the charity transfers donated goods for the trading company to sell.

This raises the question of VAT. The sale of donated goods by a charity is zero rated for VAT purposes (see *Chapter 3.6*), and the fact that the sale is a bulk sale to a trading company will not alter this. Hence the sale of donated goods by the charity to the trading company will be zero-rated. Although the sale of donated goods by a trading company can be zero rated (see *Chapter 3.6*), if the trading company has **purchased** the goods from the charity, so as to comply with the obligations of **charity law** that trustees should only dispose of assets at a proper price, the trading company will *not* be selling donated goods. It will be selling bought-in (albeit second-hand) goods and the sale of such goods is *not* zero rated! The trading company will be required to register for VAT and charge VAT on the sale proceeds if its annual turnover exceeds the VAT registration threshold (£45,000 for 1994/95). So, whilst it might appear to be sensible for a charity to pass its donated goods over to its trading company so as to minimise risk, this in turn can cause tax complications - the need to register for and charge VAT - which will force the trading company either to increase its prices or squeeze its profit margins (or both) so as to meet the VAT charge.

The position will be different if the goods are donated to the trading company, but care must be taken to ensure that is what happens - for example collecting bags should bear the trading company's name and not the charity's. It is very likely that in practice this distinction will be blurred. The shop should have a prominent notice stating that it is run by the trading company and that all profits are covenanted to the charity.

3.6. Value Added Tax

The sale of donated goods is zero rated if:

(1) The sale is made by either:
  (a) a charity; or
  (b) a taxable person who has covenanted by deed to give all the profits of the supply to a charity, and

(2) It comprises a sale of the goods; and

(3) The goods have been donated to the charity or taxable person for sale.

Hence so far as VAT is concerned, provided the trading company has entered into a deed of covenant to give 100% of its profits from selling donated goods to the charity, it makes no difference if the charity or trading company sells the donated goods. However, if there is no covenant or the trading company intends to pay over its profits by Gift Aid or dividend (see *Chapter 10.3* and *10.4*) or intends to retain all or part of its profits, this VAT relief will not apply. VAT will then have to be charged on the sale of donated goods.

Existing zero rates of VAT will continue under the transitional VAT arrangements negotiated within the European Union until 31st December 1996. The current EU Commissioner for Customs and Indirect Taxation (Madame Scrivener) is reported as saying that the current discussions concerning VAT would not interfere with provisions concerning the retention of zero rates and that they should "in no way lead to a taxation of charity sales which are currently exempt" (EFC Monitor, March 1993 p.28).

3.7. Can a charity shop also sell new goods?

A shop run by a charity which sells donated goods may also wish to sell new goods. These could range from Christmas cards in the few weeks up to Christmas each year to a complete range of bought-in new goods (baskets, carpets, etc.) throughout the year.

A number of questions are raised by this practice:

(a) **Is the activity ultra vires ?**

Charities need to have the necessary constitutional capacity to trade (see *Chapter 1*) and they can sell donated goods. But they do not usually have the constitutional capacity to undertake a regular business of selling bought in goods.

This applies whether the charity acts as principal or agent. Some charities apparently believe that it is perfectly legitimate for the charity to conduct a business of selling new goods as agent on behalf of the trading company. This also has the merit of allowing the charity to occupy the premises (hence stopping any arguments about the loss of rate relief as a result of occupation by a trading company). Unfortunately this belief is misguided. It makes no difference whether the charity receives income through selling goods it owns as principal or from *commission* received from selling goods as agent. In either case, the profits (not being derived from primary purpose trading) will be *taxable* and the charity trustees could be reprimanded by the Charity Commission and/or the Court for having allowed the charity to conduct its affairs in an ultra vires manner. Any losses sustained by the charity as a result of such ultra vires activity could be recovered from the trustees personally out of their own resources, (see *Chapter 1*).

(b) **Is rate relief obtainable on the shop premises?**

80% mandatory rate relief is obtainable if a charity "wholly or mainly" occupies a property for charitable purposes (see *Chapter 3.3*). The sale of donated goods falls within this. But when does a charity cease "mainly" to occupy a shop if it sells new goods alongside donated goods? How is the "wholly or mainly" test operated in practice? Is this based on a percentage of turnover, floor area, or what?

Since there has been no court ruling on this question, one has to rely on the varying practices of different rating authorities. These vary from place to place, so it is impossible to advise definitively on what a court might consider was an appropriate level of sales of donated goods to constitute "mainly" donated goods. However, in a case involving agricultural tenancies, *Fawcett Properties -v- Buckingham* (1960) 3A11ER 503, Lord Morton said that "mainly" probably means "more than half". On this line of argument, if 49% or less of the turnover of a charity shop is attributable to the sale of new goods, with the balance made up of the sale of donated goods, this should mean that the shop is "mainly" occupied for charitable purposes and should continue to enjoy the 80% mandatory rate exemption.

(c) **Will income tax be charged on any profits arising from the sale of bought in goods?**

As indicated in Section 3.1, the Inland Revenue will not seek to tax profits derived from the sale by a charity of donated goods. But if a charity starts selling new goods, the profits derived from that activity will be potentially taxable as "for-profit" trading - (see *Chapters 5* and *10*). In practice some inspectors of taxes operate the de minimis exemption (see chapter 5.4) in relation to new goods when sold along side donated goods.

Clearly, if the sale of the donated and new goods is undertaken

FACTOR	CHARITY	TRADING COMPANY
Rate relief	Yes	No
VAT	Zero rating on goods donated	Zero rating only if there is a Deed of Covenant for all profits to be paid back to the charity
Sale of new goods	No, unless incidental or donated	Yes
Leases	Obligations fall on charity	Obligations fall on trading company
Trading risks	Ditto	Ditto
Section 5 Charities Act 1993	Requires a statement that the organisation is a registered charity on official documents and fund-raising literature	Applies to the trading company as regards literature seeking donated goods.
Profits	Tax-free on donated goods	Tax free if all profits are covenanted back to the charity (or paid over in some other tax-effective way)

through a separate trading company and all the profits are covenanted to the charity (see *Chapter 10*), there will be no profit in the trading company upon which corporation tax can be charged, although this will cause problems with VAT and rate relief (see above).

(d) **Will the VAT zero rating apply to the sale of the new goods?**

The zero rating for donated goods does not apply to any new goods sold in the shop (unless these are zero-rated for other reasons, e.g. books or if new goods have been donated to the charity). If the total sales of new and donated goods exceed the VAT registration threshold (£45,000 for 1994/95) then VAT will have to be charged on the sale of new goods. The VAT registration requirement depends on the level of taxable supplies made and this includes sales of zero-rated donated goods as well as standard-rated new goods.

3.8. Charities Act 1993 requirements

Under Section 5 of the Charities Act 1993, a registered charity with a gross income in its last financial year of more than £5,000 must state in English or Welsh in legible characters the fact that it is a registered charity on various documents and, in particular, "on all .... receipts".

This means that if a registered charity runs a shop selling donated goods, the till receipts must contain the magic phrase "a registered charity".

Equally all cheques and orders for goods must contain the same phrase, as must any circulars, notices or advertisements asking the public to donate goods to the charity. If a trading company owned by a charity sells donated goods it will encourage donors to give goods to the trading company - for the benefit of the charity. Where the goods are being solicited by the trading company, such an advertisement will probably be treated as being issued "on behalf of" the charity and should comply with Section 5, notwithstanding that the notice or advertisement is published by the trading company. Breach of Section 5 is a *criminal* offence. The offence will be committed (in the case of a cheque or order) by the person who *signs* the offending item, and in the case of receipts or notices soliciting donations of goods, by the person who *issues* or *authorises the issue* of the relevant document. The maximum penalty is a fine of £1,000.

3.9. Conclusion

The sale of donated goods by a charity is not treated as trading.

A large number of UK charities run thrift shops directly, rather than using a separate trading company (e.g. Oxfam; British Red Cross Society; Sue Ryder Homes; Notting Hill Housing Trust; Imperial Cancer Research Fund). All these shops are run by the charities themselves.

The profits from the sale of donated goods by a charity are exempt from income or corporation tax. The sale of donated goods by a charity is zero-rated for VAT. Not all these advantages are available to trading companies which sell donated goods (see table).

Some charities have used trading companies to sell donated goods and have been fortunate enough to obtain rate relief to which they are not in law entitled.

If a trading company is used it is vital that a covenant stripping out 100% of the taxable profits is in place, otherwise if its annual turnover exceeds £45,000 (1994 figure), zero-rated status for VAT will be lost.

Chapter 4
PRIMARY PURPOSE TRADING

This Chapter discusses when a charity can trade in fulfilment of its primary purposes, and the position with regard to relief from taxation on primary purpose trading, rate relief on premises occupied for such trading and VAT.

4.1. What is primary purpose trading?

A charity can carry on a trade in fulfilment of its main or primary purpose. In other words, if a charity is established to run a hospital, it is perfectly legitimate for the charity to charge its patients for the supply of medical facilities, even with a view to making a surplus, The London Clinic does just that. It is a famous "private" hospital, but is also a registered charity.

The following list illustrates the range of trading activities which charities undertake in the course of fulfilling their primary purposes. It is not comprehensive. It aims to show the wide variety of ways in which charities trade. We have divided the charities into the four "heads" of charity as defined in *ITC Special Commissioners -v- Pemsel (1891) AC 531,* and a charity means any body of persons or trust established for charitable purposes only (Section 506(1) Income and Corporation Taxes Act, 1988).

(a) **The relief of poverty**
Examples of trading:

    (i) **Workshops for the poor**: the sale of goods by the beneficiaries of a charity established in the United Kingdom to relieve poverty. The sale of goods made by the poor in a workshop in India run by a charity established in the United Kingdom and sold by that charity in the United Kingdom

    (ii) **Almshouses**: An almshouse is a house provided for the reception or relief of poor persons, and an almshouse charity may charge maintenance contributions in return for the services provided to the residents.

(b) **The advancement of education**
Examples of trading:

    (i) **University presses and others**: A number of universities have their own publishing arms which carry on the trade of commissioning, publishing and selling books so as to advance education. (e.g. Oxford University Press and Cambridge University Press).

(ii) **Musical societies**: In *IRC -v- Glasgow Musical Festival Association* (1926) SG 920, the Association was established to promote and conduct choirs and singing and obtained an income from admission fees which were charged to people who attended its annual musical festival, where choirs and singers competed. The Inland Revenue challenged the tax treatment of the profits derived from running the festival, but it was held that the Association was trading in fulfilment of its primary purposes.

(iii) **Opera houses and theatres**: The Royal Opera House and the English National Opera are both charities which carry on a trade in fulfilment of their primary purposes by selling opera tickets, programmes and auxiliary catering. So too is that bastion of the rich, Glyndebourne! The Royal National Theatre and the Royal Shakespeare Company are educational charities which carry on primary purpose trading by selling theatre tickets.

(iv) **Universities and charitable private schools**: Universities, public schools and certain other charitable educational institutions carry on a primary purpose trade by virtue of providing educational places in return for fees. Sometimes these fees are wholly or partly paid by a local educational authority (university fees or the assisted places scheme). Sometimes the institution will offer bursaries to students who cannot afford to meet the full fees.

(v) **Museums and heritage sites**: Many museum and heritage charities charge admission fees (e.g. the Natural History Museum, the National Trust).

(c) **The advancement of religion**
Examples of trading:

(i) **Retreat Centres**: Many religious charities run retreat centres which charge fees for courses, meals and accommodation.

(ii) **Religious publications**: The commissioning, publication and sale of printed matter such as prayer books and religious literature, or of cassettes, CDs and videos of services and religious music.

(iii) **Coffee shops**: some religious groups run coffee shops as a form of outreach into the community where people can drop in, receive counselling and witness the particular faith in action.

(d) **Other charitable purposes beneficial to the community**
Examples of trading:

The potential list of examples under this category of charities which trade in fulfilment of their primary purposes is long; the following are but a few examples:-

(i) **Health services**: Fee charging by independent charitable hospitals (e.g. the London Clinic). Fee charging by charitable nursing homes. Fee charging by charitable family planning services (e.g. Marie Stopes Clinic, Family Planning Association);

(ii) **Care services**: Charities which charge local authorities for the provision of care services under contract.

(iii) **Animal welfare**: An animal rescue charity selling recovered pets to new homes.

(iv) **Recreational services**: A city farm charging for riding lessons.

(v) **Environmental charities**: An environmental charity charging for attendance on conservation weekends. A wildlife centre charging for admission to its site.

(vi) **Support and advice services to charities**: The provision of training, information and advice to other charities (e.g. Charities Aid Foundation; Charities Advisory Trust; Directory of Social Change).

4.2. Relief from tax on profit from primary purpose trading

When a trade is carried on by a charity the profits are taxable unless the statutory exemptions explained below apply. Hence in *Grove -v- Young Men's Christian Association* (1903) 4TC 613 the YMCA ran a restaurant on commercial lines and it was open to the public. Although the profits were *applied* for charitable purposes, the trading activity (running a restaurant) was not in fulfilment of the charity's primary purpose and hence the profits were taxable.

The same point is illustrated by *Religious Trust & Book Society of Scotland -v- Forbes* (1896) 3 TC 415. The Society sold religious books at shops in Edinburgh and Belfast. The Society also sent out salesmen or colporteurs to sell the Society's books and pamphlets and to act as missionaries. The Inland Revenue challenged the computation of the Society's profits from its shop. The Society had deducted as expenses the costs of the colporteurs. The General Commissioners decided that the business of the shops was in the nature of trade and had to be distinguished from the colportage work. The fact that the profits from the shop were applied to charitable purposes did not exempt them from tax.

As the law now stands it would be possible to reconstruct the Society's objects so that it was established solely to advance religion. For example, the Society for the Propagation of Christian Knowledge is established for that very purpose. The profits from the sale of the books and other items would thus be derived from fulfilling a primary purpose of the charity and would be exempt from tax. The key point from the religious books and the YMCA cases is that just because profits derived from trading are used for charitable purposes does not mean that they will be exempt from tax. If profits are to be exempt from tax they must fall within the statutory exemptions set out in *Chapter 4.3.*

4.3. The statutory exemptions

Section 505(1)(e) of the Income and Corporation Taxes Act 1988 provides for:

"exemption from tax under Schedule D in respect of the profits of any trade carried on by a charity, if the profits are applied solely to the purposes of the charity and either:

(i)   the trade is exercised in the course of the actual carrying out of a primary purpose of the charity; or

(ii) the work in connection with the trade is mainly carried out by beneficiaries."

The reference to *"tax"* is to either income tax or corporation tax. Income tax is charged on charitable trusts, whereas corporation tax is charged on limited companies, other forms of corporations, unincorporated associations and industrial and provident societies.

The reference to a *charity* is to a charity established in the United Kingdom. The exemption contained in Section 505 does not apply to income arising in the United Kingdom of a charity established abroad. This was decided by the House of Lords in *Camille and Henry Dreyfus Foundation, Inc. -v- IRC;* (1955) 3A11ER 97.

The Foundation was incorporated under the laws of the state of New York, USA. It received substantial royalties from a company resident in the United Kingdom and claimed that it was entitled to receive the royalties free from tax as it was established for charitable purposes only. But the House of Lords ruled categorically that the exemption from tax was only available to a charity established in the United Kingdom. Hence income derived from primary purposes trading in the UK by a French charity such as Medecins sans Frontieres, would be taxable; of course if the French charity established a local UK charity to carry out its primary purposes trading work in the UK, the profits of that charity would be eligible for relief from taxation.

Thus two tests have to be satisfied to obtain the exemption from taxation of profits:

The profits must be applied solely to the purposes of the charity

The profits cannot be distributed to the members or trustees by way of dividends, bonuses, etc. In other words, a charity can be a "for profit" organisation (and any profits will be free of tax). It is not a question of whether a charity makes a profit, but what it does with that profit. It *must* be a *non-profit distributing* organisation. Incidentally, this does not mean that a charity cannot pay its employees a surplus-related bonus - in theory it can do this and pay employees under the Profit Related Pay arrangements.

If the profits were to be misapplied, for example, if they were not used solely for the purposes of the charity but on an overtly party political campaign in breach of the Charity Commissioners' guidelines on political activity, the exemption from tax on the profits might be lost. The Inland Revenue could demand that the charity pay tax on the profits which had been so spent. If so the charity trustees could be ordered to pay the charity the tax it had incurred as a result of their having sanctioned the charity engaging in an ultra vires activity - that is because a trustee of a charity is personally liable for losses suffered by a charity as a result of his or her breach of trust.

and either:

(i) **The trade is exercised in the course of the actual carrying out of a primary purpose of the charity**

It is necessary to establish that the profits have been derived from the actual carrying out of one of the primary purposes of the charity. The only way to establish the primary purposes of the charity is to look at the *objects clause* in its constitution whatever this document is called, (trust deed, constitution, charter, memorandum of association or rules). If the trade is not in fulfilment of one of the charity's primary purposes as set out in the *objects clause*, the profits will be taxable. Hence an educational charity set up to run a school would be exempt from income or corporation tax on profits derived from selling educational services. But if it ran a regular series of money raising dances (not a one-off fund-raising event) the profits from that activity would be taxable *even if those profits were applied for the purposes of the charity,* because they would not have been derived from the "actual carrying out a primary purpose of the charity". This is as for the YMCA case (see *Chapter 4.2*) and in the Oxfam case (see *Chapter 2.2*). If it sold educational material and this was not a primary purpose, profits from this activity would also be taxable, even though the activity itself would be capable of being undertaken by a charity whose constitution so provided.

In *British Legion, Peterhead Branch, Remembrance and Welcome Fund -v- IRC* (1953) 3STC 84 the British Legion was a branch of a charity registered under the War Charities Act 1940. Its objects were to perpetuate the memory of local men and women who fell in the war, to further the social and recreational welfare of survivors and to assist needy dependants. The Branch raised money by running dances at the local drill hall every Saturday night for three years. The dances were not only open to survivors of the war. The hall was let at a nominal rent; the admission charge was 2s 6d but was often added to by donations and the dances were run by volunteers from the British Legion. If the dances had been run on normal commercial lines the profits would have been greatly reduced by expenses.

Tax Assessments were raised on the profits from the dances. These Assessments were upheld by the Special Commissioners who found the branch was carrying on a trade in respect of which it was liable to tax. Hence although there was evidence that the profits had been used for the Branch's charitable purposes, this did not exempt the profits from tax - and the fact that the profits were higher because voluntary labour had been used was *not* taken into account in assessing the taxable profits.

or

(ii) **The work in connection with the trade is mainly carried out by beneficiaries of the charity.**

"Mainly" was defined by Lord Morton in *Fawcett Properties -v- Buckingham* (1960) 3A11ER 503 at 512 as being "probably ... more than half". In other words, to fall within this exemption, not *all the work* in connection with the trade has to be carried out by beneficiaries, but only *a majority of the work.*

Examples of where such work is carried out include:

(i) The sale by a charity established to help disabled people of goods produced by such people in a workshop

(ii) The sale of tickets for a play put on by trainee actors.

(iii) The sale, in a centre established to educate people in the art of painting, of postcards produced by the students.

(iv) The sale of goods produced by poor people in a developing country in a project organised by a charity to alleviate poverty and to train local people in relevant work skills.

(v) The provision of services or the sale of products by training schemes for unemployed young people, e.g. printing or data processing work.

4.4. Value Added Tax

There is no *general* exemption from VAT for charities which undertake trading activities. The trading activities of many charities will fall within the definition of business supplies for VAT even though charities do not pursue a "profit motive". VAT is a tax on *turnover* not profits. Whether VAT is payable or not usually depends on the nature of what is supplied and not on the status of the supplier.

Charities also have to pay VAT on goods and services which they purchase, just like anyone else. VAT paid on purchases is called "input tax". The problem for most charities is that this input VAT is not recoverable if the charity is not registered for VAT, or if it is a purchase in connection with an exempt supply by the charity or a non-business activity such as fund-raising; or it may be only partially recoverable in certain circumstances.

Most charities are not able to recover all of the input tax they pay, either because they are not registered for VAT, or because of the type of services they supply, or because part of their work is subsidised by grants and donations. The amount of irrecoverable VAT *paid* by the charity sector may now exceed the value of the income and corporation tax advantages enjoyed by charities!

A charity (like any other organisation or individual) is required to register for VAT if it makes taxable supplies of more than the VAT registration threshold in any year. (£45,000 for 1994/95). Where a charity is registered for VAT, it must charge output VAT on the taxable supplies, of goods and services that it makes, but it can then reclaim input tax on purchases made in connection with such supplies

A "taxable supply" is defined as "a supply of goods or services made in the United Kingdom, *other than an exempt supply*". This therefore *includes* zero-rated supplies, which count towards the £45,000 per annum VAT registration threshold.

There are a number of *exemptions* from VAT which are significant for charities. The list of exempt activities is detailed, and covers supplies such as:

CHAPTER 4 – PRIMARY PURPOSE TRADING

(a) Land

(b) Insurance

(c) Postal services

(d) Betting, gaming and lotteries

(e) Finance

(f) Education

(g) Health and welfare

(h) Burial and cremation

(i) Trade unions and professional bodies

(j) Sports competitions

(k) Works of art

(l) Fund-raising events

If a supply is *exempt* from VAT certain consequences follow:

(i) No VAT is charged on such supplies.

(ii) Any input VAT incurred in making an exempt supply is not recoverable.

(iii) Exempt supplies are ignored for the purpose of calculating whether or not a trader is making "taxable supplies" and turnover from exempt supplies does not count towards the VAT registration threshold.

Hence if a charity is trading but only making exempt supplies, it will *not* be able to register for VAT whatever its turnover.

The type of exempt supplies which are most likely to be provided by charities are education, research and vocational training; health and welfare; and fund-raising events. Each of these is considered in the following paragraphs, other than fund-raising (see *Chapter 2.4*).

4.4. The VAT position on educational supplies

For the purposes of VAT, "education" has a wider meaning than pure academic study. One tribunal considered that it should be given its normal everyday meaning and adopted the definition given in the Russell Report, which it paraphrased as: "activities and processes involving learning and concerned with developing the ability of individuals to understand and to articulate, to reason and to make judgements and to develop sensitivity and creativity". *(De Voil: Value Added Tax Vol. 1 para 9.36).*

Education is exempt from VAT if it is provided by an *eligible body* i.e.:

(a) **A school**: that is an institution which provides primary and/or secondary education and is either:

   (i) local authority maintained; or

   (ii) a special school; or

   (iii) a voluntary school; or

   (iv) an independent school; or

   (v) a public school; or

   (vi) a grant maintained school; or

(b) **A university**, any college, institution, school or hall of such a university; or

(c) **An eligible institution**: this includes state-funded institutions of higher education and Cambridge Institute of Education, the Royal College of Art and the Cranfield Institute of Technology; or

(d) **An eligible body which provides education of a kind provided by a school or university otherwise than for profit.** This means that the *eligible body* is precluded from distributing and does not distribute any profit it makes and applies any profits made from supplies within Group 6 (i.e. education) to the continuance or improvement of such supplies. This relief does not extend to education which includes provision of tuition in, or facilities for recreation and sporting activities except as part of a general educational curriculum.

An charity will be operating otherwise than for profit for the purposes of VAT, even if it budgets for a surplus, if it is prevented by its constitution from distributing the surplus by way of dividend, bonus etc., to its members or trustees. Again, as with the exemption from income and corporation tax, for educational services to be exempt from VAT a charity must not *distribute* its profits. It can *make* a surplus but it must not distribute it to its members or trustees. Many educational charities are deemed to be exempt from VAT because of these provisions. If a charity is established under more than one head of charity (e.g. to advance education and to relieve poverty), any surplus from the educational activity must be ploughed back into educational activities, and if the surplus is used to relieve poverty the VAT exemption will be lost. This illustrates the need for a charity in such a situation to monitor closely its income and expenditure so as to be able to prove that it has re-invested any surplus in educational activities. This obligation to re-invest any surplus in educational activities applies equally to training (see below) and research.

The provision of vocational training or retraining for any trade, profession or employment or for any vocational work connected with:

(a) education, health, safety or welfare;or

(b) the carrying out of activities of a charitable nature

is also exempt when it is provided by an *eligible body*. This includes courses, conferences or seminars which train participants for future work or add to their knowledge in order to improve their performance in their current work.

Accordingly, training courses for charity trustees are exempt from VAT.

The provision of goods and services (e.g. materials, catering and accommodation) which are incidental to such education, training or retraining are exempt from VAT if:

(a) The supply is made by the person providing the education, training or retraining; and

(b) The recipient is either:

(i) a student of the person making the supply; or

(ii) another person who provides such training or retraining, and the goods are directly used by the students of that person.

Hence, if the University of London runs an educational conference and provides a luncheon for the participants, the supply of the lunch will be exempt from VAT as it is incidental to the training. The supply of alcohol with the meal will bear VAT at the standard rate. If outside caterers are employed, the position is different. If the outside caterer is VAT registered, it will be supplying food and alcohol (if any) to the conference organiser rather than to the students and will charge VAT on that supply, because in this case the goods and services are not supplied by the person who is putting on the training or retraining. If the supply is simply a supply of food rather than a supply of a catering service, then VAT will not be chargeable on the supply of cold food, which is zero-rated. To qualify, the food must be supplied packed to be set out by the conference organiser; it would count as the supply of a catering service if the food was arranged on platters covered with cling film.

These points show that detail is all important with VAT and professional advice should be sought.

4.5. The VAT position on the supply of research

Research means original investigation undertaken in order to gain knowledge and understanding. It includes using existing knowledge in experimental development to produce new or substantially improved materials, devices, products and processes including design and production. Research is exempt from VAT if it is carried on by an *eligible body* and supplied to an *eligible body* (see *Chapter 4.4*).

The position is different if the research is not 'original investigation'. The routine listing and analysis of materials, components and processes is not VAT exempt, and will bear VAT at the standard rate.

If research by the charity is funded by a third party, for example by way of a grant which does not confer any interest in the research on the grantor, then no supply is made and the grant itself is non-business income outside the scope of VAT. If on the other hand the research is funded by a client which is not an *eligible body*, this will constitute a supply of a taxable service by the university or school, and will be subject to VAT at the standard rate. The question as to whether a charitable school or university has the constitutional capacity to undertake such private research, or whether it is ultra vires also needs to be considered (see *Chapter 6.9*).

4.6. The VAT position on the supply of health and welfare services

If a charity supplies any of the following "welfare services" otherwise than for profit, the supply is exempt from VAT, (Value Added Tax Act 1994, Schedule 9, Part II, Group 7, item 9). For this purpose, "otherwise than for profit" has the same meaning as for an educational supply - see *Chapter 4.4*.

(a) Providing care, treatment or instruction designed to promote the physical or mental welfare of elderly, sick, distressed or disabled persons.

(b) Protecting children and young persons.

(c) Spiritual welfare provided by a religious institution as part of a course of instruction or retreat which, in either case, is not designed primarily as a recreation or holiday.

Primary purpose trading by a charity in these areas conducted otherwise than for profit will be exempt from VAT. Supplies which have been exempted under this include: residential accommodation at a centre for the study and practice of yoga, and the supply of food at a convention run by Jehovah's Witnesses.

4.7. Zero rating and charities

To make zero-rated supplies is the most favourable position for VAT purposes. A supplier can claim back input VAT from Customs & Excise but does not have to charge output VAT.

The key areas of zero-rated suppliers for charities undertaking trading activities (whether as primary purpose trading or for-profit trading through a separate trading company) are:

Group 3: (Value Added Tax Act 1994 Schedule 8): The supply of books; booklets, brochures, pamphlets and leaflets, newspapers, journals and periodicals, children's picture books and painting books, music, maps, charts and topographical plans.

Group 4: The supply of talking books for the blind and handicapped and wireless sets for the blind.

Group 16: The sale of donated goods (see *Chapter 3*). The export of any goods by a charity to a place outside the European Community.

4.8. What happens if a taxable person fails to register for VAT?

A person who is making taxable supplies (including zero-rated supplies) must register for VAT if those supplies exceed the registration threshold in any year (£45,000 for 1994/95). Regulation in such circumstances is compulsory. There is no choice. Failure to register without reasonable excuse may result in far greater liabilities than, for example, in the case of failure to pay income tax on the due date. Failure to register is a criminal offence. The penalty is the greater of £50 and "the specified percentage of relevant tax".

Relevant tax is the net VAT (output tax minus input tax) which should have been paid, calculated from the date from which the trader should have registered to the date of discovery. The specified percentage is 10% (where the period of delay is less than 9 months), 20% (where the period of delay is between 9 and 18 months) and 30% in any other case. Of course the organisation also has to pay the arrears of VAT. This can build up a considerable liability. The excuse "we didn't realise we had to" is not acceptable.

4.9. Rate relief

The Local Government Finance Act 1988 S43(6) provides that where the ratepayer is:

(a) A charity; and

(b) The property is wholly or mainly used for charitable purposes, the charity will be granted 80% mandatory relief from Unified Business Rate.

A charity which is occupying premises for the purposes of carrying on primary purpose trading will be using the property wholly for charitable purposes. Hence it will be entitled to the 80% mandatory relief, and it will also be able to apply for the 20% discretionary relief available under section 47 Local Government Finance Act 1988. The granting of discretionary relief is solely at the discretion of the local authority.

If a charity occupies a rateable property wholly or mainly for fund-raising, technically the charity should not receive any rate relief, since fund-raising itself is not a charitable activity but a method of raising charitable funds. For example, a charity might run a shop selling bought in goods. If the sale of such goods is not primary purpose trading then the charity will not occupy the premises wholly or mainly for charitable purposes. This leaves aside the question whether the charity has the constitutional capacity to undertake this activity. However, in practice a local authority may not notice or overlook this, and grant rate relief.

4.10. The charity SORP

The draft Statement of Recommended Practice (known as "the charity SORP") requires that the gross income which a charity derives from primary purpose trading and the gross expenditure should be disclosed in the statement of Financial Activities. The final version of the charity SORP will be published in 1995. It is a statement of *recommended* practice, and to that extent is not binding. But auditors and other financial examiners overseeing the accounts of larger charities (whose annual turnover exceeds £100,000) and of charities constituted as companies are likely to require that the recommended practice is used in the preparation of the accounts.

4.11. Charities Act 1993

Section 5 of the 1993 Act has been discussed in *Chapter 3.8*. This applies equally to the various documents, issued by a registered charity in the course of primary purpose trading. The Section applies to any registered charity with a gross income in its last financial year of more than £5,000. It requires that the charity must state that it is a registered charity in English or Welsh in legible characters on certain documents.

"(a) in all .... documents issued by .... the charity and soliciting money .... for the benefit of the charity; and

(b) in all bills of exchange, promissory notes, endorsements, cheques and orders for money or goods purporting to be signed on behalf of the charity; and

(c) in all bills rendered by it and in all its invoices, receipts and letters of credit".

Hence a charity carrying on primary purpose trading must ensure that in particular its cheques, purchase order forms, invoices and receipts contain the magic words "a registered charity". This could be a major financial obligation for charities which sell goods in fulfilment of their main objects as it may be necessary to re-programme their tills or laboriously stamp each till receipt with the necessary words or purchase a new till capable of printing them! *Breach of section 5 is a criminal offence.* The offence is committed in the case of bills of exchange, cheques etc by the person who *signs* the relevant document. In the case of bills, invoices etc, it is committed by the person who *issues* or *authorises* the issue of a document which breaches Section 5.

Thus in the case of a shop selling donated goods where the till receipt breaches Section 5, both the trustees of the charity (who as the persons having the general control and management of the charity must be deemed in law to have authorised the issue of the receipt) and the shop assistant who issues the receipt could be charged with an offence - the maximum fine is £1000.

In the case of a registered charity which sells publications, it could be argued that each publication which bears a price "solicits money for the charity". A book is clearly a document and hence all such publications should bear the words "a registered charity". This section is already in force and perhaps charities which sell publications should have a slip stating that the charity is registered placed in each book currently on sale which was printed before these sections came into effect.

4.12. Conclusion

Many charities carry out primary purpose trading.

A charity will receive its profits from primary purpose trading free of income or corporation tax if it applies them solely to the purposes of the charity.

A charity's trading activities may be subject to VAT, or be exempt or be zero-rated, depending on the nature of the trade.

A charity which carries on primary purpose trading will be able to occupy premises with the benefit of 80% mandatory rate relief.

Chapter 5
ANCILLARY AND INCIDENTAL TRADING

This chapter discusses what ancillary or incidental trading is, whether profits arising are subject to taxation or whether they qualify for the extra-statutory concession, and the de minimis exemption where turnover is small.

5.1. Charity law

Some charities undertake trading activities which are *not* in fulfilment of one of their primary purposes, but which are in some way complimentary to or derived from those purposes.

Examples include: running a cafe open to visitors at a museum; a canteen at a youth club; selling the produce of a city farm; a school running a tuck shop. Further examples can be seen in the section on exploiting surplus assets (see *Chapter 6*).

For the purposes of *charity law* the charity does not threaten its charitable status by undertaking such ancillary trading even though the trading is itself not a charitable activity, provided its constitution gives it the necessary powers to do this. This is because the trading is conducted at a minor level and supports the charitable work of the charity. As the Charity Commissioners stated in Paragraph 8 of their 1980 Report:

"There can be no objection to transitory and incidental trading by charities, for example, by jumble sales or by the running of shops to sell articles given by charitably-minded people".

Ancillary trading cannot be or become a major part of the charity's activities. If it were to become so then the charity would be acting ultra vires, which would in turn expose its trustees to potential risks (see *Chapter 1*).

It is inevitably difficult to discern whether a particular trading activity is "ancillary" or "incidental" or is of a nature or extent which has turned it into non-primary purpose trading. Each case will depend on the particular facts.

5.2. Taxation

The Inland Revenue applies three tests to any profits derived from the trading activities of charities:

(a) **Are the profits derived from carrying out a primary purpose of the charity (see *Chapter 4*).**

(b) **If not, do the profits fall within the Extra-Statutory Concession (see *Chapter 5.3*)?**

(c) **If not, do the profits fall within the de minimis exemption (see *Chapter 5.4*)?**

If none of these apply, then the profits are **taxable**.

A good illustration of how the Inland Revenue operates is given by the YMCA case quoted in *Chapter 4.2*. On that occasion, the charity opened its restaurant to members of the public and did not confine its use to beneficiaries of the charity. It was held to carry on a trade and the profits did not fall either within the extra-statutory concession or within the de minimis exemption, which were not available in 1903. If the restaurant had been open only to beneficiaries of the charity, the Inland Revenue would probably have treated any profits as derived from primary purpose trading and would not have sought to tax them.

5.3. The Extra-Statutory Concession

The Inland Revenue recognises that profits generated from non-primary purpose trading activities are frequently small and are reliant upon the free time of volunteers and other forms of gratuitous support.

Consequently, the Inland Revenue has issued Extra Statutory Concession C4 (1988), entitled *"Trading Activities for Charitable Purposes"*, and an explanatory pamphlet *"Fund-Raising for Charity"* (1994).

This states:

"Bazaars, jumble sales, gymkhanas, carnivals, firework displays and similar activities arranged by voluntary organisations or charities for the purposes of raising funds for charity may fall within the definition of 'trade' in Section 832 Income and Corporation Taxes Act 1988 with the result that any profits will be liable to corporation tax. Tax is not, however, charged on such profits provided the following conditions are satisfied:

(a) the organisation or charity is not regularly carrying on these trading activities;

(b) the trading is not in competition with other traders;

(c) the activities are supported substantially because the public are aware that any profits will be devoted to charity; and

(d) the profits are transferred to charities or otherwise applied for charitable purposes."

It should be noted that all of the four conditions have to be met in order for a charity to be able to claim that the profits from a fund-raising activity fall within the extra-statutory concession. The whole thrust of the concession is to exempt profits derived from one-off fund-raising events of the type mentioned at the beginning (e.g. bazaars, jumble sales, etc.) Recent guidance from The Inland Revenue pamphlet indicates that other events, such as concerts, dinner-dances, and sports matches, can be included, and the exemption includes all income raised at the event including sale of advertising space and programmes. Clearly, most questions will arise over paragraphs (a) and (b).

What amounts to "not regularly carrying on"? An annual fete or annual bazaar is carried on "regularly" at regular twelve month intervals, but does that amount to carrying on *regular trading activities?* In this context "regularly" appears to mean in the course of a regular or on-going business rather than at regular intervals.

The Inland Revenue pamphlet states:

"The concession does not apply to activities which are carried on on a regular or frequent basis. Normally, any event which takes place more than three times a year in the locality is regarded as 'regularly carried on'. For this purpose each type of event is considered separately so that it would be acceptable to arrange three gymkhanas and three firework displays in the same year. The size of the locality would vary from case to case according to the catchment areas of the particular events.

A two or three day series of concerts or other events for which there is a single admission charge would be regarded as a single event notwithstanding that the number of concerts within the series exceeds three. But where there is a separate admission charge payable for each day or for each concert the series as a whole cannot be regarded as a single event. The concession does not extend to a programme of events for which patrons can buy a season ticket but where each event can properly be regarded as standing on its own."

The Inland Revenue pamphlet makes it clear that the concession is restricted to activities which are reasonably small in scale. Factors to be taken into account in considering whether an activity is small in scale include:

- the degree of commercialisation involved;

- the level of input by professional organisers and celebrities (including those giving their services on a voluntary basis);

- the number of people attending;

The pamphlet states:

"All the relevant factors need to be considered together to determine whether a particular event falls within the scope of the concession. For example, a major gala or charity opening night organised on fully commercial lines at a recognised and regular venue for the activity concerned would be unlikely to fall within the concession. On the other hand, for example, a performance given to a small group of people might well come within the concession even though the performer is well known."

This statement is less than helpful. Many charities, for example, run gala nights at theatres or opera houses. The theatre is a "recognised and regular venue" for the activity concerned (i.e. putting on plays). But on the wording of the pamphlet, the gala night would be a trading activity and hence any profits would fall outside the extra-statutory concession. In a recent case (unreported), the Inland Revenue has claimed tax on the profits of a charity opening night performance of a film at a leading West End cinema which illustrates the possible risk with this type of activity.

If the extra-statutory concession does apply then all the profits of the event are covered, such as admission charges, sale of refreshments, raffle tickets, programmes and advertising space.

"Each ancillary source of income must properly form part of the event and must not constitute a separate profit-making activity. For instance, if a programme or brochure is primarily a vehicle for advertisements rather than a way of informing people about the event, it will be treated as a separate profit-making activity.

The turnover of the ancillary source of income must be sufficiently modest so that it can properly be regarded as incidental to the main event." (Inland Revenue explanatory pamphlet.)

When a fund-raising event falls outside the extra-statutory concession, it is open to the organisers to set a basic minimum charge and to invite those attending the event to supplement this with a voluntary donation. The additional contributions will not be taxable if all the following conditions are met;

- it is clearly stated on all publicity material, including tickets, that anyone paying only the minimum charge will be admitted without further payment;

- the additional payment does not secure any particular benefit (for example, admission to a better seat in the auditorium);

- the extent of further contributions is ultimately left to ticket-holders to decide (even if the organiser indicates a desired level of donation);

- for film or theatre performances, concerts, sporting fixtures and similar events if the minimum is not less than the usual price for the particular seats at a normal commercial event of the same type;

- for dances, dinners and similar functions the sum of the basic minimum charge is not less than the total costs incurred in arranging the event.

The extra-statutory concession is just that; it is a concession. There is no right of appeal against the refusal of the Inland Revenue to grant a charity the benefit of the concession.

It should be emphasised that the sale of Christmas Cards or the operation of a bar open to the general public would *not* fall within the concession both because they are done regularly *and* because the activity is in competition with other traders.

5.4. The de minimis exemption

If a charity carries on trading activities which are not in fulfilment of a primary purpose or are not eligible for exemption under the extra-statutory concession (perhaps because they are undertaken "regularly"), any profits resulting from that trade will be liable to be taxed. The level of the profits will need to be calculated. This means that once the true costs of undertaking the trade are offset against the gross profits, the taxable profit will be lower than the gross profits. A charity faced with a demand for tax on its for-profit trading activities should take professional advice on the calculation of the relevant taxable profits so as to ensure that all properly attributable expenses and charges including overheads and reliefs have been claimed against the profits.

The Inland Revenue has operated a non-statutory de minimis exemption for many years. This has been applied in cases such as charitable schools or museums which undertake primary purpose trading, but which undertake non-primary purpose trading as well (e.g. a school which runs a tuck shop, or a shop in a museum which sells not only books and educational materials, but also films, tee-shirts and fluffy toys). The Inland Revenue has allowed such charities to have a turnover from the non-primary purpose trading of up to 10% of the total combined turnover of primary and non-primary purposes trading before it seeks to tax the profits derived from non-primary purpose trading. However, this is also subject to the scale of each particular case, as the turnover from non primary purpose trading must be small in absolute terms. For example, if a charitable school is turning over £6 million per annum (excluding income from grants or donations), its de minimis exemption would be £600,000 of which the taxable profits could be, say, £100,000. Corporation tax would be levied at 25% (1994|95 rates) and would amount to £25,000. This would be too much tax for the Inland Revenue to forgo lightly! If the net profit figure is small (e.g. less than £2,000), the Inland Revenue will *probably not* seek payment of the tax due there on (£500) on the basis that the tax involved is much too small to worry about. However, this will depend entirely on the attitude taken by individual inspectors of taxes in any particular case. There is no formal de minimis exemption allowed by the Inland Revenue. Technically, all profits generated from for-profit trading *(however small)* are taxable unless the extra-statutory concession applies. The Inland Revenue are currently (1994) reviewing this concession and will (it is understood) refer to it for the first time in a guidance which will be published shortly.

It should be emphasised that the 10% figure is based on the turnover from primary purpose trading and not on the total level of income from all sources (whether from grants, gifts or from trade).

5.5. What profit?

If a charity undertakes trading activities and makes profits which are not exempt from tax either under the extra statutory concession or the de minimis exemption, the charity must work out the actual taxable profits. In assessing the profits of the trade, a charity should make sure that all proper costs and expenses attributable to the trading activity are offset against the profits generated. It should take proper professional advice on this. In particular, it may be possible for a charity to claim that if its profits are partly attributable to voluntary labour, the notional costs of the volunteers' time should be taken into account as a business expense in computing the tax due on the trading activity. Complex questions may also arise about the attribution of fixed overheads, and the reader is referred to *Chapter 6.8.* It may find when the costs of the trade are fully accounted for, that there is no, or only a small, taxable profit.

5.6. General

The Inland Revenue has six years in which to make a tax assessment.

Hence, an assessment for the 1987-88 tax year must be made by 5th April 1994. If the Inland Revenue satisfies the Inland Revenue Commissioners that it has reasonable grounds to believe that tax has been lost due to fraud or wilful default, an assessment may be made for any year back to 1937.

Where a charity has made a tax return to the Inland Revenue, it should set aside a sufficient reserve to meet the tax which it estimates will be payable pursuant to the tax return.

5.7. Conclusion

A charity may undertake some small or minor non- primary purpose trading without running the risk of breaking charity law or being confronted with a tax bill. However, each case will depend on its facts and it is dangerous to generalise.

Charities, their advisers and the authorities need to keep a sense of balance and proportion. Although it is necessary to establish a trading company to undertake for-profit trading activities in certain circumstances (see *Chapter 6*) it is wise not to rush into this structure. In one case a city farm (which was a charity) owned a cow. It sold the cow's milk. It was told by the Charity Commission that this "trading" activity would have to be run through a separate, non charitable trading company! But it could have been argued perfectly reasonably:

(a) That the trade was ancillary, so far as charity law was concerned, and thus within the charity's constitutional capacity; and

(b) That the profits (if any, after taking into account a proper apportionment of overheads etc) were so small (or even non-existent) as to be within the de minimis exemption from taxation.

Chapter 6
PROBLEM AREAS WITH TRADING

This chapter covers problem areas in trading. If a charity encounters any of these problems, it should consider establishing a separate trading company. The key problem areas are: public versus private benefit; sponsorship; sale of Christmas cards; catalogue sales; affinity cards; bars; exploitation of surplus assets; and research.

6.1. Fund-raising or trading?

As has already been discussed, for a charity to obtain tax relief on the profits derived from a trade, the trade must be carried on in fulfilment of a primary purpose of the charity or be wholly or mainly carried out by beneficiaries of the charity (see *chapter 4*). This rule is easily stated, but in practice it is at times hard to apply. Many charities undertake a mixture of trading activities. Some are in fulfilment of a primary purpose (e.g. running a charity theatre), and some are not (e.g. running a bar in the theatre which is open to the general public as well as to theatre-goers). In addition it may undertake fund-raising activities.

The difficulty of drawing a line between fund-raising, primary purposes trading and for-profit trading is illustrated by the following quotation from Paragraph 8 of the 1980 Report of the Charity Commissioners:

"Drawing the line between the charity which is merely raising funds and furthering its activities by trading and what is in substance a trading institution wearing a charitable mantle is not easy: each case must be considered on its own facts. There can be no objection to transitory and incidental trading by charities, for example, by jumble sales or by the running of shops to sell articles given by charitably minded people. But running a shop to make a profit from goods specially bought for the purpose or other trading on a permanent basis, if permitted by the trusts *(that is, the constitution of the charity)* (author's italics), might mean that the institution was not established for exclusively charitable purposes."

Just because a charity applies the profits of a trade to charitable purposes **does not exempt those profits from tax**. The *British Legion, Peterhead Branch* case (see *Chapter 4.3*) clearly illustrates this. The trade has to be in fulfilment of a primary purpose of the charity for any profits derived from the trade to be exempt from tax. A good example of primary purposes trading is given by the case of *Dean Leigh Temperance Canteen Trustees -v- IRC* (1958) 38 TC315. The charity in this case was established to promote temperance. It ran a canteen for non-alcoholic drinks in a cattle market so as to encourage temperance. It was ruled by an Inland Revenue tribunal that the profits derived from the sale of such non-alcoholic drinks were exempt from tax on the basis that the sale of such drinks was in fulfilment of the primary purpose of the charity (to encourage temperance).

If a charity undertakes a profitable for-profit trading activity which is *not* in fulfilment of a primary purpose, the charity will be taxed on those profits (subject to the de minimus exemption and the Extra-Statutory Concession discussed in *Chapter 5*).

Trustees of a charity are under a duty to exercise sensible tax planning. Paragraph 44 of the Charity Commissioners' Report for 1988 states:

"Trustees .... may be personally liable to account for taxation liabilities which are unnecessarily incurred directly or indirectly as a result of the inefficient administration of the charity".

Clearly, this means that if a charity does undertake profitable for-profit trading it should see that this is done via the most tax-effective legal structure - for example (if appropriate) through a separate trading company (see *Chapter 7*).

6.2. Public versus private benefit

A difficult question faced in some circumstances is the degree to which the trading activity is charitable. An activity only qualifies as charitable if it is undertaken for the benefit of the public. In *Educational Grants Association -v- IRC (1967) Ch 993,* a company was established for charitable purposes to promote education, but confined its activities almost entirely to making grants for the education of children of employees of a single company or group of companies. It was held that the income had not been applied for charitable purposes as there was not sufficient public benefit.

It is difficult in any particular case to determine whether a charity's activities actually provide only "incidental" or a preponderance of private benefit. If the private benefit is "incidental", there are no problems; but if the private benefit is preponderant (or to put it another way, if there is insufficient public benefit), there can be problems.

Take a hypothetical example. A charity, which has as its main object the improvement of the natural environment, is employed for a fee to re-landscape a back garden. The re-planting is done in an ecologically sensitive manner. Native trees and shrubs are planted to attract birds and insects so as to encourage as rich a diversity of nature as possible. The environment has been improved as a result of the charity's work. Therefore, it can be claimed, there has been public benefit and the charity has traded in fulfilment of its primary purpose. But the owner of the back garden has also enjoyed a considerable benefit. He or she has a much better back garden. Has the work been done for the benefit of the public or the benefit of the landowner? Would the position be different if the works had been to his or her front garden, which abutted a busy road, with many passers-by? There is authority for arguing that if an operation is undertaken to relieve a charitable need, then any *incidental* private benefit does not matter. But is the private benefit in this case incidental? To answer these questions the charity has to ask itself why it is undertaking the particular operation: is it doing it in order to raise funds by making use of skills it has developed (in which case it would not be a mainstream charitable activity)? Or is it doing it to provide public benefit?

It is worth mentioning that in *Joseph Rowntree Trust -v- Attorney General (1983)* 1 A11ER 288, it was emphasised that in respect of whether a charity is acting within its powers, incidental private benefit arising from the fulfilment by a charity of its primary purposes does not affect the position. This is equally true of the provision of education by a fee-paying school, where the pupils (presumably) benefit.

It is easy to ask these questions. But it is much more difficult for a charity, given any particular set of circumstances, to answer them. The charity may have a mixture of motives - both the desire to fulfil its charitable objects and the ever-present need to cover costs and raise funds.

The Charity Commission considers that any trading activity where the preponderance of benefit is private cannot be undertaken by a charity. This apparently simple rule presents huge problems in practice, as the hypothetical example given above seeks to illustrate. How does one determine the preponderance of benefits? This will vary and be dependent on the facts of the particular case.

The very term "private benefit" can be fraught with difficulties. Take a public limited company, such as Marks & Spencer. Environmental improvement works done on its land, where there would be a preponderance of benefit to Marks & Spencer, would be work carried out on what is "private" land for the purposes of charity law, albeit that it is owned by a public company. Similar work carried out on the grounds of a "private" hospital will have no "private benefit" implications if the "private" hospital is (as many are) a charity (and therefore a species of public body)! Clearly environmental improvement works on common land raise no problems of "private benefit".

The question of "private benefit" can arise in a number of other areas such as the provision by a charity (in fulfilment of its main objects) of advice to an employer, for example, on how to meet its statutory obligations under the Health and Safety at Work legislation, or in providing training in First Aid at work. Another example would be the provision by a charity of First Aid cover at events, such as at races and football matches, so as to allow the owner of the ground to meet the legal obligation to have such cover available. In all these cases it can be argued that, *in providing these services, a charity is fulfilling its objects, whilst at the same time enabling the purchaser of the service to meet its legal obligations* - in the examples for the benefit of the public! Accordingly the benefit derived by the employer or promoter of the event is incidental and not sufficient to disqualify the activity from being charitable. But this is a contentious area, where each case needs to be considered separately.

Does the question of "private benefit" arise in the case of a charity which contracts with a local authority or a health authority to run a care service? In such cases the charity is helping the relevant authority to fulfil its statutory obligations, but as both a local and a health authority are public bodies the question of "private benefit" does not arise.

The question of whether the activity is charitable, and therefore intra vires must be considered. If the trustees reasonably believe that it is, and have taken professional advice where in doubt, then there will be no problem. If the Charity Commission decides that it is not, it will simply ask the charity to modify its activities. The important point to remember is that *if* it is established that the preponderance of benefit from a particular activity is *private*, then any profits derived from that activity will be *taxable*. Hence, charities will be well advised to consider putting those trading activities where the private benefit is or may be preponderant into a *separate* trading company.

Charities undertaking research may also face problems in determining whether the activity is for public or private benefit (see *Chapter 6.9*).

6.3. Sponsorship

"Sponsorship" is a term much used in the voluntary sector, often with different meanings. There are "sponsored" walks and "sponsored" swims. Runners in the London Marathon seek "sponsorship" from "sponsors". In these cases the sponsor is merely a giver or donor. Such sponsorship does not amount to trading.

But a sponsor can also be someone who supports an event in return for publicity - for example the official sponsor of the London Marathon or a sponsor of an opera at Covent Garden. Here there is a supply of a service, and once again one runs into the distinctions between fund-raising, primary purposes trading and for-profit trading.

The sponsorship may only really be a straight cash donation to the charity. The term "sponsorship" might have been used to make the application seem more important, and there may have been nothing offered in return other than reasonable recognition of the support. But increasingly "sponsors" are looking for something extra in return for their "donation", which raises important issues for charities.

A sponsor may make a contribution to a charity, for example, to underwrite a concert of classical music, on condition that the sponsor's name or logo is advertised or promoted at the concert (e.g. as a backdrop to the orchestra or on the back of the conductor's jacket). This has *VAT implications*. If the charity receives a donation and merely provides a simple acknowledgement of the sponsor's contribution (for example in the programme), the donation is *outside* the scope of VAT. For these purposes a simple acknowledgement will amount to printing the name, address and logo of the sponsor in small type. But if the sponsor's name is extensively advertised or promoted, or if the sponsor receives some benefit, for example, free tickets, preferential booking rights or free advertising space in a programme, then the sponsorship *is deemed to be a payment made for the supply of services by the charity*, be it advertising or the provision of tickets to an entertainment. In this case VAT must be charged by the charity on the amount of the sponsorship.

With VAT the question arises as to what is meant by a simple acknowledgement. How big and bold can the typeface be? What information can be provided about the sponsor? How prominent can the display be?

The Customs and Excise pamphlet on sponsorship states that "if your only acknowledgement of the sponsor's contribution is a simple mention in the programme or annual report and nothing else is required of you, it is still outside the scope of VAT". But if the acknowledgement is more than that then VAT will be chargeable, provided the charity is registered for VAT (i.e., it has a total VATable turnover, including moneys from the supply of services in return for the sponsorship, of £45,000). If the supply is subject to VAT, then VAT must be charged regardless of the status of the sponsor, be it an individual, a charity, a government department or a commercial organisation.

In addition to these VAT consequences, sponsorship income can potentially be liable to income or corporation tax on the profits arising to the charity. In the case of a straight donation or a donation coupled with a simple acknowledgement in a programme, no questions of direct taxation arise. The sponsor will, if a UK taxpayer, seek to make the payment in a tax-efficient manner - using Gift Aid or a Deed of Covenant (and make the payment net of income tax). A Covenant or Gift Aid payment has to be an act of pure bounty (i.e. the donor must get nothing in return). A simple acknowledgement of the sponsor's donation is permitted, as for VAT.

For most "sponsorships", where the sponsor wants more than a simple acknowledgement, the sponsor will seek to claim the sponsorship as a tax deductible payment to be offset against the sponsor's pre-tax profits, for the purposes of calculating its corporation or income tax liability. The payment will be tax deductible if it has been incurred "wholly and exclusively" in connection with the sponsor's business. For example, if the payment is treated in the sponsor's hands as a payment for advertising or public relation services, it will be tax deductible.

Given that the sponsor has treated the sponsorship as a form of business expense in its own accounts, how should the payment be treated by the charity?

Firstly the charity will have to charge VAT if it is registered or obliged to register as a result of the supply of the sponsorship (see above). This in itself indicates that this particular sponsorship is a trading activity. But is this primary purpose trading?

A charity cannot, as one of its primary purposes, run an advertising services business. In taking "sponsorship" money in return for linking the sponsor's name with the event in a prominent manner, the charity is providing a form of advertising service. In one well publicised case a leading performing arts organisation (which was a charity) raised a considerable amount of sponsorship income so as to make up for a shortfall on its grant income. It received considerable plaudits for doing this. Much to its consternation, it then received a tax demand from the Inland Revenue for tax due on the profits derived from the non-primary purpose trading activity of providing advertising services! In this particular case the Revenue did not press their claim. However, in the light of this case and based on the principles outlined in this book, charities are recommended to put all forms of sponsorship income which are not pure gifts (i.e., those eligible for relief from VAT and paid under Gift Aid or Deeds of Covenant) through a separate non-charitable trading company unless the profits derived from the sponsorship (after allowing for all reasonable expenses) are small and fall within the rules of the de minimis exemption (see *Chapter 5*).

6.4. The sale of Christmas cards

Probably the most common form of trading by charities is the sale of Christmas cards. The scale of this activity varies from the sale of a few cards made by pupils of a school to the very high volume of cards sold on behalf of leading national charities.

First, it is important to note that for some charities (and only for some) the sale of Christmas cards can constitute primary purpose trading. The following are some examples. Where a museum, set up to educate the public, sells cards illustrated by pictures from its collection, it can be argued that the card is a form of educational material and its sale is in fulfilment of the charity's primary purpose. This would apply to the National Gallery, the Tate Gallery, etc. Or a charity may be established to educate the public in the work of local artists, and the sale of cards designed by such local artists would be in fulfilment of a primary purpose. Alternatively, a charity may sell cards which have been designed or made by beneficiaries of the charity - the cards might have been drawn by clients of an art therapy charity or pupils at a school.

The circumstances in which a sale of cards is a primary purpose activity are fairly limited. In most cases the sale of the cards will be undertaken to raise money for the charity. This is not primary purpose trading. In theory the sale of Christmas cards should then be handled by a separate non-charitable trading company. However, before a charity decides to organise itself in this way (and it must consider the matters raised in *Chapter 7*) it should first determine whether or not it makes any profit *at all* from the sale of the cards. It should attribute the proper costs of the sales, including a fair apportionment of overheads and staff time, against the profits. Once this has been done, it may find that there are no profits at all or else these are very small. If that is the case then it is probably not worth going to the expense and complexity of setting up a separate trading company, as the Inland Revenue operates in practice a de minimis approach to the taxation of profit (see *Chapter 5.4*).

If the true analysis of the profits arising from the sale of Christmas cards reveals that the charity is making a loss, the trustees should review the position carefully. It could be argued that selling Christmas cards at a loss is a breach of their duty as trustees to act in the best interests of the charity. Against this it might be argued (perfectly legitimately) that although the sale of cards is run at a loss, the intangible benefit of the publicity which the charity gains as a result more than outweighs the loss. In any event the trustees of the charity should monitor and review regularly any such loss-making sales.

If the sale of Christmas cards is generating profits (after the deduction of all properly-incurred expenses) which are above the de minimis level (see *Chapter 5.4*), then the charity should transfer the business of selling cards to a separate non-charitable trading company. How should such a transfer be arranged? A charity must always have an arms length relationship with its trading company (see *Chapter 7*). It should not give away its property, but should charge a fair price to the trading company for the stock and other assets transferred.

Christmas cards and the Charities Act 1993

As mentioned (see *Chapters 3.8* and *4.12*), Section 5 of the 1993 Act provides that a registered charity with a gross income in its last financial year of more than £5,000 must state the fact that it is a registered charity in English or Welsh in legible characters:

"(a) in all notices, advertisements and documents issued by or on behalf of the charity and soliciting money or other property for the benefit of the charity."

Does this requirement apply to cards sold on behalf of a charity? It all depends on who issues the card and what is printed on it. Consider the following examples:-

(a) The sale of a card by the XYZ Gallery, a charity, using a picture in the Gallery's collection, which states: *"Sold in aid of the XYZ Gallery"*. Is the card "a notice, advertisement" or "other document" issued "by or on behalf of the charity"?

A notice has a definite legal meaning which would not include a card. But although an "advertisement" has not apparently been defined at common law, various statutes give it a very wide meaning such as "every form of advertising" (London Cab Act 1968 and Consumer Credit Act 1974). Equally, "document" has been generously interpreted. "I should say that any written thing capable of being evidence is properly described as a document" (Darling J in *R -v- Daye* (1908) 2K333 at 340.Iin that case it was ruled that a sealed envelope was a document).

A few years ago a popular card in Japan showed Santa Claus - on the Cross. This mixture of Christian and pagan symbols in Great Britain might be claimed to be blasphemous, which could give rise to a prosecution at common law! Equally a card could be defamatory.

Hence a card could be produced in court as evidence and thus is a document and potentially subject to Section 5, Charities Act 1993.

But for Section 5 to apply the advertisement or document also has to "solicit money or other property". Does the phrase "sold in aid of" solicit money or other property for the benefit of the charity?

Bearing in mind that Section 5 (2) Charities Act 1993 states that this subsection has effect whether the solicitation is *express* or *implied*, it is the author's view that it *does*. People are encouraged to purchase the card by the statement that the card is sold *in aid* of the charity. The statement may well affect a consumer's decision which card to buy when faced with a choice between a "charity" card and a "commercial" card. The card solicits money for the charity. Thus, the card should comply with Section 5 and state the fact that XYZ charity is a registered charity.

(b) What if the card states "the XYZ Gallery" and nothing else?

Section 5 (3) Charities Act 1993 states that Section 5(2) applies "whether the solicitation is express or implied". Does the phrase "the XYZ Gallery" amount to an implied solicitation that the price of the card will be applied "for the benefit of the charity"? For the reasons set out above the fact that the charity's name appears on the card is an inducement to the purchaser to buy the card. Hence the author considers that this is an implied solicitation, and the card must comply with Section 5 and state "XYZ Gallery, a registered charity".

(c) Section 5 also applies to a trading company owned by a charity which sells cards which state "sold in aid of XYZ Charity". This is because since the card bears the charity's name it will be deemed to be issued "on behalf of the charity" (see Section 5(2)) and the analysis at paragraph (a) will apply.

The reader is also referred to the section on Commercial Participators in *Chapter 9*.

6.5. Catalogue sales

Mail order catalogues have become an important source of trading income for some charities. As with Christmas cards, in some cases the sale through a catalogue of various items may constitute primary purpose trading. Hence a museum might offer educational items based on its exhibits (such as maps, models, educational books, videos and charts) etc. In some cases a borderline may have to be drawn between those items which are clearly educational (such as books), and non-educational items (such as key-rings, tee-shirts, pens and pencils, fluffy toys, etc.). If both categories of item are sold, the charity will be undertaking *both* primary purpose trading and for-profit trading through the same catalogue! It may be possible for the charity to argue that it derives no or only very limited profits from the sale of the non-educational items, and so it does not need to set up a separate trading company (see *Chapter 5*). But if the profits from the sale of the non-educational lines are more than de minimis, it would be advisable to carry out this trade through a separate trading company.

In most cases a charity will find it hard to argue that the sale of goods through a catalogue constitutes primary purposes trading. A charity established for the relief of poverty which sells bought-in goods (even from less-developed countries) will *not* be able to argue that this constitutes primary purposes trading. In this case the sale of goods via the catalogue should be carried out through a separate trading company.

Many charities arrange their catalogue sales through arrangements with a specialist mail order distribution company, which buys in the goods and handles sales. In this case, the charity should ensure that the contract is between its trading company and the distributor. The charity should act very carefully in handling these arrangements. Some such catalogues blur the distinction between the charity, its trading company and the specialist distributor to the extent that a consumer may well (and quite reasonably) think that he or she is contracting with the charity. This can have serious implications in connection with the sale of goods. Say they are defective: does the purchaser have any recourse against the charity? Some catalogues contain a "guarantee" about refunds of goods or money, but the identity of the guarantor may be difficult to discern! In some cases the charity could be held to have given the guarantee, although in law a charity cannot underwrite the obligations of a commercial third party! This could result in a claim under the purported guarantee being successfully rebutted by the charity on technical legal grounds, unless the charity is a limited company.

A particular area of concern with such catalogue selling, whether organised by an independent specialist distributor or by the charity's trading company, is the status of donations to the charity which are paid at the same time as a purchase order for goods is placed. These donations are frequently paid on the same cheque as the payment for the goods. The cheque is then paid into the distributor's or trading company's bank account, mixed with its moneys and only subsequently paid to the charity. If the distributor or trading company goes into liquidation, the charity may never receive the outstanding donations due to it. They will have been swallowed up by the distributors' or trading company's need for immediate cash. This has happened on a number of occasions. To protect their donors' interest charities should as best practice insist that the catalogue stipulates that donations be made by means of a separate cheque or by credit card debit made to the charity directly, so as to ensure that the donations are not paid to the distributor. If this is impractical, as an alternative the charity could stipulate that all donations must be paid over to the charity each day or when donations reach a certain level, e.g., £100.

The same practice should be adopted even where the charity's own trading company runs the catalogue operation as the same problem could arise if the trading company were to be forced into receivership or liquidation (and this has also happened on a number of occasions).

6.6. Affinity cards

Many charities have entered into arrangements with banks and other financial institutions, whereby the financial institution issues a credit card which bears the name and/or logo of the charity. Such cards are known as **affinity cards**. Supporters of the charity are encouraged to take out such cards because a fee for every card issued plus a percentage of the total expenditure on the card is paid to the charity by the bank. The bank will be given access to the names and address of the charities' supporters/donors for the purposes of marketing the card. This is a joint promotional arrangement which benefits both parties.

Charities Act 1993

Once again issues arise under the Charities Act 1993 (see *Chapter 6.4*). Is an affinity card an "advertisement" for the purposes of Section 5?. The affinity card will bear the charity's name and logo. Section 5 applies to any advertisement issued "by or on behalf of the charity". It is considered that an affinity card could constitute an advertisement (see *Chapter 6.4*). It is issued by the bank and not by the charity, but nonetheless pursuant to an agreement with the charity. Hence it is reasonable to conclude that the card is issued "on behalf of" the charity. But does the card "solicit money ... for the benefit of the charity"? Under the usual arrangements the charity has a continuing financial interest in the use of the card. Each time the card holder uses it, the charity gets its cut. It would be different if the charity only received a one-off payment (as a fee for access to its list of supporters) before the promotion was begun.

A card holder may have more than one credit card. As the card holder flips through his or her wallet, he or she has a choice whether to use one of the cards, write a cheque or use cash. The charity's logo on the affinity card might induce him or her to use that card. Hence he or she would be solicited to use that card. Moreover Section 5(3) states that a solicitation can be express or implied. At the very least, the fact that the affinity card bears the charity's name or logo must amount to an implied solicitation, with the result that Section 5 must be considered as applying to an affinity card. This means that the words "a registered charity" must appear on the card, possibly on the back. The words do not have to be adjacent or close to the charity's name.

The actual licensing of the charity's name to the financial institution may be undertaken by the charity itself without fear of adverse tax consequences, provided the arrangement is properly structured (see below). However the charity should bear in mind the comments of the Charity Commissioners in their 1991 Report (see *Chapter 8*).

Affinity cards and charity law

The licensing by a charity of access to its database of members or supporters and the use of its name and logo on the credit card and promotional literature to a financial institution constitutes a form of for-profit trading. If the "badges of trade" are applied, it is clear there will be repetition (details of new members/supporters will almost certainly be supplied to the financial institution); there is a profit motive; there may be a selling organisation (the charity might establish a marketing department); and data is regularly sold in the commercial world. Moreover, the charity may undertake to market the affinity cards *directly* to its members. **Such activities will constitute for-profit trading and will not be primary purpose trading.** Therefore the charity should put these promotional activities through a separate trading company.

In setting up an affinity card scheme, a charity will need to ensure that *two* agreements are entered into: one between the financial institution and itself for licensing the use of its name; and the other between its trading company and the financial institution for the provision of promotional services.

Affinity cards and VAT

In May 1990, the Charities Tax Reform Group issued a press notice clarifying the position in relation to VAT and affinity cards:

"1. Customs are prepared to accept, however, that only that proportion of the income which is payment for the promotional services provided by the charity to the financial institutions concerned need be the consideration for these supplies. In effect, Customs are agreeing to a split between a payment for services (provision of mailing lists etc), which will be subject to VAT at the standard rate and additional contributions *for which the charity does nothing in return*. These additional contributions would then be outside the scope of the tax.

2. It has to be possible to distinguish between the additional contributions and the payments for services and the contract must

not link the additional payments with any promotional or other activity on the part of the charity. Customs would have no objection if the additional payments were arrived at through informal discussions, are mentioned in publicity for such schemes, or are set out in a legally binding agreement, providing they were divorced from anything which the charity was obliged to do.

3.   If a charity sets up, or uses an existing trading company whose role will be to supply mailing lists and offer other promotional benefits to the financial institution the payments for these services would be the consideration for a taxable supply. Charities may decide to use such a trading company to contract with the credit card issuer to provide the active promotional services, and to receive the additional payments in the charity. Although the use of a trading company provides an acceptable solution to the Revenue, and may indeed be highly desirable for direct tax reasons, Customs have said that, from their point of view, there is no necessity to use trading companies.

4.   Customs, like the Revenue, do not wish to pronounce on the exact price put on the promotional services supplied by the charity or trading company except to say they would require it to be realistic and reasonable. As a guide Customs have indicated that of the fixed sum paid to the charity for each credit card application, one fifth might be seen as consideration for promotional services and that all subsequent income might be outside the scope of the tax."

Thus for the purposes of VAT, there is no need to put the affinity card income through a trading company.

For VAT purposes, the payment by the financial institution to the charity for the use of the charity's name is treated as a *donation* for which the charity must do "nothing in return". This is somewhat strange. The very act by the charity of licensing its name in return for a payment is to give something (the use of its name) in return for the payment! Nonetheless Customs and Excise appear not to push this point.

Moreover, Customs and Excise have indicated that only 20% of the initial payment per card application will be attributable to promotional services, and none of the subsequent income - even though there may well be ongoing promotional activities!

Affinity cards and income and corporation tax

At the same time as Customs and Excise clarified the position on VAT, HM Inland Revenue stated:

"1.   The tax liability can be avoided by arranging for trading subsidiaries to carry out all chargeable activities. Given that some charities are unhappy about transferring the rights in their names and logos to subsidiaries - and because of potential VAT liabilities - it was proposed that the contracts be re-negotiated with the card issuers to create two separate agreements as follows:

(i) One agreement between the card issuer and trading subsidiary for exploitation of mailing lists and the provision of assistance in promotional work etc;

(ii) The other agreement between the card issuer and the charity for exploitation of the charity's name and logo.

2. The Revenue have given their broad approval to the treatment of income arising under contract 2 as Schedule D Case III Royalty income in the hands of charities. This is on the basis that the royalties will be paid under a legal obligation, will be annually recurring and will be pure income profit.

3. The Revenue have pointed out that the first two requirements pose little difficulty but have said that care must be taken to comply with the criteria for pure income profit. In essence the contracts in point 2 must be isolated from any other agreements for the provision of services and the charities must not assume any reciprocal obligations which might deprive payments of the nature of pure income. The inclusion in the contract of a clause which specifies that the charity must not enter into any arrangement with other financial institutions would not breach this rule. Neither would the Revenue object to a clause which provided for the charity approving all literature which bore its name and logo.

4. The Revenue have not been keen to express an opinion on the precise allocation of income between the two revised agreements except to say that it must be realistic. They feel that this will inevitably depend on the level of activity agreed to by the individual charities."

Schedule D Case III deals with annual payments which are paid under an obligation by virtue of any contract "whether the same is received and payable half-yearly or at any shorter or more distant period" (Section 18(3) Income and Corporation Taxes Act 1988):

"In order to qualify as an annual payment a payment must primarily be a transfer of income from the payer to the payee and therefore be taxed in the hands of the payee. Thus the following do not qualify as annual payments:-

(a) A trade receipt;

(b) A payment which is of a kind against which the expenses of earning it may properly be set so as to calculate the net taxable income;

(c) A payment for goods or services;

(d) A subscription to a club or similar body which provides benefits".

(Simon's Taxes Volume B at para 5.304)

A payment to a charity for use of its name or logo is not treated by the Revenue as trading income, although surely if a charity was carrying on an extensive business of licensing its name and logo to a wide variety of commercial users, this would then constitute a trade. And if it did any income would be treated as a trading receipt or alternatively as a payment for services and therefore taxable. But in the context of affinity cards the Revenue accepts that payments made to a charity for use of its name and logo are annual payments even though there is no transfer of income from payer to payee which is usually a fundamental feature of an annual payment.

It is worth mentioning that in a court case involving the commercial exploitation of the rights in the famous 1950's children's character Noddy *(Noddy Subsidiary Rights Co Limited v(1966) 3 A11ER 459 Ch D)*, it was held that income from such activities *was* trading. This is in marked contrast to the ruling of the Inland Revenue concerning affinity cards. In this instance, the Revenue has not treated the fruits of the exploitation of a logo by a charity as a trading receipt.

The beauty for charities of this arrangement is that under Section 505(1)(c)(iii) of the Taxes Act 1988, an annual payment is received by a charity effectively *free of tax.* Although the payer has to deduct income tax at the standard rate when making the payment and has to pay the tax to the Revenue, the charity can reclaim the tax deducted just as with a Deed of Covenant.

The "Noddy" case illustrates the point that if a charity builds up an extensive activity of licensing its name, the profits so derived may not be treated as pure income profit but as trading income (and therefore potentially taxable). The inter-relationship between this and the controls on commercial participators contained in Part II of the Charities Act 1992 (see *Chapter 9*) needs to be carefully monitored. These controls require that all agreements concerning the use of a charity's name with a commercial partner must be between the charity and the partner. But if a charity develops an extensive business of licensing out its name and logo, then the ruling in the "Noddy" case could mean that the charity might be treated as carrying on a business of licensing its name. Consequently, the annual payment exemption would not apply. Thus in order to structure the arrangements in the most tax-efficient manner the charity would need to establish a trading company to carry on the licensing business. But this could conflict with the requirements of Part II of the Charities Act 1992, which requires that an agreement with a charity's commercial partner is made by the charity and *not* its trading company. Charities which are engaged in a number of license agreements should take appropriate professional advice on these matters.

6.7. Bars

Many charities with public facilities, such as theatres or museums, operate bars. If the bar is only used by persons attending the museum or theatre and is not open to the general public, the Inland Revenue treat any profits from the bar as having been generated in the course of the actual carrying out of a primary purpose of the charity. From the point of view of charity law the Charity Commissioners will regard this as ancillary trading within the scope of the charity's objects (see *Chapter 5*).

If, on the other hand, the bar is open to the general public, the charity will fall within the scope of the decision in *Grove -v- YMCA* (see *Chapter 4.2*) and any profits will be taxed unless the de minimis point applies (see *Chapter 5*). Moreover it would be a breach of charity law for the charity to operate such a bar. Hence, for reasons of both tax and charity law a bar open to the public should be operated by a separate trading company.

Community associations have a procedure for licensing the bar to a member's club which covenants the profits to the community association; precedents for the appropriate club rules, licence and covenant are available from Community Matters of 89 Upper Street, London NI 0PQ (telephone 071 226 0189).

6.8. Exploitation of under-used assets

Some charities have assets which they do not utilise to the full in fulfilment of their charitable purposes. School facilities stand empty during holidays; a Women's Institute hall may be used only once a week by the Women's Institute; a historic building may be the perfect venue for a "dream function". Clearly the charity trustees' primary duty is to utilise the charity's assets to fulfil its primary purposes. Charity trustees are bound to use such due diligence and care in the management of the charity's assets as men and women of ordinary prudence and vigilance would use in the management of their own affairs.

This means that trustees should consider, if they cannot fully use the charity's assets to fulfil its purposes, whether or not they should exploit *commercially* the charity's under-used assets so as to generate more income which could be applied in fulfilling the charity's objects or in meeting the charity's costs. In deciding to utilise the charity's assets in this way, the trustees must be sensitive to the charity's reputation and not do anything which could damage it (e.g., by a religious charity hiring out a building for the recording of a pornographic film). They should also consider whether the need to generate additional income is distorting their judgement as to whether the assets could be further used for the charity's charitable purposes. It may be more difficult and even require additional fund-raising, but if the charity's assets can possibly be used for the charity's charitable purposes, the trustees should strive to see that they are.

What are the legal consequences if trustees do decide to exploit such surplus assets by, e.g., renting them out to non-charitable organisations or to charities with different objectives from their own?

It should be emphasised that if charity A owns a hall and allows Charity B to use it, and Charity A and B share common objectives then Charity A need not charge a full commercial rate (or indeed anything at all) for the use of the hall. In allowing Charity B to use the hall, Charity A will, albeit indirectly, be fulfilling its own objectives. If A and B have some overlapping objects then again A could allow B to use the hall free of charge or at a reduced rate *provided* that B's use of the premises was solely in accordance with those parts of its objects shared with A.

What is the position if a charity hires out its buildings for one-off use (for example by the day, half day or evening) for commercial rather than charitable reasons? Will income derived from such activities be treated as rent or as trading income? Rents and profits from the exploitation of "lands, tenements, heriditaments or heritages belonging to a hospital, public school or almshouse or vested in trustees for charitable purposes, so far as the same are applied to charitable purposes only" are exempt from taxation under Section 505(1)(a) Taxes Act 1988. Although "rents" are not defined in the Taxes Act, it is considered that it means payments reserved by a landlord on the grant of a lease. A day's hiring fee is not a rent.

This point is illustrated by *Coman -v- Governors of the Rotunda Hospital, Dublin* (1921) AC1. The Governors of the Hospital let out certain rooms for entertainments for periods varying from one night to six months at charges which included the use of heating and seating, and applied the profits from the lettings to the support of the hospital. The House of Lords ruled that the hospital was carrying on a trade and the profits derived from that trade were taxable and not within any of the exemptions from income tax.

Profits derived from the commercial exploitation of under-used assets are potentially taxable, if the profits are neither "rent" nor derived from primary purposes trading. Any charity which is considering commercial exploitation of its assets must consider whether or not it is making a profit from the activity (see *Chapter 5.4*). It should attribute a proper proportion of overheads and expenses against the income derived from the exploitation of its surplus assets. It may be that when this is done there will be no taxable profits.

For example, an Oxford College might hire out the college for non-educational courses (e.g., an "Inspector Morse Murder Weekend"). Can the college charge a fair and reasonable proportion of its overheads against the income derived from that activity, including items such as maintenance of the grounds and upkeep of the fabric of the building which it would incur in any event? Or can it only charge against those profits the marginal costs of running the commercial weekend event (the costs of staff, meals, heat, light, etc.)?

To try to answer these questions, the Inland Revenue conducted an enquiry into the trading activities of five universities in 1992 and considered, in particular, the question of vacation lettings.

The Revenue concluded that in most cases the vacation lettings of universities do not amount to trade because the activity was not being conducted on a truely commercial basis and none of the sample universities had yet made any taxable profits from vacation lettings. The Revenue further advised that unless a university is recovering at least 75% of the direct and *attributable* costs of vacation lettings, it will not regard such activity as conducted on a commercial basis and as trade.

◆ ◆ *example*

UNIVERSITY OF RUTLAND

Income from vacation lettings		**£20,000**
Cost of lettings		
Direct costs attributable to activity	£10.000	
Indirect costs attributable (9% of gardening, maintenance & central services)	£20,000	**£30,000**
Loss on lettings (after expenses)		**£10,000**

The University only recovered 66% of the direct and attributable costs, and hence there was no tax liability.

The 75% rule is somewhat strange. Why not 100%? The answer is probably that the Revenue was under pressure to come up with a solution satisfactory to all parties at a time when the universities' income from exploitation was increasing and where it was public (government) policy to encourage such exploitation.

If the activity does show a profit after deducting 75% of all attributable expenses and offsetting other losses, then the resulting profits will be taxable. In these circumstances the charity should establish a separate trading company (if it does not already have one) to act as its agent for exploiting the surplus assets. The trading company should pay a fee to the charity in return for the grant of this right, as the charity cannot give away its assets nor can it give the right to exploit them to a non-charity for nothing (even where that body is its own wholly-owned trading subsidiary).

That fee should be structured as an annual payment and should represent a proper fee for use of the assets (see *Chapter 6.6*). The fee will attract VAT if it brings the charity above the VAT registration limit unless the charity and the trading company are part of the same VAT Group (see *Chapter 7*).

An interesting and topical example of a charity exploiting an asset for commercial purposes involved All Saint's Church at Harborough Magna (1992) WLR 1235.

In this case the church had to go to a local Consistory Court for consent to put two aerials and a communications dish on the tower of a church and appropriate power and radio units in the church porch. The court gave its consent and laid down useful guidelines as to how the licence by the church to the communications company should be structured, and in particular it dealt with the need to bar the use of certain telephone numbers which could be used for pornographic purposes.

This case vividly illustrates the point that in exploiting surplus assets charities should *not* hire them out for activities which are inimical to the charity's own purposes. Moreover, trustees should always examine first how they might use such surplus assets to fulfil the charity's own primary purposes *before* deciding whether to exploit them for commercial purposes; and if they do, any commercial exploitation must be consistent with the charity's own purposes.

6.9.   Research

Considerable concern has arisen recently concerning research undertaken by education and research charities funded by non-charitable sponsors and partners. The Charity Commission is considering guidance notes on this subject.

The particular problems facing research charities impinge on primary purposes trading, charitable status and the relationship with a trading company.

A charity established to carry out educational research is under a duty to publish or make available the useful results of that research.

But when should the research be published or made available? It seems that it should be made *available* with reasonable promptness, but that charities do not have to *publish* the results of their work. They merely have to make them available to any interested party who wishes to inspect those results. The charity should make the public broadly aware of what results have been produced and the information which has resulted from the research.

Moreover charities do not have to make the results of their research available free of charge, provided the charge is reasonable and does not effectively debar public access to the fruits of the research. Such charging would be a form of primary purpose trading.

More difficult questions arise when the research has led to the charity possessing information which may be exploited commercially. For example, it has developed a new drug. Can a charity delay publication of the results of research whilst it patents its discovery? The answer appears to be that the Charity Commission will sanction such a delay so as to allow a charity to protect its intellectual property rights - even though possession of the patent will give the charity a legal monopoly which might, at first glance, seem to clash with the notion of a charity being established for the public benefit.

Research if carried out by a school or university or institute is exempt from VAT, and is also exempt if not carried out by a school or university or institute, but is of a type undertaken by a school and or university otherwise than for profit. As a charity is banned from distributing its profits to its members, it will provide such research "otherwise than for profit" (see *Chapter 4*). But can a charity carry out "bespoke" research where it is commissioned to do the work by a private company? Will not the preponderance of benefit be private rather than public? Whether or not a charity can enter into a contract to supply bespoke research will depend on the terms of the contract. If the sponsor is unwilling to commit itself either to reasonably prompt patenting or publication through other means (conventionally through academic journals), the charity should *not* enter into the contract, as there will be insufficient public benefit. However, its trading company may be able to do so.

It may seem strange that reasonably prompt patenting of an invention by a sponsor might constitute sufficient evidence of "public benefit". However, the Charity Commission justifies this view on the basis that many useful inventions are "killed" by commercial organisations as they may threaten the commercial success of other products. The everlasting lightbulb is a good example. By patenting an invention the owner of the invention is making public the invention, albeit that no one else can use that expression or form of the invention without the consent of the patent owner (see *Chapter 8*). But that will not stop another invention seeking to achieve the same result albeit by a different method or someone seeking to obtain a licence from the patent owner to exploit the patent.

If most of the fruits of the commissioned research were to be utilised privately by the sponsor and no patent application was made, the charity could still enter into the contract provided that the contract gave the charity the right to publish the results of the research in an academic journal. It appears that the charity may be justified in agreeing to a period of up to a year (but more usually six months) from the conclusion of the research in which it would not publish the results so as to allow the sponsor a lead time to exploit the research, either by commencing a patent application or by making commercial use of the research.

When contemplating whether a charity should undertake commissioned research, trustees need to bear in mind at all times their duties to ensure the survival of the charity and to maximise the public benefit through pursuit of the charity's charitable purposes. They also need to preserve the academic health of the charity by ensuring that research undertaken preserves and enhances the charity's reputation and that particular programmes and specialists benefit, rather than being purely seen as a means of raising money.

Notwithstanding the obligations on charities to act in the public interest, trustees are free to reach such arrangements concerning the exploitation of intellectual property rights as best serve the charity's purposes according to the particular circumstances. This means that charities may negotiate shared ownership of intellectual property rights or royalty arrangements, or the granting of all rights to exploitation to the sponsor in return for the sponsorship and the right to publish in academic journals.

In certain circumstances, it may be necessary for a charity to carry out research activities through a separate trading company. For example, many contracts with government agencies (for example in the area of defence) stipulate that there can be no publication whatsoever of the research so as to preserve secrecy. Such a stipulation is inimical to a charity, established as it is for public benefit. A commercial sponsor may insist on granting only very limited and delayed publication rights. Again, a charity should not accede to such a demand although its trading company could. In deciding to pass a prospective contract to its own trading company, a charity will need to bear the following points in mind:

(a) **It should not transfer any intellectual property rights free of charge to the trading company** - the trustees have a duty to get the best price for the charity's assets. The trustees should ensure that the trading company pays a proper price. This could be by way of a capital sum - in practice highly unlikely as the company is unlikely to have any free capital allowing it to fund such a payment. Alternatively (and more likely), it could be by way of a *royalty* - structured as an annual payment.

(b) **The trading company should pay a proper charge for use of the charity's assets.**

(c) **The trustees should be very cautious in allocating contracts to the trading company**, lest the whole balance of the charity is not undermined by excessive use of the charity's assets for non-charitable purposes, even though the charity benefits from a flow of income from the trading company.

6.10. Conclusion

If a charity faces any of the issues raised in this chapter it may need to consider establishing a separate trading company to undertake that activity. But each case must be dealt with in accordance with its particular facts, and it is advised that appropriate professional advice be taken.

Chapter 7
ESTABLISHING A TRADING COMPANY

This chapter covers all aspects of setting up and running a trading company including: why and when to establish a trading company, providing it with operating funds, the relationship between a charity and a trading company, and the role of the charity's trustees, and separate companies established for fund-raising.

7.1. When should a charity establish a trading company?

In chapters 4 and 6, we showed that a charity can only carry on trade directly provided certain conditions are fulfilled. These relate to whether the trading activity is a permitted activity in the context of the organisation's charitable status. There are also practical considerations such as liability to taxation on any profits earned, VAT and considerations of risk.

A charity has to consider first whether it can carry on the trade directly. *Chapter 6* shows the many areas where it can be difficult to define precisely whether an activity is permitted or not. Where it is not permitted, the charity ought to consider the consequences of trading unlawfully. The mechanism that has been developed for charity trading is to use a separately constituted and usually wholly owned trading company, which remits any profit from the trading back to the charity.

The second consideration is whether it would be more advantageous to organise the trading through a trading company in order to save tax or protect the charity's assets from risk.

Establishing a trading company is a complicated and expensive process. Before rushing to this solution, a charity should answer the following questions:

- Is the trading activity in fulfilment of a primary purpose of the charity?

Or if not:

- Is it ancillary to a primary purpose (see *Chapter 5*) ?
- Does the Extra Statutory Concession apply (see *Chapter 5*) ?

Or if not:

- Are there any taxable profits (after making proper allowance for all charges, etc.) ? Or

- Is the trade (even if ancillary) exposing the charity to risk?

If the trade is neither primary purpose nor ancillary *and* if there are taxable profits, then the charity should consider establishing a separate non-charitable trading company to undertake those trading activities.

If the trade involves *risk* the charity may wish to consider isolating the risk of that particular activity within a separate company, even where the trade itself is primary purpose or ancillary. This is a perfectly reasonable strategy. Many commercial organisations spread risk by having a large number of separate subsidiary companies each undertaking a different activity. If one business fails, this will not jeopardise the financial position of the whole group (unless guarantees have been given).

A charity may also consider establishing a trading company as a VAT saving scheme (e.g. to set up a design and build company when undertaking construction of a new building).

The Charity Commission and Inland Revenue both recognise and approve the establishment of separate for-profit trading companies. For example, in Paragraph 10 of their 1980 Report the Charity Commissioners commented

"Where a charity wishes to benefit substantially from permanent trading for the purpose of fund-raising we advise that it does so through a separate non-charitable trading company, so that its charitable status is not endangered. Such a trading company is usually wholly owned by the associated charity but is sometimes owned jointly by several charities. The questions which arise are (a) whether the charity's investment powers permit such an investment, and (b) whether a trading venture of this sort is too speculative for a charity. The share capital of such a company is usually small, perhaps £100, and the difficulties of forming the trading company may sometimes be overcome by the trustees themselves, or some well-wishers, putting up the money. If the owners of the shares in the company subsequently wish to give them to the charity, there is no reason why the charity should not retain them, provided that they are fully paid shares and any liability attached to them is limited. The trading company is not a charity and is not within our jurisdiction".

Thus the establishment of a trading company is perfectly legitimate provided that the charity has the necessary investment powers (see *Chapter 7.6*).

In this book, we use the term "trading company" and not "trading subsidiary". Any company owned by any charity (however constituted, whether as a trust or company limited by guarantee or a company with share capital) can be called a trading company whereas a trading subsidiary is, in law, a company owned by another company. Thus only a charity which is established as a limited company (such as Oxfam or Action Aid) can have a trading subsidiary. If the charity is not established as a company, then the trading company it owns cannot be referred to as a subsidiary. Hence all trading subsidiaries are trading companies but not all trading companies are trading subsidiaries.

7.2. How to form a trading company

A trading company can be established in two ways. A new company can be formed by filing the Memorandum and Articles of Association (see *Chapter 7.4*) and all the necessary ancillary documents with the Registrar of Companies in Cardiff (or Edinburgh) and paying a registration fee of £20. Alternatively, a clean new company ("never traded guv") can be purchased from specialist company formation agents (as listed in Yellow Pages) for about £250. This will come under an improbable name such as "Datepalm Limited" but it is a simple matter to change a company's name (although it will cost £20 to register the name change at Companies House). It may also be necessary to change the main objects clause (see *Chapter 7.4*).

However the company is formed, it is wise to take professional advice. Company law is complex and it is easy to make a mistake. Fines for breaking company law can be high - for example the maximum fine for filing accounts up to 12 months late is £1,000. It is worth paying some money initially to get the structure right and to have the structure you need.

7.3. What is a trading company?

A trading company will normally be established as a *company limited by shares*.

Some 20,000 charities are constituted as *companies limited by guarantee*, and many people in the voluntary sector are accustomed to operating such companies. A charity might therefore be tempted to stick with the devil it knows and establish its trading company as a company limited by guarantee. That would not be prudent, but to understand why it is necessary to understand the nature of a company limited by shares.

A company limited by shares has what is called "a share capital". For example a company may have a share capital of £100 divided into £100 shares of £1. Each £1 share gives the owner of that share a stake in the company's wealth. If 100 shares are issued the holder of one share owns 1% of the company's wealth. By owning a share a shareholder "shares" in the wealth of the company with the other shareholders - hence the term.

The shareholder has to purchase the right to share in the company's wealth; he or she receives this entitlement in return for investing money in the company. The ability to issue shares is a very useful method of financing a company. The shareholder gets a return through sharing in the profits of the company by receiving dividends. Dividends will be paid out when the company has profits available to distribute. If the company is running at a loss or has accumulated losses, the shareholders will get nothing. From the company's point of view, to issue shares is a cheap source of finance. In contrast, if it borrows money, it will normally have to pay interest on the loan from the start, and these interest charges will continue until the loan has been repaid. The company will commit itself to the interest payments and loan repayments regardless of profitability. By contrast, shares are rarely repaid - they can be only if the company issues redeemable shares or resolves to buy back its own shares

The position is different with a company limited by guarantee. It can only borrow money. It cannot issue shares. Hence one of the possible methods of financing a trading company - issuing shares - is lost if a company limited by guarantee is used.

The Constitution of a trading company will have two parts - a Memorandum of Association and Articles of Association.

7.4. Memorandum of Association

The memorandum of Association sets out what the company can do.

The objects clause

Under Section 3A of the Companies Act 1986, a company can have general trading objects such as:

"(a) The object of the company is to carry on any trade or business whatsoever; and

(b) The company has power to do all such things as are incidental or conducive to the carrying on of any trade or business by it"

It is also sensible to include a statement such as:

"The company is established to procure profits and gains for the purpose of paying the same to the charity called .... (registered charity no................)"

in order to show the close relationship between the charity and the trading company.

To amend the main objects clause requires a Special Resolution passed by 75% of the members (i.e. the shareholders) of the company present and voting at a meeting for which 21 clear days notice has been given.

Alternatively consent to hold the meeting without full notice can be given in writing by 90% of the shareholders (by value).

The capital clause

The Memorandum of Association will also contain the capital clause stating the authorised or nominal share capital. Companies usually start off with an authorised share capital of £100. The authorised share capital does not mean that £100 worth of shares have been issued: it merely means the company has the *capacity* to issue those shares. If the company wishes to increase the authorised share capital, it has to pass an Ordinary Resolution, which must be passed by a simple majority of the members present and voting at a meeting for which 14 clear days notice has been given - unless consent to short notice has been obtained.

Types of shares

A company limited by shares can issue a number of different types of shares if the Memorandum and Articles of Association give it the capacity to do so. If they do not, its constitution can be changed by a Special Resolution (see above), to empower the company to issue other types of share. The principle type of shares are:

Preference shares

As the name implies, preference shares carry some preferential rights over ordinary shares. They are designed to get around some of the risks attached to ordinary shares. The principal features are as follows:-

(a) **Type of dividend**: Preference shares are usually described as for example, 8% preference shares. This means that for each £1 invested, a dividend of 8% per annum is due. Hence the dividend is fixed, rather like an interest rate. However, unlike a loan, the dividend on preference shares will only be paid where there are profits available for distribution.

(b) **Preferential dividend**: The dividends on preference shares are paid before the dividends on ordinary shares. If there are accumulated arrears of the preferential dividends, those too must be paid off prior to paying a dividend on the ordinary shares.

(c) **Preferential rights in a winding-up**: If a limited company is wound up, the ordinary shareholders will get paid out last (if there is any surplus after paying off the creditors). The preference shares are paid off before the ordinary shares, but after the confusingly-named preferential (e.g., Inland Revenue), secured and general creditors.

There is little point in a charity investing in its trading company by way of preference shares.

Redeemable preference shares

These are normal preference shares but with the additional feature that the company has to redeem the shares at a stated date, say after ten years. A trading company could issue redeemable preference shares to a charity, but it should be borne in mind that if this is done, the money for the redemption of the shares will have to come from company profits. This will mean that the trading company will have to retain profits and pay corporation tax on them in order to build up a fund to redeem the shares. This conflicts with the policy of many trading companies of paying 100% of the taxable profits of the trading company to the charity (see *Chapter 10*).

Ordinary shares

These are by far the most common form of shares. Ordinary shares (except in complicated share structures) give the holder of each share one vote per share (whereas a preference shareholder normally only has a vote if the dividends are in arrears). Hence, the ordinary shareholders control the affairs of the company. For a charity's trading company, all ordinary shares will normally be issued to the parent charity (in the case of a corporate charity), or held by the trustees on the charity's behalf, (in the case of an unincorporated charity).

Dividends

It is normal for a conventional commercial company to reward its ordinary shareholders by paying dividends, when there are profits available for distribution. However, in the case of a trading company owned by a charity, it is normal for the profits to be paid to the charity either by way of Gift Aid or under Deed of Covenant (see *Chapter 10*).

Company law used to require that a company had a minimum of two members or shareholders, and the protection of limited liability was lost after the company had less than two members or shareholders for more than 6 months. Hence, a company owned by a charity would have, say, ninety-nine shares registered in the name of the charity and one in the name of a nominee - usually the chairman of the charity - who would agree in a simple document to exercise his rights as a shareholder in accordance with the charity's instructions. Such an arrangement is no longer necessary. The Companies (Single Members Private Limited Companies) Regulations 1992 allow for a company to be established with one member/shareholder - hence a charity's trading company can be established with the charity as the sole shareholder.

Name

The Memorandum of Association states the trading company's name. It is worth pausing for thought, before giving the trading company a name which includes the charity's name in its title (which is the normal practice), and consider first the *purpose* of establishing the trading company. If the trading company is seen as (hopefully) a permanent contributor to the charity's funds working alongside it, then it may well be appropriate for it to *share* the charity's name. But it may be that the particular activities of the trading company can be built up and after a few years the charity may be able to cash in its investment by selling the trading company to a commercial purchaser. At that point, the name and goodwill of the trading company may be too intimately connected with the charity's name to be disentangled. Allowing a third party organisation to own a company which includes the charity's name in its title could bring the reputation of the charity into disrepute or at very least cause public confusion.

An example of this is the charity Beauty Without Cruelty. The charity set up a cosmetics firm with the same name in 1963, but sold it in 1980. By 1993 public confusion about the purpose of the two organisations - which still had identical names - forced the charity to review its name. This could be a very expensive business - the launch of "a new corporate image" for some major charities has cost over £200,000! Hence trustees would be well advised, if they consider there is a chance that the trading company might be sold off, to give it a name which does not incorporate the charity's name.

Another problem occurs if the trading company intends to undertake high-risk activities which could lead to it becoming insolvent. Here it would be advisable to give the trading company a name which did not include the charity's, so as to lessen the damage to the charity's reputation if the trading company were to fail.

7.5. Articles of Association

The Articles of Association set out the rules for the running of the company. Most companies use standard Articles based on a model contained, in a statutory instrument issued pursuant to the Companies Act 1986 called the Companies (Tables A to F) Regulations 1986. This model has served its function well, having been used (albeit amended from time to time) since 1862. For a charity establishing a trading company the following points need to be considered:-

(a) **What is the authorised share capital?**
(see *Chapter 7.4*: both the Memorandum and the Articles of Association refer to the authorised share capital)

(b) **What is the share structure?**
Will the company issue preference shares, redeemable shares or ordinary shares?

(c) **How are the directors to be appointed?**
Do one third have to retire by rotation each year and submit themselves to re-election? Does the charity want to have a provision put into the Articles that it may dismiss any person from serving as a director by giving written notice to that effect? This would give the charity far greater control over the directors of the trading company than under company law. The Companies Act 1986 does provide a mechanism for the dismissal of a director, but it is a somewhat protracted process requiring a meeting for which 28 days notice has to be given.

7.6. Investment by a charity in a trading company

Before a charity can decide to invest any money in a trading company, whether by purchasing shares or by loan, the charity must check that it has the necessary constitutional capacity to do so. Many charities have been established with very limited powers of investment, which confine them to the investments sanctioned by the Trustee Investments Act 1961, as amended by an order which came into force on 22nd August 1994. The thrust of the order is to allow charities to make certain investments in the "relevant states" which are European Union and European Economic area countries.

If a charity's investment powers are limited by the 1961 Act, trustees can only invest in authorised investments (50% narrower range, 50% wider range) as specified in the First Schedule to the Act viz:-

(a) **Part I narrower range of investments not requiring advice.**
These are restricted to:

(i) Defence bonds; national savings certificates and bonds and Ulster saving certificates and development bonds;

(ii) Deposits in the National Savings Bank.

(b) **Part II narrower range of investments requiring advice.** These are set out in Part II of the Schedule and are mainly gilt-edged and other fixed interest securities in the UK and the relevant states. Part II also includes authorised gilt-edged unit trusts and mortgages on freehold property or leasehold property in England or Wales or Northern Ireland, having an unexpired term of 60 years at the time of investment.

(c) **Part III wider range of investments.** These are set out in Part III of the Schedule and include securities issued in the UK, or a relevant state, by a company incorporated in the UK, or a relevant state, and quoted on a recognised investment exchange within the meaning of the Financial Services Act 1986, and with a paid-up share capital of at least the currency equivalent of £1 million, which has paid a dividend in each of the five previous years, shares in a building society (UK), units of an authorised unit trust scheme within the meaning of the Financial Services Act 1986, and units of a European Union Common Investment Trust (EUCITs), which are sold across Europe.

As can be seen, the powers of investments under the Trustee Investment Act do not extend to allowing investment in a private company (such as a trading company). The powers of investment available to the trustees in the trust instrument may be wider than those available under the Trustee Investments Act, and may permit an investment in a private company. If there are no wider investment powers, the charity's Constitution may contain a power to amend its administrative provisions, which may be used to widen the investment powers. If the trust instrument contains *no* power to amend the constitution, then it will be necessary to obtain consent of the Charity Commission by a scheme to extend the powers of investment. The Commission confirmed in their 1985 Report that they will consider such applications.

The Charity Commissioner's 1980 Report stated that, there are, in particular, two factors which charity trustees must consider when setting up a trading company:

(a) Whether the charity's investment powers permit such an investment; and

(b) Whether a trading venture of this sort is too speculative for a charity.

As the 1980 Report makes clear, if a charity does not have sufficiently wide investment powers to invest in the private company and the charity does not extend those investment powers either by amending its constitution or by a scheme of the Charity Commission, it can still obtain such shares if a well-wisher or supporter establishes the trading company and donates the shares (fully paid) to the charity. However, this means that the trading company will only have a limited paid-up share capital and the charity will not be able subsequently to purchase further shares in it to increase its capital base or lend it money by way of loan.

7.7. Trustees' duties when investing

Trustees must exercise the duty of care required of trustees when making investments as follows:-

Diversification

S.6(1) of the Trustee Investment Act 1961 provides:-

" In the exercise of his powers of investment a trustee shall have regard:-

(i)   to the need for diversification of investments of the trusts, in so far as is appropriate to the circumstances of the trust;

(ii) to the suitability to the trust of investments of the description of the investment proposed and of the investment proposed as an investment of that description."

This duty applies to all trustees including charity trustees and to any exercise of the power of investment - it does not just apply to investments made in the categories stipulated in the 1961 Act.

Not to take risks

In addition to this statutory duty, case law imposes a general duty of care on all trustees including charity trustees. The first requirement is that a trustee should avoid investments of a hazardous or speculative nature.

In Re. *Whiteley (1886) 33 Ch D 347* at page 355 Lindley L.J., confirming the earlier decision of *Speight v. Gaunt (1883) 22 Ch D 727,* which required a trustee to act as an ordinary prudent man of business when considering investments, stated:

"Care must be taken not to lose sight of the fact that the business of the trustee.....is the business of investing money for the benefit of persons who are to enjoy it at some future time, and not for the sole benefit of the person entitled to the present income. The duty of a trustee is not to take such care only as a prudent man would take if he had only himself to consider; the duty rather is to take such care as an ordinary prudent man would take if he were minded to make an investment for the benefit of other people for whom he felt morally bound to provide."

On appeal to the House of Lords *(Learoyd v. Whiteley (1887) 12 App Cases 72)* Lord Watson added on page 733:

"Businessmen of ordinary prudence may, and frequently do, select investments which are more or less of a speculative character; but it is the duty of the trustee to confine himself to the powers of investment which are permitted by the trust, and likewise to avoid all investments of that class which are attended with hazard."

It follows from this that even where the trust instrument confers the investment powers of an absolute beneficial owner, not all investments which an individual would be at liberty to make will be open to trustees. In *Bartlett v. Barclays Bank Trust Company Limited (1980) 1 A11ER 139,* the trustees had such a power, but Brightman J. took the view that they were personally liable for hazarding money in a private company which engaged in a building development project and which turned out to be a "white elephant". Brightman J. said of the project:

"The Old Bailey project was a gamble because it involved buying into the site at prices in excess of the investment value of the properties, with no certainty or probability, with no more than a chance, that planning permission could be obtained for a financially viable redevelopment, that the numerous proprietors would agree to sell out or to join in the scheme, that finance would be available on acceptable terms, and that the development would be completed, or at least become a marketable asset, before the time came to start winding-up the trust. However one looks at it, the project was a hazardous speculation on which no trustee could properly have ventured without explicit authority in the trust instrument. I therefore hold that the entire expenditure in the Old Bailey project would have been incurred in breach of the trust."

In this case the trustees had to reimburse the trust for the loss it suffered as a result of their actions.

Hence, if charity trustees are considering investing in a trading company, they must act in accordance with the duties imposed upon them both by the general law and the particular constitutional restraints of their charity.

Non-financial considerations

One other relevant factor for some charity trustees in considering an investment in a trading company is the fact that the trading company itself may be undertaking activities which compliment those of the charity. For example, Oxfam Activities Limited is a trading company owned by Oxfam. It sells many products which have been manufactured in developing countries and hence are complimentary to Oxfam's own charitable activities in seeking to relieve poverty in such countries. Equally, a charitable theatre will need a bar to offer sustenance to its customers but may improve its financial viability by opening the bar to the general public. Such a bar will need to be run by a separate trading company in line with the decision in *Grove v. YMCA* (see *Chapter 4.2*). But the bar will enhance the theatre even if it is not a great financial success. Can the trustees take such non-financial considerations into account when investing? In the case of the theatre bar the question is easily answered. If the bar enhances the theatre so more tickets are sold, then even if the bar is not a great financial success in its own right, the enhanced revenue of the charity (via ticket sales) will justify the trustees' decision.

The example of the sale of goods from the developing world may pose more difficult questions. Suppose a trading company owned by a charity established to relieve poverty in developing countries pursues a deliberate policy of purchasing goods from manufacturers who pay proper wages and do not exploit child labour. This could well mean that the trading company paid more for its stock than if it had purchased them from "sweat shops". This in turn could mean that the trading company was financially more vulnerable, as it might trade on narrower profit margins than it would do if it bought "sweated" goods. Are the trustees of the charity entitled to invest in the trading company given that its humane buying policy make it more financially hazardous? In other words, can the trustees take *ethical* questions into consideration when investing?

In their 1987 Report the Charity Commissioners accepted that the concept of ethical investment will in some circumstances be relevant to charity funds. In paragraphs 43 to 45 of that Report, the Commissioners stated:-

Paragraph 43: "We agreed that unlike a private trust the purpose of which is solely to generate funds for its beneficiaries a charity has a public purpose and object. Consequently, whilst the normal duty of charity trustees in exercising their investment powers is to provide the greatest financial benefits for present and future beneficiaries, financial return is not in all cases the sole consideration which the trustee should bear in mind. Charity trustees should not invest in companies pursuing activities which are directly contrary to the purposes or trusts of their charity and they should have the discretion to decline to invest in companies pursuing activities which are inimical to its purposes. It would, for example, be entirely appropriate for the trustees of cancer relief charities to decline to invest in tobacco companies, for the trustees of charities of the Society of Friends to decline to invest in the arms industry and for trustees of temperance charities to decline to invest in breweries."

Paragraph 44: "We thought that it should be possible to determine with reasonable activity whether an investment should be directly contrary, or inimical, to a charity's trust or purposes. We envisaged considerable difficulty however if investment policy were to be placed on more subjective criteria such as that an investment would "undermine" or "be inconsistent with" a charity's purposes. In such cases, because the criteria would be so much a matter of professional opinion, trustees' own moral or political views could dictate investment policy in place of an objective assessment. This could leave a charity open to manipulation for political or ethical reasons unconnected with its purposes. This was not to say however that where there was strong and definitive evidence that the supporters might be alienated with a resulting substantial fall in donations, trustees should not take cognizance of the fact."

Paragraph 45: "We also took the cognizance of the fact, also recognised in *Cowan v. Scargill,* that although charity trustees were under a duty to seek the best investments for their charity, it was open to trustees, given the vast range of investment opportunities available, to select some investments in place of others and that the selection could not be effectively challenged provided that the choice was not detrimental to the charity and was based upon sound investment considerations and not preconceived social and political programmes."

In 1991, the Bishop of Oxford sought declarations from the Court in relation to the investment policy of the Church Commissioners. The Court's decision offers guidance on the question of an ethical investment policy by charity trustees and was summarised in the Charity Commissioners' 1991 Report. The Commissioners noted that the key criteria are:

(a) "Any decision by charity trustees to exclude from consideration a particular range of investments must be centred on the beneficiaries of the charity rather than on the trustees. The trustees should not use powers of investments for the purpose of giving expression to their views on moral or political questions. If trustees decide to exclude a particular range of investments from their consideration, they should do so only on the basis of consideration of the interest of the charity's beneficiaries;"

(b) "Generally the purposes of a charity are best served by the trustees seeking to obtain the best economic return (consistent with commercial prudence) from the exercise of investment powers; this objective is not, usually, consistent with the exclusion from consideration of investments which would be within the powers of the trustees to select;"

(c) "If trustees are satisfied that a particular range of investments would directly impede the effective furtherance of the objects of the charity, then they can properly exclude that range of investments from consideration. Such action was justified even if it involved, in terms only of investment, a financial risk. The impediment might take the form of a loss of financial support from subscribers, or of an adverse reaction from beneficiaries to an operation which was financed in a manner considered to involve a denial of the charity's objects;"

(d) "The greater the risk of financial detriment the clearer the evidence that is required of the impediment to the furtherance of the charity's objects......"

In the light of these quotations it is fair to conclude that trustees may, in considering a proposed investment, take ethical issues into account provided that the decision to invest is sound. In the "sweat shop" case it could be argued that for Oxfam to invest in a trading company which purchased goods produced in sweat shops would be analogous to the trustees of charities of the Society of Friends investing in the armaments industry.

However, that is not an end to the issue. The Commissioner's guidelines address the question of trustees *excluding* certain types of investment (in other words a *negative* approach) rather than justifying a *positive*, if higher risk investment, such as in the case of the trading company which has lower profit margins because it pursues an ethical policy of dealing only with suppliers with good labour relations. The trustees can argue (perfectly rightly) that it would be detrimental to the charity's reputation for it to support a sweat shop - but it is more difficult to justify the high risk investment in the low margin business. Such an investment might cause problems with the Charity Commission were they to investigate.

The decision to invest

How do trustees decide to invest in practice? Like any prudent businessman who is contemplating an investment the trustees must request that they be provided with sufficiently detailed information to allow them to make a sound and proper decision. Such information may well include:

(a) Market research (unless it is a question of the charity hiving off to a separate trading company a business which it has already built up);

(b) A proposed budget showing projected capital and on-going expenditure and income;

(c) A cash flow forecast for at least 2 years;

(d) A business plan, showing how it is proposed to develop and market the business;

(e) An analysis of working capital requirements.

The trustees should consider this information carefully and in detail, mindful of their duty to act in accordance with their various obligations listed above. The minutes of the trustees' meeting should record the terms of any resolution to invest in a trading company and should refer to the documents which the trustees have reviewed in reaching their decision. Those documents should be annexed to the minutes, so that if the trustees' decision to invest is ever challenged, evidence will be available to justify the trustees' action. The wording of the resolution should be carefully drawn up - it should not commit the charity to an open ended commitment to finance the trading company and should address the duties imposed on the trustees by Section 6 (1) of the Trustee Investments Act 1961 mentioned above. It is advisable to consider taking advice from a suitably qualified professional adviser.

It is important that such evidence is available. The Charity Commissioners have begun a number of enquiries into the relationship between charities and their trading companies. In the past a number of charities have written off large loans to trading companies without comment from the Charity Commissioners and the Inland Revenue. But the Commissioners are now taking a much more active stance and are less willing to turn a Nelsonian blind eye.

♦♦ *example*

The Commissioners considered demanding that the trustees of a charity which had to write off a £250,000 loan to a trading company should repay the moneys so lost out of their own pockets.

This example illustrates the point that the consequence of a breach by the trustees of their duty to invest prudently is that they can be made personally liable for any loss suffered by the charity. If this is the case, the protections of limited liability (if the charity is a limited liability company, industrial and provident society or corporation established by Royal Charter) are of no avail. The veil of incorporation is lifted and the trustees can be made personally liable for any loss that the charity has suffered as a result of their breach of trust.

Paragraph 52 of the Charity Commissioners' Report for 1990 mentions "an investment of substantial sums of charity money in a trading company connected with the deceased founder of the charity. The investment had been largely lost as a result of substantial trading losses in the company. The case, which was referred to the Attorney General, was subsequently settled by a substantial payment by the trustees to the charity in restitution. Further payment by way of a contribution to costs is being made and an undertaking by the trustees to discharge personally all tax liabilities resulting from the use of tax relieved income or gains in relation to the improper investments has been given."

Although this did not involve a loan to a trading company, it illustrates the principle that trustees can incur personal liabilities through acting negligently when making an investment.

7.8. How to invest: loans by the charity

Once the trustees have decided that they will sanction an investment in a trading company, the next issue to be resolved is to how that investment is to be structured.

It is normal practice for the charity's investment to take the form of a loan. The Charity Commissioners said in paragraph 11 of their 1980 Report:

"The trading company normally covenants to pay all or a major part of its profits to the charity or charities in proportion to their shareholdings, thus gaining exemption from corporation tax on the amount covenanted. Where such a trading company pays over the whole of its net profits it will need to borrow funds from time to time. But the trading company is not an arm or subsidiary of the charity and funds needed to sustain or expand the activities of the trading company should normally be borrowed from commercial sources. However, if it is proposed that such funds should be provided by the associated charity, we can consider this is only permissible if the loan can be regarded as a reasonable investment and if a proper market rate of interest is charged; and the charity's powers of investments are sufficiently wide to sanction such an investment. Even where charities do have wide powers of investment, they should not make loans to prop up unprofitable concerns and they have a duty to pay proper regard to the suitability of the investment proposed in the interests of the charity."

This statement does contain an error - many trading companies *are* subsidiaries of charities - (see *Chapter 7.1*), but that mistake does not detract from the authority of this statement on the question of investments.

The Charity Commissioners returned to this topic in their 1988 Report where they commented at paragraph 44

".....Normally funds needed to sustain or expand the activities of an associated trading company should be borrowed from commercial sources."

This statement needs to be evaluated in the light of the particular facts of the proposed investment - if a trading company has a good track record or prospects (based on realistic appraisals), it may well be sensible for the charity to lend money for working capital so as to keep the interest paid within the charity rather than have it paid away to a commercial lender. If the interest is paid to the charity, this will increase the return on the investment. Indeed if a bank would lend on the proposal it should be a good one, thus allowing the trustees to claim it would be reasonable for the charity to lend the money!

Moreover most banks will not lend money to a start-up company unless adequate security is given - they will not regard (in many cases) a charge over the trading company's assets as adequate security and demand a guarantee from the charity (see *Chapter 7.10*).

In their 1980 Report (paragraph 11), the Charity Commissioners recommended that if the charity lends money to the trading company it should:

(a) **Charge a proper rate of interest;**

(b) **Take security for the loan;**

(c) **Lay down terms for repayment of the loan.**

Taking these in turn:

A proper rate of interest

Some charities (in breach of the Charity Commission guidelines) make interest-free loans to their trading companies but then receive the profits under a covenant. It could be argued that the sums covenanted are not "pure income profit" in the hands of the charity, but a payment in lieu of interest forgone. The Inland Revenue could argue that the covenanted payment falls outside the definition of "a covenanted payment to charity" contained in Section 660(3) Income and Corporation Taxes Act 1988 which states:

"a payment made under a covenant *otherwise than for consideration in money or moneys worth* in favour of a body of persons or trust established for charitable purposes only."

Thus, if a charity makes an interest free loan to its trading company it runs the risk that tax deducted by the trading company, on sums paid under a Deed of Covenant to the charity will not be recoverable on the basis that the Inland Revenue will claim that the payment by the trading company under the covenant to the charity is, in reality, in return for the loan.

So far as the covenanted profits of the trading company are concerned, it does not matter if the charity charges interest. It merely means that the charity receives the money from the trading company in two forms, as interest and the reduced taxable profits (if any) under the deed of covenant.

What is "a proper rate of interest"? When considering making a loan to a trading company, the trustees should weigh up a number of factors:-

(a) **Risk:** commercial lenders charge higher rates of interest to riskier customers and charity trustees should bear this in mind;

(b) **Rate:** what rate could the trustees obtain by depositing surplus cash with a conventional commercial borrower? Say the normal deposit rate was 2% below a bank's Base Rate but the charity charged the trading company 2% over a bank's Base Rate, the charity would be receiving a 4% greater yield on its cash deposits which could justify a decision by the trustees' to make a loan to the trading company - given that a simple 4% yield on investments is regarded by fund managers as acceptable in current market conditions (in 1994).

NB. It should be noted that the interest should be *physically paid* by drawing a cheque on the trading company's bank account and clearing it through the charity's bank account.

◆◆ *example*

MINSHAM PROPERTIES LTD V. PRICE (INSPECTOR OF TAXES) 1990 STC 718.

This case involved the administration of a loan of £270,000 by a charity to its wholly owned trading company. A loan account was opened in the books of each company; a charge for interest was periodically entered in the account. The subsidiary claimed relief from corporation tax in respect of the interest charges. In order to qualify for relief the interest must have been paid out of the company's profits. It was held that the periodic journal entries, in which the interest charges were credited to the charity's account and debited to the subsidiary's account did not amount to evidence that the interest had been paid. The entries merely amounted to evidence that the interest had not been paid. Thus the relief from corporation tax was not available.

The Charity Commissioners could allege that operating in this manner, whereby corporation tax relief was lost with the result that the charity re-ceived less money from the trading company, amounted to a breach of trust by the trustees for which the trustees could be made personally liable - see paragraph 44 of the Charity Commissioners Report for 1988 quoted in *Chapter 6.1* above.

If the loan stipulates interest is payable and is not recovered, the Commissioners may step in. In one case, noted in paragraph 53 of the Charity Commissioner's Report for 1990, a charity had lent moneys to three non-charitable associated trading companies. The Charity Commissioners noted:

"We have been able to secure a repayment of £139,711 to the charity which represents unpaid interest on these loans."

Security for a loan

The Charity Commissioners require that the trading company executes a charge or mortgage in favour of the charity to secure the loan. The charge will be over all the trading company's assets - thus, it should be a fixed charge over any land, buildings, plant, machinery, intellectual property rights, etc., and a floating charge over stock and other items which change in the course of trade. This is, of course, subject to the assumption that no charge has been given to any other party (e.g. a bank).

The reason for taking a charge is that if the trading company should be unable to pay its debts, the charity will be able to appoint a Receiver who will sell the items subject to the charge and pay the proceeds of sale to the charity thus cutting out the other creditors, (other than preferential creditors in the case of a floating charge). By having a charge the charity will have priority over the assets of the company in the event of a liquidation of the trading company.

However, this security may be more apparent than real, as in many cases the assets of a trading company may amount to very little, other than some unsold stock (e.g. last year's Christmas cards) and debts due.

This is because the trading company will pay over all its taxable profits each year to the charity, hence having no retained earnings with which to purchase fixed assets, plant or machinery or to build up reserves (see *Chapter 10*).

Repayment of the loan

The repayment of loans made by charities to trading companies is fraught with difficulties. The Charity Commissioners (perfectly reasonably) demand that when a loan is sanctioned the trustees should stipulate repayment terms. Usually the loan is repayable on demand but repayment is rarely demanded.

The problem with the repayment of a loan is that it comes out of taxable profits. The payment of interest is a tax-deductible item for the purposes of calculating taxable profits which will be subject to Corporation Tax, but the repayment of the capital element of a loan is not.

◆◆ *example*

XYZ Trading Limited borrows £50,000 from XYZ Charity @ 10% per annum interest.

Trading company's taxable profits after all deductions (other than interest)	£45,000
Less interest	£ 5,000
Taxable Profit	£40,000
Corporation Tax @ 25%	£10,000
Payment to XYZ Charity under covenant	£30,000

But XYZ Trading Limited covenants all its taxable profits to XYZ charity. Hence it pays away all £40,000 to XYZ Charity and the Inland Revenue. It has no retained profits from which it could repay the loan.

If it retained some of the profits in order to be able to repay the loan, it would pay Corporation Tax on that part of the profits it retained. But for so long as it is locked into a 100% Deed of Covenant, it cannot retain any profits. Thus the loan remains outstanding. The only way in which the trading company will be able to repay the loan will be to await the end of the Deed of Covenant and then give a lesser proportion of profits either by Covenant or Gift Aid to XYZ Charity and retain the balance. It will pay Corporation Tax on the retained profits. From the retained cash net of tax, it could begin to repay the loan (whether in whole or in part).

Can these problems be avoided if the loan to the trading company is repaid within the trading company's financial year so that the loan is not on the books of the trading company at its year end?

◆◆ *example*

XYZ Trading Limited borrows £20,000 from XYZ Charity on 1st January 1993

It repays it on 30th October 1993

Its financial year end is 31st December 1993

Its taxable profits are £100,000

It covenants 100% of its taxable profits to XYZ Charity

The receipt of the loan will appear as a form of income in the profit and loss account whilst the repayment of the loan should appear as one of the items of expenditure in the profit and loss account or alternatively as an extraordinary item.

The repayment of the loan will not reduce the taxable profits. But the repayment is relevant to cash-flow. Having repaid the loan, will XYZ Trading Limited have sufficient cash to honour the obligation under the deed of covenant to pay 100% of its taxable profits to XYZ Charity? It will have to find £120,000 in cash by 31 December to repay the loan and pay over 100% of its taxable profits (£100,000 + £200,000). In reality it may not be able to do this. This subject is dealt with further in *Chapter 10.6*.

Some charities are also believed to engage in more questionable behaviour. As indicated above the Charity Commission monitors (and in the future will probably monitor more carefully) loans made to trading companies. In order to disguise this, some charities apparently do the following:

◆◆ *example*

XYZ Charity lends £100,000 to XYZ Trading Limited on 1st January 1993 (the first day of its financial year).

On 30th December 1993 XYZ Trading Limited borrows £100,000 from its bankers. It repays £100,000 to XYZ Charity.

On 31st December 1993 (the financial year end of the charity and the trading company) their balance sheets will show:-

XYZ Charity:
loans to XYZ Trading Limited: NIL

XYZ Trading Limited:
Creditors: sum due to Bank: £100,000

Then on 1st January XYZ Charity lends £100,000 to XYZ Trading Limited, which repays the bank! Hence for 363 days of the year the charity is financing the trading company but the year end accounts do not show this. In the case of unincorporated charities, prior to the implementation of Section 43 of the Charities Act 1993, there has been no obligation to have *audited* accounts unless there was an express obligation contained in the charity's constitution. Hence this type of arrangement, which would require a note in the audited accounts of a limited company, often escaped notice in the case of unincorporated charities. In the case of a charity which had to have its accounts audited (either because its constitution so stipulated or because of company law), it was much more likely that this type of arrangement would be picked up and an appropriate note made to the accounts to draw attention to this post-balance sheet event.

Once Section 43 of the Charities Act 1993 comes into effect, unincorporated charities will be in the same position.

Qualifying Expenditure and loans

Before making a loan to a trading company, charity trustees also have to consider whether or not the loan constitutes *qualifying expenditure* for the purposes of Section 505(3) Taxes Act 1988. That Section, together with Section 506, contains curbs on charities which have tax-free income of over £10,000 in a 12 month period. If such a charity incurs *"non-qualifying expenditure"* the charity will lose tax relief (and hence pay tax) on the amount of its income and gains which equals its non-qualifying expenditure in that period.

◆◆ *example*

XYZ Charity has tax-free income and gains of £1,000,000 in year ended 31st December 1993

Its qualifying expenditure is £800,000

Its non qualifying expenditure is £100,000

It retains £100,000 of its tax-free income

The charity will pay tax at the appropriate rate (corporation tax if it is a company or an unincorporated association or income tax if it is a trust) on £100,000 (the amount of its non-qualifying expenditure). Hence at corporation tax rates it would pay £25,000 tax.

Qualifying expenditure means expenditure incurred for charitable purposes only. (Section 506(1) Taxes Act 1988). *Non-qualifying expenditure* means expenditure which is not qualifying expenditure, for example, money spent on a party political campaign or on a non-qualifying loan.

Section 506(4) Taxes Act 1988, states that if a charity makes a loan which is not *a qualifying loan* then the amount so lent shall be treated as *non-qualifying expenditure*, with the adverse tax consequences mentioned above. What is a *qualifying loan?*' Paragraph 10 Schedule 20 Taxes Act 1988 defines it as:

(a) A loan made to another charity for charitable purposes only; or

(b) A loan to a beneficiary of a charity which is made in the course of carrying out the purposes of the charity; or

(c) Money placed on current account with an institution authorised under the Banking Act 1987; or

(d) Any other loan as to which the Board of the Inland Revenue are satisfied on a claim made to them in that behalf, that the loan is made for the benefit of the charity and not for the avoidance of tax.

A loan by the charity to its trading company will not fall within paras (a), (b) or (c). Can such a loan come within (d)? At first glance it would seen unlikely. After all the very purpose of the charity making the loan is to provide working capital to the trading company which will allow it to generate taxable profits which will be covenanted to the charity, thus avoiding tax! In practice the Revenue does not appear to apply this argument. In many cases it has agreed that a loan by a charity to its trading company is a qualifying loan. Although there is no mechanism for seeking prior approval of loans from the Inland Revenue, the Revenue will give an opinion if asked.

Moreover in IR75 *"Tax Relief for Charities"*, the prime example of "qualifying expenditure" is the expenditure of a charity setting up a subsidiary company to carry on a trade for fund-raising purposes. Nonetheless paragraph 43 of the Charity Commissioners 1988 Report states:

"Arrangements whether strictly contractual or not, which involve a trading company associated with a charity paying over to the charity (usually with the assistance of a very short term loan from the bank) a greater proportion of its profits than it can commercially afford may be viewed by the Inland Revenue as an artificial attempt to secure a tax advantage. This is particularly the case where, in order to maximise the tax relief obtainable, payments are made on the basis that the charity will immediately make a payment back to the company by way of reinvestment of an appropriate amount to finance its stock of working capital and debtors etc. As such there are several bases on which the tax effectiveness of the arrangements might be challenged. Attention is however particularly drawn to the provisions of Section 506 and Schedule 20, paragraph 9(1) of the Income and Corporation Taxes Act 1988 under which an investment made for the purpose of the avoidance of tax by a charity (some improper element of private benefit is not necessary) may be treated as non-qualifying."

7.9. How to invest: shares purchased by the charity

If a charity has the appropriate investment powers it may consider purchasing shares in the trading company rather than making a loan. The trustees should bear in mind the following, when considering such a proposed investment:

(a) **As a private company there is no market for the shares.**

They are not quoted on any Stock Exchange. Hence the charity's moneys are locked in. The charity will only be able to realise its investment if it sells all its shares in the company in a private sale, or if the company is able to build up sufficient reserves to buy back the charity's shares. Buying back the shares is highly unlikely, as the only way in which a company can buy back shares is to have available profits retained in the company. As retained profits are taxed, the company will probably want to covenant 100% of its profits over to the charity hence leaving the trading company without any retained profits from which it could buy back the charity's shares.

(b) **Shareholders are paid out last on a liquidation of a company.** If a charity takes a charge to secure a loan it will gain priority in the payment of debts in a liquidation (see *Chapter 7.8*). But as a shareholder the charity will be paid out last, after the preferential creditors, and after the secured and the unsecured creditors. The chances of the charity recovering its money in an insolvent liquidation will be very small.

(c) **It is therefore sensible for trustees to consider making a loan to the trading company in accordance with the Charity Commission's guidelines when financing a start-up.** When the risk is at its greatest in the early years, the charity thereby stands a better chance of getting its money back in the event of failure. The loan will appear as a liability on the trading company's balance sheet. Once the trading company has built up a track record and, hopefully, paid money to the charity by way of Gift Aid or covenanted donation, the trustees can consider converting the loan into shares in the trading company. They must consider any such proposal in accordance with their investment duties outlined in *Chapter 7.7*. If they decide to do so, this will strengthen the trading company's balance sheet. Creditors will be reduced by an amount equal to the loan and will be matched by an increase in shareholders' funds. The charity's balance sheet will no longer show the trading company as a debtor; instead its investments will have increased. The trading company's strengthened balance sheet and the fact that the charge in favour of the charity will have been removed (as the loan which the charge secured will have been converted into shares) will mean that the trading company may be able to borrow money from a commercial source, hence diversifying the financing of the trading company and removing some of the charity's risk. There will be a price to be paid; namely the interest that will be paid to the bank which had hitherto gone to the charity.

(d) **A trading company does not need to be owned one hundred per cent by the charity.** Although this is the normal practice, it does not need to be the case. Some charities have established joint ventures with commercial partners whereby the ownership of the trading company is shared. This can have considerable potential advantages:

   (i) The risk of the trading activity is spread between the charity and the commercial partner;

   (ii) The commercial partner should be chosen for the expertise and skills it has which should enhance the potential success of the company - the trading company should benefit from management, marketing and financial skills.

On the other hand the charity should be aware of:-

(i) The risk of associating its name with that of a commercial partner. The name and reputation of a charity are its most precious assets and they could easily be damaged if the partner is criticised. Charities should bear in mind the complex tentacles of modern business life. The UK company with which the charity has an agreement may have a subsidiary or associate which operates under less scrupulous standards of management. The activities of that company, if publicised, could rebound to the detriment of the charity. A charity needs to be very cautious about entering into an agreement with a commercial partner. This point is examined in further detail in *Chapter 8.3*.

(ii) The possible advantage of operating the joint venture under a name which does not include the charity's - both to address the point raised in (i) and the question of the goodwill of the trading company (see *Chapter 7.4*). In the case of a joint venture there may well be provision for the purchase of the charity's interest in the trading company after an agreed period which could result in the commercial partner owning a company which included the charity's name, unless this point is addressed from the start.

If a charity is thinking of establishing a joint venture, it should take proper professional advice to ensure that there is an adequate agreement regulating such matters as:

• Minimum financial commitments by both parties;

• The composition of the board of directors;

• Share capital structure;

• non-competition;

• The price of services and/or management charges rendered to the joint venture by the partners;

- Licences of intellectual property rights;

- Share transfers and valuations and termination.

This is a short list of the main factors to consider and is not comprehensive. Similar points will apply if two or more charities decide to co-operate and set up a jointly owned trading company.

7.10. Loans from commercial sources

It has already been noted that in their 1988 Report the Charity Commissioners commented that funds needed to sustain or expand an associated trading company should be borrowed from commercial sources. However, this statement begs a number of questions.

Firstly, it assumes that a trading company will be able to borrow from a commercial source. Many trading companies may only need a relatively small amount of money (e.g. £100,000), and it is well known that it is harder to borrow a small sum than a big one. Expensive overdraft finance may be the only possibility. In evaluating whether or not to lend money commercial lenders will look (just as the Charity Commissioners recommend a charity) for:-

(a) A proper rate of interest which can be met by the borrower;

(b) Reasonable certainty that the borrower will repay the loan.

(c) Security.

Clearly the trading company must be able to pay a proper rate of interest. But so far as repayment of the capital is concerned, this will require the trading company to retain profits (which will be taxed) in order to give it enough cash to repay the borrowing. This requirement may well contradict the terms of a Deed of Covenant given by the trading company to the charity whereby all or a substantial proportion of the trading company's taxable profits are covenanted back to the charity. If a trading company is locked into such a Deed of Covenant, say for three more years, this may well make it impossible for the company to borrow moneys from a commercial source. And in this context it should be born in mind that paragraph 44 of the 1988 Charity Commissioners' report states:

" ..... Trustees have a duty to consider the tax effectiveness of the arrangements between them and any associated trading company and may be personally liable to account for taxation liabilities which are unnecessarily incurred directly or indirectly as the result of the inefficient administration of the charity. It makes no difference that the liabilities may arise from the disqualification of the investment made by the charity, but from the disallowance to the associated trading company of corporation tax relief."

Consequently, there is an inherent contradiction in the Charity Commissioners 1988 Report. On the one hand it demands trustees minimise the impact of taxation - which means covenanting all taxable profits to the charity (at the time of this report, Gift Aid had not been introduced although it can now be used - see *Chapter 10*).

But if a charity enters into a covenant, it will not be able to abide by the Commission's other recommendation, namely to borrow from commercial sources as it will not be able to repay the loan!

In addition security for a loan from a commercial lender could be a major problem. As indicated above (see *Chapter 7.8*), the assets of a trading company are often very few and insufficient adequately to secure a charge in favour of the lender. In such circumstances the lender may request that the charity give it a guarantee in respect of the trading company's borrowings. This is absolutely standard practice in the commercial world, where holding companies give guarantees in respect of the borrowings of subsidiary companies. This guarantee might, in turn, be backed up by a charge over the holding company's assets. Unfortunately it is outside a charity's powers to do this. A charity *does not have the legal capacity* to guarantee the debts of a non-charitable organisation.

◆◆ *example*

ROSEMARY SIMMONS MEMORIAL HOUSING ASSOCIATED LIMITED V. UNITED DOMINION TRUST LIMITED (1986) WLR 1440.

The plaintiff was an incorporated charitable Housing Association. Its rules stated that it objects were the provision of housing for the needy and aged and that it was empowered to borrow and "to do all things necessary for the fulfilment of its objects". So as to carry out a housing development in pursuance of its objects, the plaintiff Housing Association negotiated with United Dominion Trust ("UDT") for a loan by UDT to R Limited a company which was to carry out the project on behalf of the Housing Association. R Limited was not a subsidiary of the Housing Association and was not a charity. The Housing Association guaranteed to UDT to pay on demand all moneys due to UDT from R Limited and backed this up by charging certain land to UDT.

The Court ruled that the Housing Association did not have the legal capacity to give a gratuitous guarantee in respect of the liabilities of a non-charitable body with which it was not associated in any legal sense, notwithstanding that the purpose of the transaction was to promote the Housing Association's objects.

Hence both the guarantee and charge given by the Housing Association were void and could not be enforced by UDT.

Note that in this case the judge did say "had R been a subsidiary of the plaintiff the situation might have been different" (at page 1446)

It is submitted that despite this statement it would have made no difference if R had been a subsidiary of the charitable Housing Association. It could still not have given a gratuitous guarantee in respect of the debts of a commercial company, particularly given that normally a trading company is not established to promote the charity's objects. (as was the case with R).

Given the emphasise on gratuitous guarantees in the *Rosemary Simmons Memorial Housing Association* case, there might be grounds for arguing that a charity with sufficiently wide investment powers could give a guarantee *in return for* a fee e.g 3% per annum of the amount guaranteed. The fee payable by the trading company would mean that the charity was making its assets work twice - both in connection with its normal activities *and* through charging the guarantee fee. But the fee payable would have to be calculated at a reasonable level so as to be justifiable as a prudent investment by the trustees. If not, if the guarantee was called and the charity paid up under it, the trustees could find themselves criticised for breach of their duty as trustees and exposed to the risk of being held personally liable for the loss suffered by the charity in honouring the guarantee.

A charity may also be asked to give a comfort letter to a lender who is advancing money to the charity's trading company - such a comfort letter may or may not be legally enforceable - it all depends on the wording. Such a letter might mention that the charity is aware of the trading company's borrowings and that the charity would not wish to see it go into liquidation.

If it is legally enforceable, then it constitutes a guarantee with all the implications analysed above. If it is not legally enforceable it may still cause the charity considerable moral difficulties. The practice was criticised in paragraph 9.35 of the Charity Commissioner's Report on *The Royal British Legion:*

"A letter of comfort is what it says. It is a document which whilst it does not bind the writer legally gives to the recipient the assurance that a third party has the backing and support of the writer. There is no doubt that without such a letter Legion Leasehold Housing Association would have found it difficult to borrow from financial institutions. It also has the effect of confusing the boundary between the charity and its non-charitable associates."

Paragraph 2.5 of the Report recommended:

"That the Board of Commissioners consider as a matter of policy whether it is appropriate for a charity to issue a letter of comfort on behalf of a non-charitable associated organisation to a bank or other institution and so lend its name to that organisation's financial credibility."

7.11. VAT and VAT groups

A charity may wish to set up a "VAT Group" with its trading company. This has the great advantage that all transactions (e.g. management charges) within the VAT group are VAT-free. Only bodies corporate are eligible to be treated as members of a VAT group. Hence an unincorporated association or trust with a trading company cannot be members of the same VAT group as they are not bodies corporate. For these purposes a body corporate includes limited or unlimited companies (whether limited by shares or guarantee), Industrial and Provident Societies and bodies incorporated by Royal Charter.

The big problem for charities with VAT groups is that all members of the VAT group are jointly and severally liable for any tax due from the representative member (Section 43(1) Value Added Tax Act 1994). The representative member is one of the members of the VAT group who is so named on the application for VAT group status. Any business carried on by a member of the group shall be treated as carried on by the representative member. Hence if the trading company is the "representative member" the trading company will be jointly and severally liable for any VAT due from the charity to Customs & Excise. If on the other hand the charity is the representative member it will be liable for all VAT due from the members of the group. And if the representative member fails to pay the VAT due each other member of the VAT Group is liable for the VAT owed by the members of the Group. This is perfectly normal for a commercial group of companies. But in the case of a charity, the VAT Group Registration confronts the problems of guarantees set out at *Chapter 7.1* Nonetheless the Charity Commission takes the view that given the substantial benefits charities may gain by opting for a VAT group registration it is perfectly proper for them to take on the joint and several liabilities laid down by Section 43 of the Value Added Tax Act 1994.

7.12. The role of charity trustees in relation to trading companies

When a charity establishes a trading company, it needs to resolve the precise relationship between the two entities. It may be simplistic to reiterate that the trading company has a different purpose from the charity (i.e. to carry out for-profit trading). But it is worth using that as the test for determining the structure of the management of the trading company. The trading company's board will require persons with some different skills and backgrounds from the charity trustees.

It is not advisable to have all the trustees serving as directors of the trading company. It would be sensible to have two or three trustees only (including perhaps the chairman and treasurer). The rest of the directors of the trading company should be drawn from the management of that company plus perhaps a non-executive director (if thought appropriate) with particular relevant expertise. It is not necessary for the Chief Executive of the charity to serve as a director of the trading company. It should also be born in mind that trustees of the charity cannot be paid for serving as directors of the trading company. This is based on the fundamental provision of trust law that a trustee should not benefit from his/her trust, which is linked to the notion that trustees must avoid conflicts of interest.

As paragraph 28 of the Charity Commissioners Report for 1988 states:

" ..... Their (i.e. rules against trustees benefiting) application is not confined to the circumstances where remuneration has been drawn directly from the funds of the charity for services as a trustee or employee of the charity. They also apply where the remuneration has been drawn from the assets of a trading company over which a charity has, through its shareholding, a total or substantial measure of control."

Those trustees who serve as directors of an associated trading company should not usually find that their duty (when acting as trustee) to act in the best interests of the charity will conflict with their duty to act in the best interests of the trading company (when acting as a director). However, such persons can find themselves faced with difficult choices and conflicts particularly if the trading company is undergoing financial difficulties.

◆◆ *example*

A charity's trading company is experiencing cash flow difficulties. It has insufficient cash to meet its obligations and there is in consequence concern over its financial viability. The Inland Revenue and Customs & Excise are both owed considerable sums and are pressing for payment. The Board of the trading company requests the charity to lend it a sufficient sum to pay off the pressing creditors and give it some working capital.

The directors of the trading company will be concerned, from their own personal point of view that the charity backs the trading company. If the charity does not, it will be clear the company is insolvent as it cannot pay its debts as they fall due. This means the company will have to be placed in insolvent liquidation, which raises the possibility that aggrieved creditors might petition the liquidator of the trading company to initiate wrongful trading proceedings against the directors of the insolvent trading company (see *Chapter 13*). If a court held that any of the directors had been guilty of wrongful trading, it can order that the directors concerned should make a contribution from their personal assets towards paying the creditors of the insolvent company. Hence the directors of the trading company will have a direct financial interest in seeing that the charity gives financial support to the trading company, although this may not be in the best interests of the charity. Thus their personal wishes may conflict with their duties as trustees. In such circumstances trustees who play such a dual role should be advised to declare their interest at any trustees' meeting in any proposal for the charity to give financial support to the trading company. They should not vote on any such proposal.

This illustrates why it is advisable not to have all the trustees serving as directors of the trading company, since if they do, it will not be possible for independent trustees to consider such a request for financial support to the trading company in such circumstances.

7.13. The relationship between charity and trading company

Charities must bear in mind at all times that trading companies are separate legal entities distinct from the charity, and the relationship between the two organisations should be at arms length. This means in practice that there should be no subsidy whatsoever by the charity of the trading company for use of shared facilities, equipment or staff, etc. The charity should ensure that it recovers the proper costs of any of its assets used by the trading company, and this should include not only direct costs (e.g. staff salaries), but indirect costs as well (e.g. a proper attribution of overheads). The charity should render this charge to the trading company on a regular basis. This may well demand sophisticated apportionments of employees' time (where an employee works for both organisations) and of overheads (probably based on a square footage basis) and for use of equipment (e.g. monitoring how much each organisation uses the photocopier). The management charge should not be so structured as to result in the charity making a profit. This is because if it were to make a profit as a result of supplying equipment, staff, etc., this profit would potentially be taxable, since it would not have been generated by primary purposes trading. Providing a management service to a commercial company cannot be a primary purpose of a charity. This may seem strange to anyone used to the commercial sector who will be accustomed to the practice of holding companies (especially in transnational groups) making management charges to subsidiaries designed to strip out profits. But the position is very different with charities.

In addition, it may be necessary to charge VAT on the management charge. This will depend upon the level of VATable turnover of the charity, whether or not it is registered for VAT and whether or not the charity and the trading company are members of the same VAT group. There can be circumstances in which charging a management fee plus VAT is beneficial to the charity. It is not always fully appreciated that the irrecoverable element of VAT may decrease proportionally as VATable supplies increase. Some charities can consequently benefit by trying to increase their VATable outputs. By charging VAT on management charges, a charity may indirectly increase the amount of input VAT it can recover. This can be an advantage of not putting the charity and the trading company into the same VAT group. Naturally, the trading company should be able to recover all the input VAT on the management charge. Whether or not this is appropriate will depend upon the particular circumstances of individual charities.

The necessity of keeping the charity and trading company at arms length means that the following points should be borne in mind at all times:

(a) The charity and trading company must have separate bank accounts. Some accountants, based on normal commercial practice, recommend that the charity and the trading company have one unified bank account - this is a complete breach of charity law. Charity funds should be kept distinct from non-charity monies in separate bank accounts in the respective names of the charity and trading company. If the trading company receives money on behalf of the charity (e.g. donations given at the same time as purchases are made through a catalogue), the money should be paid over to the charity immediately. This is on the basis that the suggestion made in the section on catalogues (see *Chapter 6.5*) is not abided by (i.e that all donations whether of cheques and/or credit card debits or cash should be made out or given directly to the charity).

(b) Separate minutes should be kept of the meetings of the Board of Directors of the trading company and those of the trustees of the charity. Although the Board of Directors may meet on the same day as the trustees of the charity, nonetheless the meeting of the Board of Directors of the trading company is a separate meeting and should be so minuted and its minutes maintained in separate statutory books as required by company law.

(c) Make sure that the proper information is put on the trading company's notepaper

   (i) Its registered name (*not* the charity's) i.e. XYZ Limited;

   (ii) Its registered office;

(iii) Its place of incorporation (i.e. England or Scotland);

(iv) Its registered company number (*not* the charity's);

(v) The names of *all* its directors or *none* of them. You cannot be selective and only put the chairman's name.

(d) It is worth considering "colour coding" the two organisations so that members of staff are constantly aware of the distinction between the two organisations - for example the charity could have buff notepaper and the trading company white paper. All purchase orders, invoices, internal memos, letters, etc. would be printed on the appropriate paper. This can be very important, for many charities set up structures which are understood by the Chief Executive and Finance Director, but not always fully understood by members of staff lower down in the organisation, which can result in confusion and problems. Although it did not involve a commercial trading company, War on Want a number of years ago was involved in an investigation by the Charity Commission when it ran a political campaign through the charity, rather than through the separate company which it had set up deliberately to undertake political campaigns (W.O.W. Campaigns Limited). This illustrates the fact that sophisticated divisions of responsibilities may not always be appreciated by members of staff. A simple system such as colour coding may help combat this.

In order to ensure that the relationship between a charity and its trading company is clear, some charities have a master agreement between the two to regulate their dealings. The topics which an agreement should cover will vary for each case but, broadly speaking, it would be sensible to consider such items as:

(a) Use of the charity's name and logo: it should be a non-exclusive licence; Are there any restrictions on the use of the name/logo (e.g. the need for prior clearance before any sub-licensing deals)?

(b) Use of the charity's mailing lists.

(c) Payment for use of the charity's name and logo: how should the payment be structured - probably as an annual payment (see *Chapter 6*) ?

(d) Payment for use of the mailing list - this should be structured on a break even basis, as any profit from exploiting rights in a data base might be taxable in the hands of the charity.

(e) Terms for use of the charity's facilities (e.g. premises, computers, machinery, equipment and staff).

(f) Accounting.

(g) Termination: How much notice should either party have to give in order to terminate the agreement? This may be somewhat unnecessary in an agreement between a charity and its trading company, but the two are separate entities, may well have different boards of directors, and it is important as well to maintain the distinction in all party's minds. It should also be remembered that the Charity Commission requires that all arrangements whereby a charity licences its name to commercial third parties should be kept under review - see paragraph 107 of their report for 1991 mentioned in *Chapter 8.3* - the ability to terminate quickly the licence to the trading company will be part of a charity's ability to review such arrangements.

7.14. Employee shareholdings/profit bonuses

Many commercial organisations over the last decade have taken advantage of legal and tax changes to set up schemes to encourage employee motivation through offering employees a stake in the business, whether through share ownership or share options (which when exercised give the employee shares in the company) or through tax efficient profit-related pay schemes. Charities with trading companies may be encouraged to consider setting up similar schemes for employees of that company, but they should be very wary about doing so. Comparisons between commercial groups of companies and charities are very often misleading and overlook the fundamental objective of a charity, namely to act for the public benefit. Many charities share some of their staff and/or premises with their trading companies. If staff who are partly engaged on the trading company's business know that they may improve their personal financial position by increasing the profits of the trading company, they may well concentrate their efforts on boosting the trading company's activities to the possible detriment of the charity. Their loyalties will be divided and they will be pulled towards the trading company.

Moreover, the trading company may need working capital to finance its activities. It may seek this from the charity. That capital may be vital to the company's success and hence to the remuneration of the employees. But who will write the report to the trustees requesting that this financial assistance be provided? It could well be employees of the charity who also work for the trading company, and who thus have a vested financial interest in the outcome of the application to the charity for working capital! What is more, the lower the rate of interest charged by the charity on a loan to the trading company, the higher the profits of the trading company might be, which may in turn result in an enhanced profit bonus for staff members! Such a conflict could lead the writer of the report to err on the side of recommending a low rate of interest which would be a breach of the Charity Commission's guidelines. It may be difficult for volunteer trustees to spot all these ramifications in a short meeting in which they are, understandably, relying on a report prepared by the staff.

This is but one example of a new commercial practice aimed at increasing motivation which could have serious knock on effects in the very different world of charities. Consequently charities should act with considerable caution in this area.

7.15. Fund-raising companies

Chapter 2 considered fund-raising and showed that it was a different activity from trading, although at times the distinction can be hard to draw. This is especially true with major high-risk one-off fund-raising events, which could be run by the charity (because the event does not meet the 'badges' of trade) but which are instead put through a separate non-charitable fund-raising company.

Charities need to be especially careful when using such fund-raising companies to ensure that the distinction between the charity and the company is maintained at all times.

As ever, problems arise most acutely when there is insolvency. In paragraphs 45-48 of the Charity Commissioners' Report for 1988 , they mention cases where fund-raising companies owned by charities have gone into liquidation leaving creditors of the fund-raising company unpaid.

"46 Nevertheless, the practice of raising funds through an associated trading company can give rise to misunderstanding among those supporting the charity and resentment should the trading company run into difficulties. Where assurances have been given that all donations, entrance fees, and sponsorship money would go straight to the charity, there is naturally objection to any suggestion that it should be used to pay off creditors of the trading company. In these circumstances local fund-raisers have on occasions withheld money and donated it to another charity rather than pay it over and risk it being used to pay off the company's debts. This is a mistaken course. Moneys raised for the purposes of a particular charity should be paid over to the charity trustees leaving them to resist the claims of creditors of the trading company if necessary.

47. Representations are, however, also made that where large sums of money can be raised for charity those resources should properly be made available to pay the liabilities legitimately incurred in fund-raising. In particular several creditors have expressed themselves

baffled by the situation because they thought they were dealing with the charity itself and not with a separate trading company. This has led to some adverse criticism in the press with the implication that the use of such a company in some way smacked of sharp practice and the suggestion that tradespeople and contractors could be deterred from dealing with such companies. Fund-raising companies are however set up not only to undertake trading on a scale which would not be proper for a charity, but also to shield the assets of the charity where the venture contains an element of risk. This is particularly the case where publicity and trading expenses are considerable and the return may be uncertain; for example, where reliance is placed on income from sales of memorabilia and sponsorship of promotional expenses.

48. Trustees for their part may feel torn between resisting any claim made by the associated trading company, and meeting what they may feel to be a moral obligation given the close connection between the two bodies, particularly where the collapse of the trading company might rebound to their discredit. To act in such a way, however, would not only be outside the powers of the trustees if the funds were collected on the basis that they will be paid to a charity without deduction of the expenses incurred by the company in raising the funds, but would defeat the whole object of the arrangement. We strongly advise all charities acting closely with an associated fund-raising company to ensure that in all publicity material directed to raising funds and in the contractual relationship of such companies with suppliers, the status of the two bodies is made clear."

◆◆ *example*

Trading Places (1) Ltd a company established by Breakthrough, a registered charity to organise a one day celebrity fund-raising event recently ceased trading. According to press reports (January 1994) Breakthrough itself faced a possible claim for £207,000 owed to a printing company by Trading Places (1) Ltd - whether or not a successful claim can be mounted will depend on whether or not the contract in question was with Breakthrough. If the printer alleges that Breakthrough *guaranteed* the payment of it by Trading Places 1 Ltd, it is highly unlikely that such a claim could succeed - see the analysis of the *Rosemary Simmons Memorial Housing Association* case.

This case illustrates the problem highlighted in the quotation from the Charity Commissioners' Report.

7.16.   Conclusion

Trading companies are necessary to carry out for-profit non primary purpose trading and are sometimes used for fund-raising.

Charities should be especially cautious about financing trading companies. Trustees should know their investment powers and understand their trustee responsibilities.

Beware of superficial comparisons between normal commercial practice and charities - charity law imposes a range of unusual restrictions on charities, which are revealed on many issues such as loans, investments, inter-company management charges, VAT groups, guarantees to banks, incentives to staff, and use of company names.

Chapter 8
INTELLECTUAL PROPERTY RIGHTS

Intellectual property rights may be of great value to charities and/or their trading companies and should be dealt with carefully and thoroughly. This area can be highly complex and appropriate professional advice should be taken.

This chapter covers: copyright; names and logos; registration of trade and service marks; registration of patents, and use of data bases.

Commercial organisations protect their intellectual property rights assiduously through the registration of trade and service marks, by registering patents and through enforcing copyright. Similarly, charities and their associated trading companies have intellectual property rights which need to be protected. Many charities are involved in the creation of such rights through research and development, and the production of reports or publications.

8.1. Copyright

Charities and their trading companies will frequently create or commission materials which are protected by copyright. In order to protect against unauthorised use by others, they need to ensure that they deal with copyright matters effectively.

Copyright law has a wide application. By Section 1 of the Copyright Design & Patents Act 1988 it exists in:

(a) original literary, dramatic, musical or artistic works;

(b) sound recordings, films, broadcasts or cable programmes; and

(c) the typographical arrangement of published editions.

For charities carrying out primary purposes trading, copyright can be a significant consideration. For example, a research charity may be commissioned to write reports in connection with bespoke research; an educational charity commissions and publishes a book from an author (e.g. The Oxford or Cambridge University Press or the Directory of Social Change); an art gallery wishes to use a picture from its collection on a postcard or greetings card; a charitable theatre commissions designs for a stage set; a religious charity publishes religious books. Who owns the copyright in these items?

Charities trading through trading companies will similarly encounter copyright issues - e.g. on commissioning the design of Christmas cards; on commissioning market research; on designing a sales catalogue; on building up data bases of customers; on commissioning advertisements. Again, who owns the copyright?

First, it is worth emphasising a few basic principles of copyright law:

(a) **There is no copyright in an idea.** The law provides that ideas, opinions, information and facts should be freely available. Copyright law merely protects *the way* in which the author has expressed such ideas or information. There are exceptions to this depending on the circumstances. For example, an idea may be disclosed only after the receiver has signed a confidentiality undertaking whereby he or she agrees to honour the confidentiality of the idea. The owner of the idea could sue if the idea was disclosed in breach of the undertaking. Hence if someone wishes to disclose an idea to a possible investor, it is worth getting the potential investor to sign a confidentiality agreement before the idea is disclosed.

(b) **There is no central registry of copyright.** Copyright is not established by filing details with a government department; it comes into being simply by virtue of an act which contains a sufficient degree of intellectual innovation and originality to be protected by the law. The position is different in the United States of America, where there is a central registry and filing with the Registry is essential to protect copyright. The intellectual input required in order to create copyright is not usually onerous and varies with the medium concerned. For example, quite a low expectation of intellectual input is required to establish copyright in a database containing names and addresses of contacts or customers (see *Chapter 8.6*). On the other hand, a higher degree of intellectual innovation may be required in connection with the writing of a book. In England there is not even any legal obligation to put a copyright notice on copyright material although it is sensible to do so.

If an author is concerned that there could be a dispute over when a copyright work was created, he or she can send a copy of the work by recorded delivery post to an independent third party for safekeeping (e.g. a solicitor or a bank), so that there is separate independent evidence of when the copyright work was created.

(c) **An employer owns the copyright in any material produced by an employee in the course of his employment.** This can come as a considerable surprise to both employers and employees! If office work is done outside business hours, then it will be *treated* as having been done in the course of employment. The other side of the coin is that copyright in materials produced by a *consultant* (or indeed anyone who is not an employee) will vest in the author, even though the commissioned material has been paid for. This means that a charity (or its trading company) should always ensure when commissioning designs, reports or other copyright materials, that the copyright is assigned or transferred to the charity or to the trading company (as the case may be). The assignment of copyright must be in writing and be signed by the assignor. Many organisations fail to take an assignment of copyright, thinking that payment is sufficient to purchase the copyright.

◆◆ *example*

One recent court case involved an the action brought by Henry Moore's daughter against the Henry Moore Foundation (a registered charity). Henry Moore's daughter claimed that a large number of her father's sculptures did not belong to the charity but to Henry Moore personally and thus, on his death, passed to his successors under his Will. But the Court was satisfied that Mr Moore had been *employed* by the Henry Moore Foundation for many years prior to his death and thus all his works produced during the years of his employment belonged *not* to Mr Moore, and hence to his beneficiaries, but to the Henry Moore Foundation.

(d) **Copyright lasts for 50 years* from the death of the author.** Even though the copyright itself is owned by a company (which by definition cannot die) because the author was employed by a company, the copyright period is based on the life of the *author* who created it on behalf of the company. (*From 1st July 1995: 70 years from the death of the author.)

(e) **If two or more authors jointly own the copyright it will last until the end of the fifty years* from the end of the calendar year in which the last of them died.** (*From 1st July 1995: 70 years)

(f) **If copyright is breached, the copyright owner may seek an interim order in the courts so as to restrain the breach of copyright pending trial of the main action.** If the application is successful, the copyright owner will obtain an order (an injunction) banning use of the copyright material until the matter comes up for a full hearing. The full trial may not take place for at least two years after the injunction has been obtained. At trial, if successful, the copyright owner will be awarded a permanent injunction and damages. Damages are based on the depreciation caused by the infringement to the value of the copyright - hence if the defendant has dealt with the copyright work as if he had a licence, he will be ordered to pay as damages an amount equivalent to the fair fee or royalty which he would have had to pay to the copyright owner in order to be able to grant such a licence.

If the plaintiff wins an order for an injunction, he has to give an undertaking in damages to the defendant. This means that if at the trial of the main action the injunction is not maintained, the plaintiff has to indemnify the defendant for all losses incurred as a result of the injunction having been awarded, since the court will have ultimately decided that there should be no injunction and hence the original injunction should not have been given. This can be a major concern for a plaintiff.

(g) **There are no fixed rules to say how much of a book or article can be copied without infringement, but the question revolves around both quality and amount.** If a great degree of skill, judgement and effort has been invested in creating a copyright work, copying only a small part may nonetheless constitute a breach. On the other hand, it may be necessary to copy a larger part of a less inventive work to amount to a breach. There must be *actual* copying. Co-incidental creation of a similar work independently does *not* constitute infringement even though it covers the same ideas. For further information on this see *Chapter 8.6.*

(h) **It is necessary to distinguish between physical possession and legal ownership of a copyright work on the one hand and exploitation of the copyright on the other.** For example, take a picture by a recently deceased painter such as Francis Bacon. A gallery may have purchased the picture but the gallery will *not* control the copyright in the picture unless it has been assigned to it. The painter's heirs, as laid down in the painter's Will, will have the rights to exploit the copyright in the picture unless the painter assigned the copyright during his lifetime. On the other hand, once the copyright has expired, the owners of the picture can control exploitation of copies of the picture by limiting access or charging fees for taking copies etc., even though the owner no longer owns the copyright due to its expiration. Copyright will also exist in any photographs of the original, and will belong to the photographer, if he or she is the "author" of the work, which is generally the case.

(i) **Copyright is immensely flexible. It attaches to each level of creative endeavour in a finished work.** For example, a book may be adapted as a stage play and then into a television show with background music. There will be separate copyrights in the stage play, the television show, the background music, the master tape and the broadcast. For example, if a charity dedicated to the education of the public through music commissions the filming, broadcasting and recording of a public concert it will need to deal with various copyrights such as:-

(i) use of the copyright in the music (where the 50 year rule applies) both for the performance and the recording;

(ii) the musicians' performing rights;

(iii) the recording rights;

(iv) the filming rights;

(v) the broadcast rights;

(vi) the video rights.

8.2. Software and copyright

UK law recognises that computer software is protected by copyright. A charity or its trading company will deal with two types of software - bespoke software which it has commissioned and standard programmes it has bought from a supplier (such as Lotus 123). As regards standard programmes, the purchaser will *not* be able to negotiate the terms and conditions of the contract, but will have to take or leave those terms. As regards bespoke programmes, the purchaser must consider the following questions:

(a) **Who obtains copyright in the programme?** Should it be the purchaser? This will not happen unless there is an express assignment of the copyright in the programme contained in the contract with the software creator. It may be in the purchaser's interest to allow the creator of the software to retain title in the programme, so as to encourage the creator of the software to maintain it. In particular, there may be merit in allowing the creator of the software to licence it to other users (provided they are not direct competitors). In this way the software may acquire a larger number of users which at least should ensure its bugs are more quickly dealt with - and its maintenance cheaper.

(b) **Who has the copyright in a report which identifies *the need* for the bespoke programme?** The copyright will be owned by either the author (if an independent contractor) or his employer (if the author is an employee). But there will be nothing to stop the creator of the software using the *ideas* or concepts in the report, unless it has agreed not to do so by signing a confidentiality agreement.

(c) **If the copyright is not assigned, the source codes can be placed in escrow** (which is a form of safe deposit) under an agreement with, for example, the National Computing Centre. This will provide that if the creator of the software ceases to trade (and therefore to maintain or upgrade the software), the purchaser (or its agents) can obtain access to the source codes to upgrade or maintain the software.

8.3. Names and logos

A charity's most precious asset is its reputation or goodwill. Some charities have incredibly powerful brand names. Apparently in the United States of America the Red Cross ranks as the third best known brand name! Charities recognise the need for good punchy titles-hence the spawning of catchy acronyms and distinctive logos, of which the World Wide Fund for Nature's panda or the Save the Children Fund's child must be among the best known.

Names and non-artistic logos are not usually protected by copyright, but instead are treated under English law as *marks*. A mark can be registered or unregistered.

If a charity or its trading company commissions a design of a logo, it should make sure that all rights are transferred to it. Just as with copyright, the mere act of payment for design of a logo does not mean that the rights in it transfer to the purchaser. The omission to obtain a transfer of such rights can give rise to problems.

◆◆ *example*

In one case a charity commissioned a distinctive artistic logo from a designer. This was duly designed, but the charity failed to take an assignment of the rights in the logo. The logo became well known and hence valuable. As a result the designer had the charity over a barrel. Whenever the charity had to prove it had ownership of the logo (e.g. if it wanted to enter into an arrangement whereby it allowed a third party to use it), it had to obtain a licence (for a fee!) from the owner.

These problems would have been avoided if the charity had taken a transfer of all rights in the logo when it placed the order for its design with the designer - when the designer's negotiating position was much weaker than it subsequently became.

Registered marks are dealt with in *Chapter 8.4*. Even if a name is not registered as a trademark, a charity or its trading company can still protect their names by bringing a *passing off* action in the Court. Passing off occurs if there is evidence of the public being confused by the existence of two organisations with similar names. If two organisations with similar names operate in completely different markets there can be no confusion, and the law will not intervene. The plaintiff must usually show damage. This could be loss of sales, which in the case of a charity may be very difficult to prove unless it engages in primary purpose trading, but less tangible damage to reputation will also suffice.

It is sometimes claimed that the remedy of passing off is not available to charities as they have no commercial reputation to protect. This is not true. In a number of cases charities have obtained injunctions to protect their names and reputations.

◆◆ *examples*

Dr. Barnardos' Homes (now Barnardos) was able to restrain the defendant from publishing novelettes as a Barnardo publication *(Dr Barnardos Homes v. Barnardo Amalgamated Industries Limited (1949) 66 RPC 103).*

The British Legion was entitled to restrain a non-political social club from the use of "British Legion" in its name *(British Legion v. British Legion Club (Street) Limited (1931) 48 RPC 555).*

In the *British Diabetic Association v. The Diabetic Society Limited (1992)* the British Diabetic Association, a registered charity, obtained an injunction to stop the defendant (which was in the process of being registered as a charity) from using its confusingly similar name.

The recent case involving elderflower champagne *(Tattinger & Others v. Allber Limited and Others,* The Times, 28 June 1993), in which the Court of Appeal banned the use of the word "champagne" in conjunction with elderflower, may help charities in this area. The Court of Appeal was less worried about evidence of loss of sales in the near or long-term future - rather, the damage to Tattinger's interest was seen as "insidious"; in the words of Lord Justice Mann: "a gradual debasement, dilution or erosion of what was distinctive, which would be incrementally damaging to the goodwill acquired by the name."

This indicates that where sufficient *distinctiveness* is shown, the level of protection accorded is close to that available under trade mark legislation, with an automatic presumption of infringement if a distinctive term is used by others.

The Commercial Exploitation of Names

Many charities increasingly seek to exploit their names and goodwill through linking them with commercial organisations: for example - the World Wide Fund for Nature's panda appears on many a product. This trend was addressed by the Charity Commission in their 1991 Report as follows:

Paragraph 106: "We also had occasion to consider the use of charity names by commercial concerns. In our view, charity trustees should be wary of entering into arrangements whereby the charity's name is to be used by a commercial company in return for money. This might involve the endorsement of a commercial product by a charity or the use of the charity's name in relation to a commercial product. There are cases when a charity can properly associate with a commercial organisation to their mutual benefit but care must be taken to protect the interests of the charity and to ensure that the relationship is, and remains, appropriate."

Paragraph 107: "The charity's name is a valuable asset. It is the means by which it is identified in the Central Register of Charities and to the public. Before allowing the use of a charity name on a commercial basis, charity trustees must first consider the needs of the charity, and whether funds could be raised by other methods. The name of a charity must not be exploited for non-charitable purposes. If a charity's name is used commercially it must be shown that the arrangement is expedient, in the interests of the charity and on terms which are advantageous to the charity. Any such arrangement must be precisely defined by the charity trustees in every detail and kept under review. They must ensure that there is no misuse of the charity name nor any improper exploitation of its association with a commercial organisation and that the arrangements made allow them to prevent any such misuse."

A careful analysis reveals that this statement is less than helpful - at one point the Commission states "The name of the charity must *not* be exploited for non-charitable purposes" but then states that a charity can use its name "commercially" (which is surely a non-charitable use!). The regime introduced by the Charities Act 1992 concerning commercial participators (see *Chapter 9*) implies that a charity *can* lawfully licence its name and logo provided the safeguards laid down by the 1992 Act are complied with. Hence it is submitted the Charity Commissioners do not consider that a charity cannot exploit its name or logo commercially. In some cases a charity may appoint its trading company as its agent to exploit its name - see *Chapter 6* for further details - in which case these comments apply to the contract between the trading company and the commercial partner.

However well-drafted the agreement may be, all charities which enter into arrangements whereby their name is to be associated with the goods and/or services provided by a third party need to appreciate that there is a risk that the charity's name could be brought into disrepute through the activities of some member of the licensee's group of companies. Modern transnational companies have tentacles spread through many countries. The company with which a charity has a licensing arrangement in the United Kingdom may be involved in many different industries in many different countries of the world, and it is impossible for the charity adequately to check on the performance of all those companies prior to entering into any arrangement whereby the charity licences its name. Hence, the charity may take warranties from the licensee that, for example, in all companies controlled by it, the licensee will ensure that all employees are employed on conditions which comply with the standards laid down by the International Labour Organisation. But such a clause will not cover a joint venture where the joint venture company is not "controlled" by the licensee. Nor will it give any solace to the charity should it transpire that, for example, the licensees' subsidiary in Colombia is suddenly discovered in a world-wide blaze of publicity, to be breaking laws relating to the exploitation of child labour.

Alternatively, there could be a sudden scandal about the compliance of a product upon which the charity's logo appears with food safety legislation - such matters can blow up very quickly (e.g. the oil in Perrier scandal).

Nothing can be 100% watertight in these circumstances, and charities need to proceed with considerable caution.

Clearly, it is vital for the charity to ensure that any licence agreement contains stringent clauses to protect the charity's name such as:

(a) a clear and precise definition of the goods or services which will enjoy use of the charity's name/logo;

(b) a warranty by the licensee that neither it nor any of its associated companies (i.e. subsidiaries or joint ventures) will at any time during the duration of the agreement do anything which could bring the reputation of the charity into disrepute;

(c) a termination clause allowing the charity to terminate the licence immediately should, in its opinion, its name be brought into disrepute or if the licensee is in material breach of any of the terms of the agreement;

(d) clear terms about the method and frequency of payment - this should be structured as an annual payment (see *Chapter 6.6*);

(e) a liquidated damages clause setting out an agreed amount of damages payable to the charity in the event of breach - so as to save costly legal arguments about the amount of damage sustained by the charity (which could be very hard to prove to the satisfaction of the court).

A charity would be well advised to take professional advice on such a contract.

8.4. Trade Marks

What is a trade mark?

The law relating to trade marks has recently undergone extensive reform. A new Trade Marks Act came into effect on 31st October 1994. Consequently the following section refers to the new Trade Marks Act. The Trade Marks Act is based upon the first European Council Directive of 21st December 1988 which aims at approximating the laws of Member States of the European Community relating to trade marks. The Directive does not attempt to achieve a full scale harmonisation of national trade marks laws. Instead it aims to minimise those differences which can affect the free movement of goods and services and thus hinder the development of the single market.

A *"trade mark"* is defined as any sign capable of being represented graphically which is capable of distinguishing goods or services of one undertaking from those of other undertakings.

A trade mark may, in particular, consist of:

(a) words (including personal names);

(b) designs;

(c) letters;

(d) numerals;

(e) the shape of goods or their packaging.

The new definition is far wider than under the old Trade Marks Act 1938 which excluded, for example, the shape of goods. Hence under the old law, the distinctive Coca-Cola bottle was not registerable as a trade mark. Now it will be. Musical jingles and colours will also be registerable.

It is worth mentioning that a crucial change with the new law is that it will be easier for charities which are *not* carrying on trading activities to register trade marks. This is because section 1 of the Trade Marks Act refers to signs capable of distinguishing goods or services of an "undertaking". The word undertaking is not defined, but in other pieces of European legislation (e.g. in relation to competition law), it is treated as a wide and loose concept. An essential characteristic of an undertaking, with regard to competition law is that the activities pursued must be of an *economic* or *commercial* nature, although this is widely construed to include cultural or sporting activities. The absence of a profit motive or the absence of profits is no longer relevant, provided that the objectives of the undertaking are economic or commercial.

Under the old trade mark legislation, in order to register a service mark it was necessary for the service to be used in connection with the supply of services in consideration for money or moneys worth. This made it difficult for a charity which was not receiving direct financial reward for its activities to register a service mark (e.g., the Citizens Advice Bureau). Now it will be easier for such organisations to register trade marks. The new legislation abolishes the old distinction between trade and service marks.

What cannot be registered as a trade mark?

Certain items cannot be registered as trade marks, namely:-

(a) those which are devoid of any distinctive character;

(b) those which consist *exclusively* of signs or indications which may serve to designate the kind, quality, quantity, intended purpose, value, geographical origin at the time of production of goods or the rendering of services or other characteristics of goods or services. Hence one will not be able to register a mark which states: "The Best £5 Yorkshire Wrench".

Why have a trade mark?

The advantage of registering a trade mark is that it gives the owner of the mark an exclusive monopoly in using the mark in relation to the types of goods or services for which it is registered. Consequently, if someone is using a registered trade mark in relation to the same goods or services, it is a simple matter for the trade mark owner to obtain an injunction to restrain its wrongful use. The trade mark owner merely has to show that the defendant is *using* the registered mark.

Under the new law, a trade mark owner will also be able to obtain an injunction in relation to *similar* goods or services if there is actual or likely confusion. This is much easier than using the common law right of a passing off action to restrain a defendant from using the plaintiff's name, logo or unregistered mark. (See *Chapter 8.3*). In such cases, the plaintiff has to establish that there is at least confusion and possibly deception as a result of the use of its logo, name or unregistered mark by the defendant. This can be difficult and expensive to prove.

Obtaining an injunction should also be easier for charities which have not registered a trade mark, (although not for their trading companies), by virtue of Section 59(3) Charities Act 1992. That provides that if, on the application of a charitable institution, the court is satisfied that any person is acting as a professional fund-raiser or a commercial participator in relation to that institution without there being a Section 59(1) or (2) Agreement in force, the court will grant an injunction restraining the professional fund-raiser or commercial participator. It will not be necessary to show confusion in these circumstances but merely the act of seeking to raise funds by using the name of the charitable institution without an agreement in the prescribed form. "It will be interesting to see how widely this sub-clause is interpreted. Given the wide meaning of the word "represent" (see *Chapter 9.2* below), it should be possible for a charitable institution to argue that any commercial organisation which seeks to sell goods bearing the slogan "sold in aid of XYZ charity" or something similar should be restrained from selling those goods if it does so without the benefit of an agreement in the form laid down by Section 59(2) Charities Act 1992 (see *Chapter 9*).

It should be emphasised that this right to seek an injunction under Section 59(3) will *only* apply to *charitable institutions*. The definition of a charitable institution does not extend to a trading company owned by a charity. Hence, a trading company in these circumstances will have to rely upon its common law rights in passing off.

How do you register a trade mark?

This is not the place to go into the detailed procedure for registering a trade mark. Suffice to say that an application has to be made to the Trade Marks Registrar. There are forty-two different categories of goods and services, and multi class applications are now possible under the Trade Marks Act. The importance of registering in precisely the right class or classes is now less important, as a trade mark owner can obtain an injunction if the mark has been used on similar goods/services, provided there is evidence of actual or likely confusion. If a charity or its trading company are considering registering a trade mark, it is wise to use the services of a professional trade mark agent who will be accustomed to registering marks. Registration is a complex matter and can take up to two years. The registration of a trade mark is deemed to run from the date upon which the application was originally filed. Registration will last for ten years and is then renewable for further ten year periods.

Can you lose registration of a trade mark?

Under the new trade marks legislation it will be possible to have the registration of a trade mark revoked:

(a) if within five years following the completion of the registration it has not been put to genuine use in the United Kingdom; or

(b) if such use has been suspended for an uninterrupted period of five years and there are no proper reasons for non use; or

(c) if in consequence of acts or inactivity of the owner it has become the common name in the trade for a product or service for which it is registered; or

(d) if the trade mark was registered invalidly.

Licensing of trade marks by a charity to its trading company

It may well be that a charity may be able to register a trade mark in relation to part of its activities but it may wish to authorise its trading company to utilise the trade mark as well. The charity should give the trading company a *non-exclusive licence* to utilise the mark, since by section 24 of the Trade Marks Act, an exclusive licence means that the licensee has the sole right to use the trade mark and that would mean that the charity as the owner of the registered trade mark, could not use it! The trading company should ensure that the grant of the licence is registered with the Trade Mark Office within six months of the date of the licence. If this is not done, then the trading company as licensee will not be entitled to damages or to sue for profits in respect of any infringement of the trade mark. The charity could still seek an injunction to restrain unlawful use, but could not seek damages for loss of profits, as it would not have been conducting the business of the trading company. The trading company will be able to register the mark in its name for those classes of activities which *it* determines.

Is a trade mark valid outside the United Kingdom?

(a) **The European Union Trade Marks Regulation**

This draft Regulation of the European Community will, when adopted, establish a new property right, the Community Trade Mark, which will be effective throughout the European Union. It will be obtained by registration at the European Union Trade Marks Office which is to be set up in Alicante in Spain. The new regime is likely to be in operation by 1997. A Community trade mark will give its owner the exclusive right to use that mark throughout the *member* countries of the European Union.

Obviously it would not be reasonable for this new European trade mark to be granted if it conflicted with a similar right already being enjoyed by someone else. The existence of an earlier conflicting trade mark anywhere in the European Union will present a bar to registration. The owner of a UK trade mark will not be able validly to register it as a European trade mark if someone else has already registered an identical or similar mark for the same or related goods or services in, say, France. Once the European trade mark registration system gets under way, it will potentially offer organisations operating throughout the European Union an effective and cheaper method of registering trade marks.

(b) **The Madrid Agreement**

The Madrid Agreement of April 14th 1891 concerning the international registration of marks is an international treaty under which a national or a resident of one of the contracting states who has registered a trade mark in that state, can have it put on the international register maintained by the International Bureau of the World Intellectual Property Organisation (WIPO) in Geneva. A mark on the international register is then automatically protected in other contracting states designated by the proprietor, unless within a period of one year a state indicates that, in accordance with its national law, it refuses such protection.

The United Kingdom is not a party to the Madrid Agreement; in fact only twenty nine states are currently parties to it. However, the Trade Mark Act allows the UK to implement the 1989 Protocol to the Madrid Agreement which simplifies the Madrid Agreement. Once the new Trade Mark Act is in force, the United Kingdom will be a party to the Madrid Agreement. This will make it easier for owners of UK trade marks to obtain wider protection through registration with WIPO, and in particular should facilitate the use and protection of trade marks in Eastern Europe.

The Registrar of Trade Marks will be responsible for receiving and certifying applications for international registration which are based on UK registered trade marks or applications and forwarding them to WIPO. A fee will be charged to cover the cost of this operation.

Conclusion

A charity which is carrying on primary purpose trading or which has a trading company should consider whether or not it should register as a trade mark its name, its logo or any other items which might be registerable. Usually the charity's logo will be the property of the charity itself. In order for the charity to enable its trading company to register the name in connection with trading activities, it may need to licence its trading company to use the name and logo in connection with these trading activities, and charge an appropriate fee. The trading company will then apply to register that trade mark in connection with the trading company's own activities, so that the trading company will be the registered proprietor of the trade mark in relation to the activities. If on the other hand, the charity is the registered proprietor of the trade mark, then if it grants a licence to the trading company to utilise the trade mark in connection with the trading company's activities, that licence agreement should be registered with the Trade Mark Registry.

8.5. Patents

Patent derives from the Latin word meaning "an open letter". In the seventeenth century the Crown started to grant patents as a method of giving an inventor a monopoly. The law has been considerably refined since then, but the basic purpose of a patent remains the same - namely, to give the inventor of a new idea, which has a *practical application* in a product or process, a monopoly for a period of 20 years. Charities and their trading companies will come across questions of patents from time to time. This book does not endeavour to give a detailed explanation of the law relating to patents. If readers require detailed advice, they should seek it from an expert patent agent or solicitor specialising in intellectual property law.

Patents are a very specialised area. That said, the following key points should be borne in mind. Charities which undertake research, such as those involved with developing new drugs or universities studying industrial processes, need to be able to protect their intellectual property rights. As previously emphasised, such rights can be extremely valuable and charities need to ensure that their value is not lost.

What is a Patent?

The following are the key points to remember about patents:

(a) The first person to apply for a patent will be the person who is granted it. The first in time gets the patent. This is the case even if the person who applies for the patent is not the first person to have invented the new idea.

(b) Patents are not available to protect ideas alone. The ideas have to have a practical application (e.g. the zip fastener or velcro).

(c) A patent will not be available to cover:
  (i) A discovery (this will have no use until a practical application has been found for the discovery);
  (ii) A scientific theory (for the same reasons as a discovery);
  (iii) A literary, dramatic musical or artistic work (this is protected by copyright);
  (iv) A mathematical method;
  (v) A scheme, rule or method for performing a mental act, playing a game or doing a business (e.g. "Monopoly");
  (vi) A computer programme (protected by copyright);

(vii) The presentation of information;

(viii) The invention of a method of treatment of the human or animal body or surgery or therapy or of diagnosis;

(ix) Any variety of animal/plant nor any essentially biological process. This latter area is under scrutiny from the European Commission due to the development of biotechnology.

How should a Patent be applied for?

The patent should be applied for at an early stage in the research and development process. This will give an opportunity to search the patent register to see whether anyone else has already applied for a patent so as to avoid the costly and frustrating process of undertaking a large amount of research and development only to discover that someone else has got there first.

The following may apply for a Patent:

(a) **An employer.** Under Section 39 of the 1977 Patent Act, employers own the rights in patentable discoveries/inventions created by an employee, if carried out in the course of the employee's normal duties or in connection with duties that have been specifically assigned to the employee.

(b) **Independent consultants**, who will own the patent rights in respect of inventions that they have created even if this work is done under contract unless the contract specifically deals with the question of patent rights. Hence, if a team of experts is being built up (as is frequently the case) which may lead to the discovery of a patentable invention, the organisers of the team should ensure that all independent consultants and contractors (as opposed to employees) sign appropriate contracts assigning all intellectual property rights (including the right to apply for patents) to the organiser.

International aspects

It is possible to apply under the European Patent Convention to the European Patent Office in Munich to register a patent there, but applications have to be made for each country which is a party to the European Patent Convention. This is different from the proposals under European law for a European Union Patent Convention, whereby it will be possible, once that system has been established, to apply for one common patent which will be applicable in all member states of the European Union. This idea is still very much in the pipeline unlike the proposed European trade mark registration procedure (see *Chapter 8.4*).

Charities and patents

It may seem inconsistent that a charity, which is set up pro bono publico and operates in the public domain, should be able to own a private monopoly such as a patent. Nonetheless, the Charity Commission takes the view that, for example, a research charity which carries out research and development which leads to a patentable invention can apply for a patent. This is justified on two grounds:

(a) It actually puts the knowledge in the public domain (the patent register), albeit on terms that only the charity or its licensees can deal with it; and

(b) It allows the charity to exploit the fruits of its research and prevents that valuable (and often expensive) asset being stolen by competitors.

There is of course nothing to stop a charity which holds a patent on, for example, a life-preserving drug, from procuring that it is sold cheaper than the normal commercial price. In reality what would happen is that the charity would grant a patent licence either to a commercial operator or to its own trading company to exploit the patent. The charity would need to ensure that the payments under the patent licence are received in the most tax-effective manner. (See *Chapter 6.9*). Such a licence might stipulate the terms upon which the drug was to be sold (e.g., that it was not to exceed a certain price).

If a charity grants a licence to its trading company to exploit a patent, it should ensure that this is done in line with the principles set out in *Chapter 7*. The licence must be granted at arms length and conform to normal commercial terms. The charity should not favour its own trading company. If a trading company owned by a charity is the owner or licensee of a patent, it will be able to exploit the patent (including appointing a licensee or sub-licensees) in a normal commercial manner, depending on the terms of the patent.

8.6. Databases

Databases are becoming ever more important for charities and their associated trading companies. In 1990 the World Wide Fund for Nature reported that it cost £20 for each new supporter's name to be "captured". It also revealed that, over the eleven years the average supporter remained on its list, a net £400 would be donated, a twenty fold return on the charity's "investment". The list containing names of a charity's supporters is obviously something of value.

Charities and Non-Profit Groups in Europe (CHANGE), in their evidence to the Select Committee on the European Communities: Protection of

Personal Data, estimated that up to 70% of the voluntary income of large charities is specifically derived from direct marketing and related activities (including trading catalogues). This method of fund-raising is obviously crucial. Charities use their own in-house lists of supporters, or they use lists owned and operated by commercial broking agencies.

Electronic storage of data

The law concerning the electronic storage of data covers two distinct but inter-linked areas:

(a) intellectual property law (i.e. copyright), and how it operates to protect the rights of the "author" to repress piracy and unfair competition; and

(b) the protection of personal data and regulation of the potential conflict between the right to privacy and the right to freedom of expression including the right to seek, receive and impart information. Both of these areas are now the subject matter of draft European Union Directives. The "Proposed Directive on the Legal Protection of Databases" (SYN 393) was submitted by the European Commission on 15th April 1992, and the revised "Proposed Directive concerning the Protection of Individuals with regard to the Processing of Personal Data and on the Free Movement of such Data" (SYN 287) was submitted on 15 October 1992.

Databases and Copyright

What is a database? Dworkin and Taylor in "Blackstones Guide to the Copyright, Designs and Patent Act 1988" ("CDPA 1988") state that:

"A database is an accumulation of information stored in such a way that it can be systematically searched and retrieved by computer".

The Proposed European Directive SYN 393 (yet to be implemented) defines databases in a somewhat wider fashion to include:

"collections of work, whether literary, artistic, musical or other, or of other material such as text, sounds, images, numbers, facts, data or combinations of any of these".

The CDPA 1988 does not deal specifically with databases. Hence the general rules of copyright (see *Chapter 8.1*) apply to them.

Copyright in databases falls within Section 1 of the CDPA 1988 in the category of original literary works. Copyright arises by the creator inputting a sufficient degree of intellectual innovation and inventiveness (originality) into his or her work. The intellectual input required is not usually onerous and quite a low expectation of intellectual input is required to establish copyright in a database. There is no requirement for an inventive step - merely the compiling of information will suffice. Most databases will qualify under the CDPA 1988 as original literary works.

However, there are several unanswered questions:

(a) where a database has been constantly changed and updated, does each input of data constitute the creation of an entirely new database? This could create a situation in which copyright not only lies in the first complete database but in each updated database - assuming there is sufficient originality in each new compilation.

(b) who is the creator of the database? This could be the person who wrote the programme, the person who compiles the data, or the person who inputs the data. If a database has been created in-house by the organisation's own employees, copyright will be owned by the employer.

If a database is built up "in house" by an organisation (whether a charity or its trading company) using external consultants, the organisation should ensure that the consultant agrees by contract that he or she transfers all intellectual property in the database to the organisation. Otherwise the charity or the trading company may find that technically the part of the database created by the consultant is owned by the consultant! (See *Chapter 8.1.*) If use of a database is licensed, the licensor should undertake that it owns the copyright in the database and should agree to indemnify the user for any liabilities it may incur if the database breaches someone else's copyright.

Checklist for those compiling a database

(a) **Complete copies**

You must gain authorisation from the copyright owner to include a complete copyright work in your database (for copying only part of a copyright work, see point (c) below). Section 17(2) of the CDPA 1988 states that "copying in relation to a literary, dramatic or artistic work means reproducing the work in any material form. This includes storing the work in any medium by electronic means".

(b) **Public Domain**

Data already in the public domain may be incorporated into your database without more ado. Examples of such data are as follows:

(i) **The Electoral Register**. This is widely used in marketing and research. It can be processed and transferred from one data user to another.

(ii) **The Register of County Court Judgements**

(iii) **Public records**. Under Section 49 of the CDPA 1988, material which is comprised in public records within the meaning of the Public Records Act 1958 which are open to public inspection may be copied, and a copy may be supplied to any person, by or with the authority of any person appointed under that Act.

A privately published directory (e.g. of grant making trusts or charity advisors) is not in the public domain!

(c) **Extracts**

Where extracts from a database (or indeed from any copyright material) are taken and stored in a database there is infringement only where the whole of the work or any substantial part of it is affected - Section 16(3)(a) of the CDPA 1988. In this context what does the word *"substantial"* mean? It is now settled law that the *quality* of that which is taken is usually more important than the *quantity*. For example, sometimes the quantity of material taken may be minimal, but the value to the user of the database, and the loss of economic potential to the copyright owner may be great. Peterson J. said in *University of London Press Limited -v- University Tutorial Press Limited* (1916) 2 Ch 601 that "what is worth copying is prima facie worth protecting".

There is a real paucity of case law on this subject, which reflects the fact that it is in a rapidly developing field. However, the case of *Waterlow Directories Limited -v- Reed Information Services Limited* (1992) FSR 409 had to consider whether the part of a law directory reproduced by the defendant was "substantial". The plaintiff (Waterlows) applied for an interlocutory (interim) injunction until the matter came before a full hearing. The court came to the conclusion that there was a strong case that the part of the plaintiff's directory taken by the defendant was substantial and granted the injunction. In order to update its directory, the *defendant* had compared the plaintiff's directory with the defendant's directory and highlighted those names and addresses which appeared in the plaintiff's directory but not in the defendant's directory. The highlighted names and addresses were copied onto a word processor which was used to produce letters inviting solicitors and barristers to appear in the new edition of the defendant's directory. Out of 12,620 firms of solicitors listed in the directory, about 1,600 were highlighted in this way.

Each case will turn on its particular fact but the law directory case shows that using 12.7% of a database may amount to copying a "substantial" part. If a data user needs to copy a substantial part of another database, the user will need to obtain (and doubtless pay for if granted) a licence from the owner of that other database, in order to avoid running into claims that he is breaching copyright.

Damages

Damages for breach of copyright under CDPA 1988 are compensatory (i.e. the wronged party should be put in the same position as if the breach had not occurred). See *Chapter 8.1.*

Rights of Data Subjects

The law has the unenviable task of balancing the individual's rights of privacy and the data user's freedom of expression. As it has developed in the twentieth century, the concept of freedom of expression is often said to include freedom of information.

The Data Protection Act 1984 ("DPA 1984") introduced important new rights to protect the individual. These included:

(a) the right to see most of the information held about him/her on computer;

(b) the right to correct such information if it is inaccurate or misleading; and

(c) the right to seek compensation if the information is being or has been misused.

The Act does not cover manual files held on paper.

Any organisation that records personal details by electronic means should be *registered* under the DPA. It is an offence under Section 8 of the DPA 1984 to hold personal data without being registered or without having applied for registration. An unregistered data user becomes liable to prosecution.

Schedule 1 to the DPA 1984 sets out "the Data Protection Principles" These are as follows:

1. The information to be contained in personal data be obtained, and personal data shall be processed, fairly and lawfully.

2. Personal data shall be held only for one or more specified and lawful purposes.

3. Personal data held for any purpose or purposes shall not be used or disclosed in any manner incompatible with that purpose or those purposes.

4. Personal data held for any purpose or purposes shall be adequate, relevant and not excessive in relation to that purpose or those purposes.

5. Personal data shall be accurate and, where necessary, kept up to date.

6. Personal data held for any purpose or purposes shall not be kept for any longer than is necessary for that purpose or those purposes.

7. An individual shall be entitled:

    (a) At reasonable intervals and without undue delay or expense:-

    (i) to be informed by any data user whether he holds personal data of which that individual is the subject; and

    (ii) to have access to any such data held by a data user; and

    (b) Where appropriate, to have such data corrected or erased.

How to register under the Data Protection Act

Registration must be done on Form DPR 1. The maximum period of registration is three years, but an organisation can register for a lesser period of one or two years. Whatever the period chosen, the register must be completed and amended when necessary. You will have to detail the purposes for which the data is used; the personal data which the data user holds; the sources from which the data user intends to obtain the information; the people to whom the data user may wish to disclose the information; and any overseas countries or territories to which the data user may wish to transfer the personal data.

Personal data concerns information recorded on the computer about a living individual, where he or she can be identified from that information (or from that and other information) in the possession of the data user. This includes any expression of opinion about the individual. The data is unlikely to be personal data when the subject is not an individual (e.g., if the information relates only to a limited company or other artificial legal persons).

Mailing Lists

Charity A can only swap mailing lists with Charity B if the names and addresses on the list have been obtained fairly and lawfully, (first Data Protection Principle), and if the body or person to whom the disclosure is made is set out in the data user's register entry (e.g. an environmental charity's entry on the DPA Register may state that it can transfer the data to any other charitable/voluntary organisation). It is not necessary to specify the particular organisation concerned, merely to disclose the category.

The meaning of the words "fairly obtained" were considered by the Data Protection Tribunal in September 1993 in a case concerning a mail order and list broking company called Innovations. An enforcement notice was issued because Innovations advertised its mail order catalogues without warning customers that their names and addresses would be sold on. (Case DA/92 31/49/1) The Data Protection Tribunal found that "personal information will not be fairly obtained unless the data subject is told of the non-obvious purpose before the information is obtained". If there is no forewarning, then the data subject must give his or her consent at a later stage to any non-obvious use.

The Innovations case clearly has implications for charities who obtain names and addresses for one purpose, e.g., donations, but wish to use them for another purpose, e.g., to swop with another charity or voluntary organisation. Any advertisement whether in a newspaper or on television or radio must state whether personal details will be used for another purpose. It is not enough to notify donors at a later stage. The charity must then seek positive consent to the non-obvious use of donors' personal data.

In considering whether information has been fairly obtained, the Registrar will also consider, inter alia, whether or not the person supplying the information could reasonably be expected to appreciate the purposes for which the information would be used or disclosed. If not, why were the purposes not set out? The Registrar will be particularly concerned where the data user is given the impression that information will be kept confidential.

The proposed European Union Directive on the protection of personal data has been of much concern to charities who feared that it was not apparent whether a compulsory "opt in" box would be required, rather than a warning in the first instance. However it seems that the Directive - which is unlikely to be issued before January 1995 at the earliest - will not require data subjects to give their specific consent to their data being passed on to other organisations. Charities and their trading companies which use databases must keep an eye on European developments.

Conclusion

Charities and their trading companies compiling/using databases must ensure that:

(a) they either have/obtain copyright in the database; or

(b) obtain the necessary licence; and

(c) they are registered under the Data Protection Act 1984.

Chapter 9
CHARITIES ACT 1992 AND COMMERCIAL PARTICIPATORS

9.1. Introduction

At about the same time as the Charity Commission was expressing its concerns in its 1991 Report (published in May 1992) regarding the licensing of names and logos by charities (see *Chapter 8.3*), the Government had also acted by passing the Charities Act 1992 (in March of that year). In particular Part II of the Charities Act 1992 deals with the whole question of charities' relations with commercial third parties. The very existence of controls on "commercial participators", as defined in the Charities Act 1992, illustrates the fact that the Government is well aware that charities licence their names and logos to commercial third parties and of the need to regulate those relationships. The Act did not outlaw such arrangements, notwithstanding the statement quoted in *Chapter 8.3* from the Charity Commissioner's Report for 1991, that a charity should not exploit its name commercially!

Although Part I of the Charities Act 1992 is now consolidated in the Charities Act 1993, Part II of the Charities Act 1992 remains on the statute book. *Part II is not yet in force. It will come into effect on 1st March 1995.* To understand the drafting of the 1992 Act, it is worth going back to the Woodfield Report of 1988. That report recommended (inter alia) that whenever goods or services were offered for sale with the indication that some part of the proceeds was to be devoted to charity, there should be specified:

(a) the charity or charities that were to benefit (and, if more than one, in what proportion);

(b) the manner in which the sums they were to receive would be calculated.

In the White Paper of 1989; *"Charities; A Framework for the Future"*, the Government expressed its concern about the practicability of these proposals; and commented (at page 56):

"Basic details of the agreement reached between the charity and the 'co-venturer' should be provided, however, with some latitude being allowed as to the form of expression chosen. Under the kind of provision envisaged, charity catalogues, for example, would be required to incorporate a simple, single, statement to the effect that X per cent of net profits, gross profits or receipts would go to the named charity or charities. Some formulae may be more complex. Even so, it should be possible to give some indication of their effect, by reference , for example, to the minimum proportion going to charity."

Although there had been some doubts about the practicability of the Woodfield proposal the authors of the White Paper were sure that:

"The public, when being encouraged to make a purchase on the grounds that it will benefit the charity, have a right to certain basic information, which should not be difficult to provide."

9.2.   What is a commercial participator?

The White Paper referred to the commercial partner of a charity as a "co-venturer". When drafting the 1992 Act the Government invented a new term to add to the vocabulary of the voluntary sector: the *"commercial participator"*. In essence, a commercial participator is someone who encourages the purchase of goods or services on the grounds that some of the proceeds will go to a charitable institution.

Section 58(1) of the Charities Act 1992 defines a *commercial participator* as:

"In relation to any charitable institution..... any person who:

(a)   carries on for gain a business other than a fund-raising business, but;

(b)   in the course of that business, engages in any promotional venture in the course of which it is represented that charitable contributions are to be given to or applied for the benefit of the institution."

A *"charitable institution"* is defined as:

"A charity or an institution (other than a charity) which is established for charitable, benevolent or philanthropic purposes."

This wording follows the House to House Collections Act 1939. The definition includes registered charities and those charities which are exempt from registration under the Charities Act 1993 (such as universities). In addition to charities, the definition also covers "benevolent and philanthropic" organisations such as Amnesty International and probably environmental organisations like Greenpeace and Friends of the Earth, although there is some doubt as to whether or not they are "benevolent and philanthropic" since the word "benevolent" means "of a kindly disposition, charitable, generous" and "philanthropic" means "benevolent or humane". Can organisations such as Greenpeace or Friends of the Earth which are primarily dedicated to preserving the environment (rather than man-kind) be considered as benevolent or philanthropic? The matter has not been tested by the Courts.

A *"promotional venture"* is defined as "any advertising or sales campaign or any other venture undertaken for promotional purposes".

"Venture" has not, apparently, been defined in any statute or, remarkably enough, considered in any legal judgements. However, the Oxford English Dictionary defines "venture" as "that which is ventured or risked in a commercial enterprise or speculation".

To *"represent"* is defined extraordinarily widely by Section 58(6) as meaning to represent:

"In any manner whatever, whether expressly or implicitly and whether done by speaking directly....... or by means of a statement published in any newspaper, film, or radio or television programme or otherwise."

"Charitable contributions" is defined by Section 58(1):

"In relation to any representation made by any commercial participator or other person, means -

(a) the whole or part of:
   (i) the consideration given for goods or services sold or supplied by him, or
   (ii) any proceeds (other than such consideration) of a promotional venture undertaken by him, or

(b) sums given by him by way of donation in connection with the sale or supply of any such goods or services (whether the amount of such sums is determined by reference to the value of any such goods or services or otherwise).

"Services" is defined by Section 58(9) as including facilities and in particular:

(a) access to any premises or event;

(b) membership of any organisation;

(c) the provision of any advertising space;

(d) the provision of any financial facilities.

9.3. Examples of commercial participators

(a) **Affinity card companies** (see *Chapter 6.6*)

Banks or financial institutions issue credit cards in conjunction with a charitable institution and donate an agreed percentage of the customer's total expenditure on the card to the charitable institution. In these arrangements, the bank is:

(i) engaging in a business (running a credit card agency) which is not a fund-raising business; and

(ii) in the course of that business, engaging in a promotional venture in which it is representing that a percentage of the consideration paid by the consumer for the services provided by the credit card company will go to a charitable institution.

Hence, the credit card company is a commercial participator and will be subject to the controls set out in the 1992 Act. This is made expressly clear by Section 58(9)(d), where the definition of *"services"* includes "the provision of any financial facilities" (see above). (See also *Chapter 6.6.*)

(b) **The Glastonbury Festival**

The farmer who organises the well known Glastonbury Festival each June currently advertises that he gives the net profits of the event to Greenpeace. He used to have a similar arrangement with CND. Accordingly, provided Greenpeace is considered to be a charitable institution for the purposes of the 1992 Act (see above), the farmer is a commercial participator - as he is carrying on a business (running the Glastonbury Festival) and in the course of that business is representing that part of the price for the tickets will go to the charitable institution.

(c) **Catalogues**

Some commercial organisations distribute catalogues of merchandise coupled with the inducement that part of the profits from the activity or part of the price per item will be passed to a named charity. In this case the catalogue company is running a commercial business (selling goods by mail order) and in the course of that business is representing that part of the taxable profit or part of the price paid for each good (the situation will vary) will pass to a named charity. The catalogue company is a commercial participator.

(d) **Lotteries**

With the relaxation on small lotteries introduced by the National Lottery Act 1993, some charities will have arrangements with commercial organisations to run small local lotteries on their behalf. The lottery management company will be selling tickets to the lottery coupled with the inducement that the net proceeds from the lottery will be distributed to charitable institutions. Accordingly, the lottery management company will be a commercial participator as it is carrying on a business (managing lotteries) and in the course of that is selling tickets which state that the profits from the lottery will go to charitable institutions. The definition of *"services"* in Section 58 of the 1992 Act makes it quite clear that a *service* includes access to any event and a lottery must surely fall within the definition of an *"event"*.

(e) **Informal arrangements**

Each of the above examples are based on the formal negotiated activities of, for example, a credit card company which has an arrangement with a charity to use its logo on the credit card. Equally, a catalogue will display a charity's logo as an inducement to consumers to purchase goods from the catalogue. In each case the commercial participator has an agreement with the charity. However, the legislation on commercial participators can also bite on informal arrangements. For example, say there is an international emergency (e.g. an earthquake). Members of the public may feel moved to respond and help. A restaurant owner may decide to give, for example, £1 for every meal purchased during a two week period to the International Red Cross. If the restaurant owner advertises this (which no doubt he will do), he immediately will become a form of commercial participator although he does not have a formal agreement with a charitable institution. He is carrying on a business (a restaurant), and in the course of that is inducing people to buy his meals coupled with the statement that part of the proceeds will pass to a charitable institution (the International Red Cross). This will mean that the restaurant owner should comply with the Act as well.

9.3. Is a trading company owned by charitable institution a commercial participator?

This is one of the thorniest questions that has been thrown up by the Charities Act 1992. Companies connected with a charitable institution (which by definition will include a charity's trading company) are excluded from the definition of a professional fund-raiser under the Charities Act 1992. But this express exclusion does *not* extend to commercial participators. When the Charities Bill was discussed in the House of Lords, it was generally believed that trading companies owned by charitable institutions would not be treated as commercial participators. Despite this, the Act applies the rules relating to commercial participators to a trading company owned by a charitable institution. This was in fact consistent with the White Paper of 1989 - see the quotation at *Chapter 9.1* which referred to 'charity catalogues', which are usually issued by charities' trading companies.

The position has been clarified by Section 25 of the Deregulation and Contracting Out Act 1994 which provides that a company connected with a charitable institution is *not* a commercial participator.

9.4. Section 59 agreements

Section 59(2) of the Charities Act 1992 provides that it shall be unlawful for a commercial participator to represent that charitable contributions are to be given to or applied for the benefit of a charitable institution unless it does so in accordance with an agreement with the institution satisfying the prescribed requirements. The prescribed requirements are laid down in a statutory instrument (the charitable institutions (Fund-Raising) Regulations 1994) which states the prescribed requirements are:

(a) the names and addresses of the parties;

(b) the date when the agreement was signed by or on behalf of each party;

(c) the duration of the agreement;

(d) arrangements for early termination;

(e) any terms relating to the variation of the agreement during that period;

(f) a statement of the agreement's principal objectives and the methods to be used;

(g) arrangements for the transfer of monies to the charitable institution so that monies should be paid over within 28 days of receipt unless the agreement otherwise provides;

(h) a statement of the manner in which is to be determined:

    (i) If there is more than one charitable institution party to the agreement, the proportion in which the institutions which are so party are respectively to benefit under the agreement;

    (ii) The statement to be made under Section 60(3) Charities Act 1992 (see *Chapter 9.5*).

A breach of the requirements set out in the statutory instrument will be a criminal offence giving rise to a maximum fine of £500.

In addition, by Section 59(3), the court may grant an injunction on the application of a charitable institution if it is satisfied:

(a) that any person has breached Section 59(2); i.e., a commercial participator solicits money for the benefit of a charitable institution without having entered into a Section 59(2) Agreement; and

(b) that unless restrained such a contravention is likely to continue or be repeated.

The charitable institution may seek such an injunction from either the High Court or a County Court.

If a charitable institution enters into a Section 59(2) agreement with a commercial participator, but the agreement does not comply with the prescribed requirements as set out in the regulations, then the agreement can only be enforced by the commercial participator to such extent (if any) as may be provided by an order of the court. This will mean that the commercial participator will not be able to continue to use the charitable institution's name until the court has ordered that it can. This could mean that, for example, a commercial participator must stop using stock which bears the charitable institution's logo until the agreement satisfies the prescribed requirements.

Under Section 59(5), the commercial participator will not be entitled to receive any remuneration under a defective agreement until the agreement satisfies the prescribed requirements or a court orders that the commercial participator may be paid. It is unlikely that this provision will be of much use to charitable institutions. This is because money will normally pass from the commercial participator to the charitable institution (e.g. *"5p per bottle of water sold goes to XYZ Charity"*). In this case, sales are being made by the commercial participator, with a proportion of sales income being forwarded to the charity. It is only where moneys are going from the charitable institution *to* the commercial participator that the charitable institution could refuse to pay until the court had ordered it to do so or the agreement had been rectified so as to ensure that it complied with the prescribed requirements.

9.5.   Section 60(3) statements

Section 60(3) provides that where any representation is made by a commercial participator to the effect that charitable contributions are to be given to or applied for the benefit of one or more particular charitable institutions, the representation shall be accompanied by a statement clearly indicating:

(a)   the name or names of the institution or institutions concerned;

(b)   if there is more than one institution, the proportions in which the institutions are respectively to benefit;

(c)   (in general terms) the method by which it is to be determined;

    (i)   what proportion of the consideration given for goods or services sold or supplied by him, or of any other proceeds of a promotional venture undertaken by him, is to be given to or applied for the benefit of the institution or institutions concerned; or

    (ii)   what sums, by way of donations by him in connection with the sale or supply of any such goods or services are to be so given or applied, as the case may require.

The following points should be noted:-

(a) **any representation made by a commercial participator has to be *accompanied* by the required statement.** A representation, as we have already seen, can be made expressly or implied and can be made by speaking directly or by means of a statement published in a newspaper, film, radio or television programme or otherwise. In the case of an oral representation, this means the statement has to be made at the same time or be clearly visible at the same time. In the case of a newspaper advertisement, this means the advertisement must contain the statement. In shops it *should* be sufficient that the statement is made by a clear and legible sign, provided it is readily visible when the representation is made, (e.g. it is near the point of sale of the goods concerned, if not printed on the goods themselves).

(b) **as can be seen, there are two *different* ways in which the statement can be made "as the case may require". Unfortunately, Section 60(3) is not satisfactorily worded.**

The first possibility is that the statement indicates:

"(In general terms) the method by which it is to be determined (i) what proportion of the consideration given etc".

On close analysis this could be ludicrously easy to comply with.

◆◆ *example*

Suppose a high street retailer, ABC, with its own branded products, decides to give 5p for each bottle of ABC's water sold to XYZ Charity. The statement required under s.60(3)(c)(i) could be as general as:

"The directors of ABC shall meet each year in Monte Carlo to decide what proportion of the price paid for this bottle of water will be given to XYZ Charity a registered charity".

Such a statement does indicate in *general terms* the *method* by which it is to be determined what proportion of the price of the bottle of water will be given to XYZ Charity! Obviously this is a ridiculous example. But it illustrates one of the problems with the drafting of this sub-section of the Act. Charitable institutions negotiating arrangements with commercial participators should be advised to ignore completely the statement "in general terms the method by which it is to be determined" and seek to ensure that the statement clearly indicates what *proportion* of the consideration given for the goods or services sold will be given to the charitable institution concerned. It is also fair to assume that if this sub-section were ever to be the subject of judicial scrutiny, a court would seek to give an effective meaning to it and the generalised statement set out in the example above would surely not receive judicial approval. Moreover, there is an element of contradiction in the way in which the sub-section is drafted, because one does not need a *method* in order to determine a *proportion*, and this might also be taken into account if the wording was ever subject to scrutiny by a court. A proportion is a proportion, and no method is needed to determine a proportion!

This first type of statement is designed to cover those types of promotion where, for example, a retailer states that a certain amount for each *product* sold will go to a charitable institution (e.g. on a bottle of water or a can of lemonade). The statement has to relate *not to* the profits to be derived from the sale of that particular item, but to its *price*. This could cause problems for retailers since they will be obliged to state what percentage of the price will be given away. It could well be that a retailer will make no profit on that line because he is left with unsold stock, and hence will make a loss on the promotion.

An example of the first type of statement under Section 60(3) might be as follows. (ignoring the phrase "in general terms the method by which"!):

"For each bottle sold 5p will go to XYZ Charity a registered charity"

The second method of making the required statement under section 60(3)(c), is to state "(in general terms) the method by which it is to be determined.... what sums by way of donation by" the commercial participator in connection with the sale or supply of such goods are to be given.

The best and easiest example of this is a trading company owned by a charitable institution. In this case, the statement could be:

"100% of the taxable profits of XYZ Trading Limited are given each year by Deed of Covenant to XYZ Charity a registered charity".

That clearly states *the method* by which it is to be determined what sum by way of donations are to be given to the charitable institution concerned. However, as noted above, a company controlled by a charitable institution is exempt from the controls on commercial participators. Alternatively, the second method will cover such cases as where a manufacturer agrees to give, e.g. £1 million to a named charity and states this on a named product for the period of a promotion.

◆◆ *example*

On a drinks can; "ABC Corporation has agreed to give £500,000 to XYZ Charity, a registered charity. Each can sold helps ABC Corporation meet its target."

(c) **The sale of charity Christmas cards: Special problems will arise in relation to the sale of charity Christmas cards and controls on commercial participators.**

Section 58(6) defines "to represent or solicit" in such a wide way that the high street retailer which sells Christmas cards which bear the emblem "sold in aid of XYZ charity" will almost certainly be construed as being a commercial participator. It is carrying on a commercial business (selling cards), in the course of which it is impliedly representing that part of the proceeds of sale will go to XYZ charity. The average person in the street who buys a Christmas card in the shop will assume that part of the proceeds of sale will go to XYZ charity as a result of the statement printed on the card purchased in the retailer's shop. Hence, in theory the retailer will need to have a Section 59 Agreement and make the statement under Section 60(3). That is simply stated. But in reality the position is far more complex. The high street retailer will *not*, in many cases, pay a penny to XYZ charity despite the statement on the card.

In fact, XYZ charity will probably have set up a trading company, XYZ Trading Limited, to carry out the sale of Christmas cards (see *Chapter 6*). XYZ Charity will have licensed XYZ Trading Limited to use the charity's name on the card. XYZ Trading will then have sold the cards to a wholesaler. XYZ Trading will, hopefully, have made a profit on that transaction. After deductions of all expenses etc. XYZ Trading will covenant its profits to XYZ Charity or give them by Gift Aid. In that very limited sense the cards *are* sold in aid of XYZ Charity. The wholesaler will then sell the cards either outright or on a sale or return basis to retailers which will then seek to sell them to the public. Hence, whilst the high street retailer would *appear* to be a commercial participator, in fact it is *not* because it is not paying any part of the proceeds of sale of the Christmas card to a charitable institution, although it is impliedly representing that it is!

This means that the high street retailer will need to make it very clear that it is not a commercial participator. It will not want to put up a statement to the effect that:

"Not a single penny from the sale of these charity Christmas cards is paid by this company to any of the named charities"!

That would clearly be commercially disastrous. Instead it will want a more bland statement probably to appear on the Christmas card itself (or packet, if the cards are sold in packets) such as:-

"These cards were sold by XYZ Trading Limited which covenants all its taxable profits to XYZ Charity, a registered charity. XYZ Trading Limited took its profits on the sale of this card at that point. All subsequent sellers of this card are not commercial participators for the purposes of Part II of the Charities Act 1992".

It may well be necessary for charities' trading companies to print such a statement on Christmas cards, although to mingle such legalese with Christmas Greetings may seem highly inappropriate! Inevitably there will be old but as yet unsold stock in circulation printed prior to the legislation coming into effect. Consequently, a statement may have to be put up in shops so as to ensure that the representation made by the sale of a Christmas card which states "sold in aid of XYZ Charity" is accompanied by the statement required by Section 60(3), which in this case would be a statement to the effect that the sub-section does not apply!

(d) **Sales of publications and other items produced by charities. Another potential problem thrown up by Part II of the Charities Act 1992 arises from the sale by charities of goods produced in fulfilment of their primary purposes.** The best example is afforded by books produced by charitable publishers (e.g. Yale University Press or the Directory of Social Change). Another common example is the sale of theatre tickets (e.g. National Theatre, Royal Shakespeare Company, English National Opera or Glyndebourne).

Under Section 5 of the Charities Act 1993, all documents issued by or on behalf of a registered charity and soliciting money or other property for the benefit of the charity have to state the fact that the charity is a registered charity. A book published by a charity is "a document". It has a price printed on it. Accordingly, it can be argued that the book is a document which "solicits" money for the benefit of the charity. Hence, in future all books produced by publishers which are registered charities should state "a registered charity" in English in legible characters.

The sale of a book published by a registered charity bearing the name of the charity and the phrase "a registered charity" on the book's spine or inside cover, could well constitute a "representation" for the purposes of Section 58 of the Charities Act 1992, given its wide definition (see above)! The average consumer who buys a book bearing the name of the charity and sees the phrase "a registered charity", may well believe that part of the proceeds of sale of the book will go to the charity concerned.

However, such publications are rarely sold directly by the charitable publisher itself. Instead they are sold through commercial outlets. Is the commercial bookseller a commercial participator for the purposes of the 1992 Act? Clearly, it is carrying on a business which is not a fund-raising business and in the course of that business is engaging in a promotional venture, i.e. selling books, but is it: "representing that charitable contributions are to be given to or applied for the benefit of the (charitable) institution."? This is the definition of a commercial participator in Section 58(1) of the Act.

As previously mentioned, "to represent" has a very wide meaning. It could certainly be argued that the sale by a commercial bookseller of a book bearing the legend "a registered charity" could be an *implied* representation that part of the proceeds of sale are to be given to the registered charity concerned. It is quite likely that a consumer, faced with a choice between two books on the same subject, one produced by a commercial publisher and the other by a registered charity, might opt to purchase the one published by the charity. If this is the case, then just as with the "charity Christmas cards", books or other publications produced by publishers which are registered charities will have to bear a statement to the effect that the end retailer is not a commercial participator and that the *registered* charity concerned has already taken its reward at another point in the retail chain. Note that this argument only applies to registered charities - an exempt charity (such as Oxford University Press and Cambridge University Press) will *not* be caught by it, since as exempt charities they do not have to state 'a registered charity' on documents.

(e) **General fund-raising: One of the anomalies in Part II of the 1992 Charities Act is that the controls on commercial participators only apply if the commercial participator claims that part of the proceeds of sale of goods or services will go to a named charitable institution**. There is *no* control on a *commercial* party which seeks to sell goods or services coupled with the inducement that part of the proceeds of sale will go to a *general* charitable cause. For example "to relieve poverty in the Third world"; "to help earthquake victims"; or "to benefit children".

◆◆ *example*

The Armenian earthquake attracted widespread sympathy. A restaurant owner might have been moved to offer "£5 from every meal sold will go to help the victims of the Armenian earthquake."

Because the restaurant owner has not specified a *named* charity, he is not a commercial participator.

However, despite this oversight in the primary legislation, the Regulations issued under Section 64, charitablr institutions (Fund-Raising) contains controls on such activities. Such persons will have to make a similar statement to that under Section 60(3), and also state how the charitable contributions referred to are to be applied for those purposes and not for the benefit of any particular charitable institution or institutions.

Example of the statement required for a Non-Commercial Participator

"£5 per meal will be donated to support victims of the Armenian earthquake. These sums are not being raised for the benefit of a particular charitable institution."

Breach of these provisions will be a criminal offence giving rise to a maximum fine of £500 (second level).

(f) **The right to cancel - (for telephone sales):** If a commercial participator makes *"a representation"* (as defined in Section 58(6)) by telephone, then within seven days of any payment of £50 or more being made to the commercial participator in response to the representation, the commercial participator has to give to the purchaser a written statement complying with Section 60(3) and including full details of the right of the purchaser to cancel under Section 61(2). The payment can be made by whatever means including a credit or debit card.

The seven day period is determined as follows (Section 60(6)):

(i) if the purchaser pays in person, the seven days run from the time of payment;

(ii) if the purchaser pays by post, the seven days runs from the time of posting the payment;

(iii) if the purchaser pays via telephone or fax or other telecommunication apparatus and orders an account to be debited, the seven days run from the time such authority is given.

The purchaser then has seven days from the date he is given the written statement (Section 61(2)(b)of the Act) to exercise, if he so wishes, the right to cancel the purchase, but this is conditional, in the case of the sale of goods, on the restitution of the goods in question by him (Section 61(4)of the Act).

Does this mean that the purchaser has to be given the notice (i.e. must it be *physically* handed to him), or is the statement given when it is posted through his letterbox or when it is put into the post (if posted)?

Section 7 of the Interpretation Act 1978 provides that where an Act authorises or requires any document to be served by post (where the expression "serve" or the expression "give" is used) then, unless the contrary intention appears, the service is deemed to be effected by properly addressing, pre-paying and posting a letter containing the document and, unless the contrary is proved, to have been effected at the time when the letter would be delivered in the ordinary course of post. The implication is that "to give" is synonymous with "to serve". This is confirmed by a case under the Law of Property Act 1925 Section 36(2) which uses the phrase "give....notice in writing" in which it was held that "give" meant the same as "serve".

Section 76 of the 1992 Charities Act states that any notice or other document to be given or served under Part II may be served on or given to a person by:

(i) delivering it to that person;

(ii) leaving it at his last known address in the UK;

(iii) sending it by post to him at that address.

In the case of a body corporate (e.g. a limited company), notice is effected by delivering it or sending it by post:

(i) to the registered or principal office of the body in the UK; or

(ii) if it has no such office in the UK, to any place in the UK where it carries on business or conducts its affairs (as the case may be).

The right to cancel notice is deemed to be effected under the Interpretation Act 1978 "at the time at which the letter would be delivered in the ordinary course of post" (Section 7 of that Act). This means that delivery will be *presumed* to have taken place on the next working day or the next but one, depending on whether first or second class post is used. The court will normally assume that second class mail is used.

◆◆ *example*

Gullible responds to a telephone sales campaign run by Rip Off Merchandising Company in which it is represented that 10% of the price for a shell-suit will be given to XYZ Charity. Gullible sends £100 to purchase the shell-suit by post on 1st May to Rip Off. Rip Off receives the payment on 3rd May. Rip Off has to give Gullible the right to cancel notice within seven days (Section 60(5)) of the post mark on Gullible's letter - Section 60(6)

---

states that the payment shall be regarded as made at the time when it is posted (i.e. the notice must be given by 7th May).

Rip Off posts the right to cancel notice on 7th May. Gullible will be deemed to have received the notice two working days after the 7th May unless the "contrary" is proved - Interpretation Act 1978 Section 7. If he receives the notice, Gullible must exercise his right to cancel within seven days of being given the right to cancel notice. If he receives the notice on 9th May, he will have to post his notice exercising his right to cancel and return the goods by 16th May (letter posted on 7th May and deemed to be served on 9th May).

There is no approved format for the notice exercising the right to cancel, it merely has to indicate the donor's *intention* to cancel.

The commercial participator may deduct administrative expenses reasonably incurred by him in connection with the making of the refund - see Section 61(4) of the Act. Viscount Astor explained in the House of Lords:

"Administrative expenses is intended to cover the direct costs of refunding the payment, for costs such as staff time, postage, bank charges and so forth. It will also cover the costs of dealing with any notice of cancellation of an agreement to make payment". (House of Lords Debate 4535 Col.1215 (18th February 1992))

If a commercial participator makes a solicitation in the course of a television or radio programme and states that payment can be made by credit or debit card, the commercial participator *must,* in addition to the statement required under Section 60(3), make it clear that the consumer has the right to cancel if he makes a payment of **£50 or more**.

9.6. Relationship between charities, trading companies and commercial participator legislation

Many charities have appointed their trading companies as licensees to exploit commercially the charity's name and logo in order to avoid any possible tax liability that could arise, since the commercial exploitation of a charity's logo and goodwill is not primary purpose trading (see *Chapter 6*).

However, Section 59(2) of the Charities Act 1992 makes it absolutely clear that the agreement in relation to the exploitation of the name of a charitable institution has to be between the *institution* and the *commercial* participator. It *cannot* be between the charitable institution's trading company and the commercial participator. However, this also means that monies which flow to a charity from the commercial participator should be structured in an appropriate manner or it may be taxed, since those profits will not have been derived from primary purposes trading. As already discussed in the case of affinity cards (see *Chapter 6.6*), payments by a commercial participator to a charity *must* be constructed as an annual payment so as to allow the charity to receive that income *free of tax*. However, if the agreement with the commercial participator covers *more* than use of the charity's name and logo (e.g., use of a mailing list of supporters), any payments to the charity in respect of the use of those rights cannot be treated as pure income profit. In such a case there will have to be two agreements (as with the affinity card arrangement) one whereby the charity receives payment from the commercial participator for use of its name and logo as an annual payment, and a separate contract between the trading company and the commercial participator in respect of access to the trading company's database, etc. It should also be remembered that the method of treating licence income as an annual payment may not always be available - see the discussion in *Chapter 6.6*. In any event VAT will have to be charged on the licence fee and any fees paid for the use of the database.

9.7.   Breach of Section 60 - criminal sanction

Section 60(7) of the Charities Act 1992 imposes a strict criminal liability on a commercial participator who is in breach of Section 60 (i.e. a commercial participator who fails to make the statements required under Section 60(3), (4) or (5)). The maximum fine is currently £5,000. It should be noted that the liability will arise on the commercial participator and not the charitable institution. Technically the fine could be imposed for each offence (i.e. for each item sold without the requisite statement being made), so that the fines could mount up very rapidly. In order not to damage potentially valuable commercial relationships with commercial participators, charities will need to ensure that the requirements of Section 60 are strictly adhered to. It could be very damaging to a charity's reputation for its commercial partner to be found guilty of breaching the requirements of the Charities Act 1992.

Much British legislation is under-enforced. However, there are indications that the introduction of some form of incentive payment to Trading Standards Officers is increasing the rigour of their performance, which could mean that legislation such as that contained in Part II of the Charities Act 1992 will be more widely enforced in the future.

It will be a *defence* for a person charged with any offence under Section 60:

"To prove that he took all reasonable precautions and exercised all due diligence to avoid the commission of the offence". (Section 60(8))

This is similar to a phrase used in the Trade Descriptions Act 1968, Section 24. It shifts the burden of proof from the prosecution, who would, under normal rules of criminal law, have to prove that the defendant had mens rea and committed the offence, on to the defendant who has to show that he took all reasonable precautions etc. That is a heavy burden. However, in one case under the Trade Descriptions Act 1968, *Tesco Supermarkets v. Nattrass* (1972) AC153, the House of Lords ruled that the defendant's employer had exercised all due diligence by devising a proper system for the operation of its supermarkets and securing implementation as far as was reasonably practicable and, in that case, the employer was not held liable for the negligent act of its employee.

Thus commercial participators will need to ensure that they have proper procedures adequately monitored to ensure that their staff comply with the requirements of Section 60. If they do not, they will be unable to establish that they have taken all reasonable precautions and exercised all due diligence. When the matter was debated in the House of Lords, Viscount Astor commented:

"In order to avail himself of this defence, the person charged must establish, on the balance of probabilities, that he was not negligent in failing to avoid the commission of the offence". (House of Lords Debate, Vol.535 Col.1210 (18th February 1992))

Under Section 60(9), where there is a breach of Section 60 which is due to the act or default of some other person, that other person (e.g. an employee) shall be guilty of the offence. The same defence of having taken all reasonable precautions etc. can be pleaded. The sub-section is designed to allow criminal charges to be brought against employees who break the requirements of the Act in breach, for example, of their employer's rule book.

Conclusion

Part II of the Charities Act 1992, once it is in force, will effect a number of the commercial activities of charities and their trading companies. It will be prudent for charities to review such arrangements in the light of the Regulations as soon as possible, as it may well be necessary for charities to renegotiate agreements, reprint catalogues, train staff and print notices as required by the 1992 Act in time for the Act coming into force on March 1 1995.

Chapter 10
TRADING COMPANIES TAXATION AND ACCOUNTING

This chapter covers the questions of how the profits of a for-profit trading company owned by a charity are taxed. Points considered include: management charges and the payment of profits to the charity by dividend, gift aid or deed of covenant.

10.1. Taxation of profits

As already seen in Chapter 4, charities enjoy a privileged position so far as direct tax is concerned, as the profits from primary purposes trading are tax free. Trading companies owned by charities will be subject to the normal rules of corporation tax and will pay tax on taxable profits as follows (1994/95 rates):

25% on the first £300,000;

33% on profits over £1,500,000;

a marginal rate of 35% on profits between £500,000 and £1,500,000.

However, if the trading company can reduce its taxable profits by paying them away to the charity which controls the trading company, the position changes. There will be *less* or *no* corporation tax to be paid, depending on the level of taxable profits remaining in the trading company as at its corporation tax date. The corporation tax year starts on 1st April (and not 6th April as for other taxes). Corporation tax is charged on the actual profits of each accounting period. This will usually coincide with the period for which the company prepares its annual accounts, but it cannot exceed 12 months.

◆◆ *example*

A trading company prepares its audited accounts for the year 1st July 1993 to 30th June 1994. Its profits were £100,000. It pays Corporation Tax (CT) as follows:-

CT year 1 from 1 April 1993 to 31 March 1994: CT rate 25%

CT year 2 from 1 April 1994 to 31 March 1995: CT rate 25%

CT payable for year 1: £100,000 x 9/12 x 25%		£18,750
CT payable for year 2: £100,000 x 3/12 x 25%		£ 6,250
	TOTAL	£25,000

Corporation tax has to be paid nine months after the end of the accounting period. In this example, the accounting period ended on 30th June 1994. Tax must be paid by 31st March 1995, even if no tax assessment has been received.

10.2. Shedding profits by management charges

It is standard practice in the commercial world for subsidiary companies to pay a management charge to the holding company in return for the provision of head office and other services. The charge has to be fair and reasonable - if it is excessive, the charge will not be treated as a tax deductible expense in the hands of the subsidiary company (see Section 74 Income and Corporation Taxes Act 1988 ("the ICTA")). But subject to that caveat, some charity finance directors, accustomed to the practices of the commercial world, may suggest that the simplest method of stripping out taxable profits from the trading company and putting them in the parent charity is for the charity to charge the trading company a management fee.

This practice could cause problems for the charity. Firstly, the charity may have a "vires" or capacity problem - charities do not have the legal capacity to carry on the business of rendering management services to commercial companies. The Charity Commission and the Inland Revenue could (perfectly correctly) question the basis on which the charity was rendering such services.

Secondly, the profits that the charity made on such activities would be *taxable* in the hands of the charity since the rendering of management services would *not* be in fulfilment of a primary purpose of the charity.

10.3. Payment of profit by way of dividends

It used to be the case that a trading company could transfer away its profits to its parent charity, in a tax-efficient manner by declaring a dividend. This only applied if the trading company paid corporation tax at the small companies rate (25%) - otherwise there could be a loss of tax relief of up to 8% of the taxable profits of the trading company.

However, the March 1993 Budget made the payment of dividends by a trading company to its parent charity, tax-inefficient. In that Budget the Chancellor reduced the value of the tax credit on dividends paid by UK companies from 25% to 20% for dividends paid after 5th April 1993, subject to transitional relief (see below). Previously the tax credit (known as Advance Corporation Tax or "ACT") had been the same as the small companies rate of Corporation Tax.

◆◆ *example*

XYZ Trading Limited taxable profits
for the year ended 31 March 1993: £100,000

Tax payable on the profit
(Corporation Tax at 25%):   £ 25,000

Net profit after tax   £ 75,000

XYZ Trading Limited declares a 100% dividend
and gives to XYZ Charity, its parent charity:

A cash dividend of: £75,000

An ACT Voucher for: £25,000   (for dividends paid up
                                                    to 5th April 1993)

XYZ Trading pays the corporation tax to the Inland Revenue and XYZ charity, as a charity, could recover the full amount of the ACT (£25,000) from the Inland Revenue.

When the small companies' Corporation Tax Rate and the ACT rate were the same there was no adverse tax impact for the trading company to pay a dividend to the charity. But with the reduction of ACT to 20%, in the example above, XYZ Charity will only receive an ACT Voucher for £20,000 and recover £20,000 from the Inland Revenue. This leaves £5,000 of tax to be paid (£25,000 of tax on the profits less £20,000).

For a transitional period of 4 years from 6th April 1993 charities will be able to claim additional payments, designed to ease the transition to the new reduced value of the ACT tax credit. The transitional relief is as follows:

- for 1993-94 : 1/15 of dividend which equates to a tax credit of 24%

- for 1994-95 : 1/20 of dividend which equates to a tax credit of 23%

- for 1995-96 : 1/30 of dividend which equates to a tax credit of 22%

- for 1996-97 : 1/60 of dividend which equates to a tax credit of 21%

The payment of a dividend by a trading company to its parent charity is no longer a tax-efficient method of transferring profits from the trading company. The Charity Commissioners in paragraph 44 of their 1988 Report stated:

"Trustees have a duty to consider the tax effectiveness of the arrangements between them and any associated trading company, and they may be personally liable to account for taxation liabilities which are unnecessarily incurred directly or indirectly as a result of inefficient administration of the charity."

In the light of this statement and the March 1993 Budget, trustees should now be *very cautious* about using dividends to strip out profits from a trading company.

10.4. Payment of profit using Gift Aid

Gift Aid was introduced in the 1990 Budget, as a tax-effective mechanism for making *single* payments to charity (Deeds of Covenant are tax efficient for *regular* payments). The minimum qualifying level for Gift Aid payments has been reduced in subsequent Budgets. Where a UK tax-payer makes a gift of more than £250 to a charity, that payment will be treated as having been made net of basic rate tax (25%). If the donor is a tax payer or has deducted income tax at the basic rate when making the payment, and if the donor signs the required form (form R190SD for individual donors or form R240SD for companies), the charity can then claim repayment of the tax paid or deducted by the donor in exactly the same way as for Deeds of Covenant.

◆◆ *example*

XYZ Trading Limited estimates it will make taxable profits of £100,000 in the financial year ended 31st December 1993. Prior to 31st December 1993, it issues a cheque to XYZ Charity for £75,000. The cheque must be cleared through XYZ Charity's bank account before 31st December 1993. XYZ Trading Limited pays £25,000 to the Inland Revenue (basic rate income tax of 25% on £100,000). This tax must be paid by 15th January 1994 (within 15 days of the end of the quarter in which the tax was deducted from the Gift Aid payment). XYZ Trading signs a form R240SD and returns this to XYZ Charity confirming the £75,000 Gift Aid payment on which tax has been deducted and accounted for.

XYZ Charity recovers the £25,000 from the Inland Revenue.

In order to qualify for Gift Aid certain conditions must be met:

(a) **The donation must be more than £250 (after deducting basic rate income tax).**

(b) **The donation must be in money.** The legislation refers to the "payment of a sum of money". Notwithstanding any legal argument as to what constitutes payment, the Inland Revenue explanatory booklet 1R 113 confirms that a loan waiver will not satisfy this requirement.

(c) **The donation must not be linked in any way or linked with the acquisition of any property by the charity or the supply of services to the donor** - this is another reason why the relationship between the charity and its trading company needs to be at arm's length (see *Chapter 7*). This is especially relevant with a trading company owned by a charity as it will almost certainly be a "Close Company" for the purposes of the taxes legislation. A "Close Company" is defined as a company which is under the control of five or fewer participators. A "Close Company" which makes a donation under Gift Aid must not receive a benefit exceeding 2.5% of the amount of the gift, subject to an overall ceiling of £250 in consequence of making the gift. Hence there must be no hostages to fortune in the relationship between the charity and the trading company in terms of unpaid benefits received by the trading company from the charity, which could lead the Inland Revenue to disallow a claim for repayment of income tax deducted under Gift Aid.

(d) **The payment must be made net of basic rate income tax (25% - 1994 figure).**

Problems with Gift Aid

At first glance Gift Aid appears the perfect method of passing taxable profits free of tax to a charity. It is flexible and simple; it requires no binding long-term legal agreement. But it has disadvantages:-

(a) **No retrospective adjustment**

With a payment under a Deed of Covenant a charity can make a retrospective adjustment (see *Chapter 10.5*). With Gift Aid this is **not** possible. This can present problems.

◆◆ *example*

XYZ Trading Limited makes a £100,000 donation under Gift Aid to XYZ Charity based on an estimate of taxable profits. It deducts £25,000 tax at the basic rate and pays this to the Revenue.

It transpires that the estimate was wrong. Taxable profits were only £50,000. XYZ Trading has had to pay £25,000 of income tax to the Inland Revenue under the Gift Aid payment but only saves £12,500 of corporation tax. It will be initially out of pocket by £50,000 as its profits were not sufficient to cover the Gift Aid payment.

But XYZ Charity will not be able to repay to XYZ Trading the £37,500 which was overpaid although XYZ Trading should be able to recover the £12,500 of income tax paid by XYZ Trading and recovered by XYZ Charity in respect of this payment provided XYZ Charity repays it to the Inland Revenue..

XYZ Trading Limited will have paid over all its taxable profits plus a further £37,500. XYZ Trading Limited's balance sheet will show a deficit of £37,500. Worse still, this loss cannot be carried forward by XYZ Trading Limited to offset against future profits as it is not a trading loss.

This accumulated loss has two consequences:

(i) Under Section 263 Companies Act 1985, a company cannot make a *"distribution"* save out of "profits available for distribution".

"A distribution" is defined very widely and includes "every description of distribution of a company's assets to its members, whether in cash or otherwise". It is fair to conclude that a payment of its taxable profits, whether by Deed of Covenant or Gift Aid by a trading company to its sole member (the charity), is a distribution of the company's assets to its members.

"A company's profits available for distribution are its accumulated, realised profits so far as not previously utilised by distribution or capitalisation, less its accumulated, realised losses". (Section 263(3), Companies Act 1985)

Hence, once XYZ Trading Limited has accumulated losses, it can only make a distribution once it has cleared off those accumulated losses, by retaining profits which will be taxed at the appropriate rate. In the example XYZ Trading Limited will need to retain taxable profits of £50,000, pay tax of £12,500 (at 25%) leaving a net sum of £37,500 on the balance sheet to "soak up" the accumulated loss. Only then will XYZ Trading Limited be able to make a fresh *distribution to* XYZ Charity.

(ii) If a company makes an unlawful distribution, by Section 277 of the Companies Acts 1985, if a shareholder or member knew or had reasonable grounds for believing that the distribution was unlawful, the member is liable to repay the amount of the distribution pursuant to Section 277. The directors of the trading company who sanctioned the unlawful distribution will themselves be jointly and severally (i.e. individually) liable to repay to the company the amount of the unlawful distribution. Thus, if the charity is unable to repay the excess *Gift Aid* payment, the directors could incur personal liability.

If a trading company is obliged by a *Deed of Covenant* to pay its profits to the charity but is prevented from doing so by Section 277, the charity cannot claim there has been a breach of the covenant, because if the company honoured the covenant, the charity could be forced to repay the covenanted sum under Section 277. Given the joint and several liability of the directors of the trading company to repay the unlawful distribution as well, it is possible to conceive of a conflict between the interests of the charity which would be to force the directors of the trading company to repay the distribution and the personal interests of those directors. The author is not aware of any such case having occurred but it is possible to envisage it happening.

(b) **Donated Goods: liability to VAT**

The sale of donated goods by a trading company will be zero-rated for VAT only if the company **covenants** all its profits to charity. A Gift Aid payment will not suffice. Where there is no Deed of Covenant and no covenant of all the profits to the parent charity, the zero-rating concession on donated goods (if the goods are sold by the trading company) will not apply, and VAT will be payable in respect of any such sales (provided that the trading company's taxable turnover is sufficient for VAT registration).

Procedures

The procedures for making a Gift Aid payment are as follows

(a) The donor company must certify the Gift Aid payment on form R240(SD).

(b) The tax deducted by the donor company must be paid over to the Inland Revenue on form CT61(2) within 14 days of the end of the relevant CT61(2) Return Period.

(c) The charity recovers the tax paid to the Inland Revenue.

However, despite the drawbacks with Gift Aid mentioned above, some trading companies find it a more flexible method of giving than the traditional Deed of Covenant.

10.5. Payment of profit using a Deed of Covenant

The Deed of Covenant is probably the method most widely used by trading companies to pay taxable profits to their parent charities.

A Deed of Covenant is a binding obligation on the part of the donor to give an agreed sum of money, or a sum calculated in accordance with a fixed formula, to a body of persons established for charitable purposes. Certain points must be noted:

(a) **It must be clearly stated on the face of the Deed that it is a deed.**

(b) **The Deed must be signed and "delivered" and the signature must be witnessed in England and Wales.** In the case of a trading company, this means that the deed should be signed on behalf of the company by two directors, or one director and the company secretary, of the trading company and their signatures should be witnessed. Delivery requires the wording "signed and delivered" above the signatures. A witness is not needed in the case of a Deed of Covenant executed under Scottish law. In Northern Ireland (but not in England, Wales or Scotland) the Deed must be physically "sealed".

(c) **A Deed of Covenant must be for a period which is capable of exceeding three years.** A Deed of Covenant made after 6th May 1992, which is expressed to last for four years or until the occurrence of a specified later event, will continue to be treated as valid after the end of the four year period until the occurrence of the specified event or until the covenantor exercises his power to terminate it, provided he cannot exercise this power within the initial four year period.

(d) **Tax relief is not due on payments under a Deed of Covenant unless the payments are actually made.**

A sample Deed of Covenant for use by a trading company covenanting all its profits to a charity is shown on the opposite page.

The following points should be noted:-

(a) **Is this tax evasion?**

The notion of a profit-shedding covenant may seem like tax avoidance, especially as many charities may lend back moneys to the trading company (see the section on cash flow, at *Chapter 10.6). Nonetheless,* the Inland Revenue has expressly approved these arrangements in their Statement of Practice SP3/87.

(b) **Definition of Profits**

The definition of Annual profits is crucial. Clause 3 of the Sample Deed refers to the income *and* chargeable gains, of the company on which corporation tax falls finally to be borne. If it does not refer to chargeable gains then chargeable gains made by the trading company which would be subject to Capital Gains Tax would not be covered by the Deed of Covenant; they would remain in the trading company and be subject to Capital Gains Tax.

The definition of profits refers to the deduction of disallowed expenditure. One of the problems experienced by trading companies with deeds of covenant is caused by the distinction between accounting profits and taxable profits. Accountants have their own methods of calculating the net profits of a business which are different from the taxman's. For example, the taxman will not

DEED OF CHARITABLE COVENANT

DATED _____

PARTIES

1. _____ Limited whose registered office is at

   _____ CRN

   _____ ("the Company").

2. _____

   Registered Charity No. _____ ("the Charity").

BACKGROUND

1.1 The Charity is a body established for charitable purposes only.

1.2 The Company wishes to make a covenanted donation to charity within the meaning of the Income and Corporation Taxes Act 1988 Sections 338, 339 and 660(3).

TERMS AND CONDITIONS

1. **Covenant to Pay**

   The Company shall pay to the Charity in each accounting period for the purposes of corporation tax in accordance with the provisions of this Deed an annual sum equal to the Annual Profits of the Company as defined in Clause 3 for that period (less income tax at the basic rate for the time being in force).

2. **Commencement and Termination**

   This Covenant shall commence within and include the accounting period during which this Deed is executed and shall as a minimum continue until and include the accounting period ending on or after the   day of 19

   This Covenant may be terminated after that date by written notice served on the Charity in accordance with Section 671 Income and Corporation Taxes Act 1988 (as amended by Finance Act 1992).

3. **Definition of Annual Profits**

   "The Annual Profits of the Company" for an accounting period means and shall be the income and chargeable gains of the Company for that period on which Corporation tax falls finally to be borne but without deducting:-

   (i)   the amount of the Corporation tax which but for Section 339 of that Act would be payable in respect of such income or chargeable gains **or**

   (ii) the annual sum payable under this Covenant;

   Less such amount as is (after deduction of Corporation Tax at the rate applicable to the relevant accounting period) equivalent to the aggregate of the items of expenditure properly included in the Profit and Loss Account of the Company in accordance with ordinary principles of commercial accountancy for the relevant accounting period disallowed from being deductible expenditure of the Company for Corporation Tax purposes.

4. **Manner of Payment**

   Payments shall be made annually at least 7 days before the end of each accounting period of a sum (less income tax at the basic rate for the time being in force) equal to the profits of the Company of that period as then estimated. In the event of any overpayment the excess shall be refunded at or after the end of the said period and in the event of any underpayment the shortfall shall be made good (less income tax at the basic rate for the time being in force) before the end of the said period.

5. **Nature of Payment**

   No payment shall be charged to capital and all payments shall be applied by the Charity for the purposes of the Charity.

AS WITNESSED whereof this Deed was executed and delivered as a Deed on the day and year first above written.

EXECUTED as a Deed on behalf of the Company by

_____ Director

_____ Director/Secretary

Name: _____

Address: _____

Occupation: _____

allow a business to deduct all expenses of entertainment, whereas accountancy standards do. Accountants take into account a depreciation charge when calculating profits. The taxman does not allow a depreciation charge, but he does allow capital allowances.

◆◆ *example*

XYZ Trading Limited has £100,000 of income and chargeable gains on which Corporation Tax will be due, for the financial period to 31.12.93.

Accounting profits are £80,000. The £20,000 difference is made up of disallowed expenditure.

Although this expenditure is disallowed for tax purposes, XYZ Trading has had to pay for these items in cash.

Hence the covenant provides for XYZ Trading to pay to XYZ Charity:

Income and chargeable gains	£100,000
Less non-allowable expenditure	£ 26,667

(this is the non-allowable expenditure of £20,000 grossed up at the appropriate rate of corporation tax - 25%)

Annual profits after disallowed expenditure	£ 73,333

From this, XYZ Trading Company Limited will deduct 25% basic rate income tax (£18,333.25) and pay that to the Inland Revenue. XYZ Charity will receive £54,999.75 in cash from XYZ Trading Limited and recover the basic rate tax deducted from the Inland Revenue.

XYZ Trading will then pay corporation tax of £6,667 to the Inland Revenue on the £20,000 profits it "retained" and did not pay to XYZ Charity. By doing this the XYZ trading was left with sufficient cash to pay the tax due on the disallowed expenditure. If the covenant is not sophisticated enough to cover this point, the trading company will find it has paid all the taxable profits over to the charity (in the example £100,000) but may well not have the cash to meet the payment under the covenant, bearing in mind, that although the taxable profits are £100,000, in cash terms (leaving aside depreciation) the trading company has only made £80,000 profit.

(c) **When should the payment be made?**

Clause 4 of the Sample Deed makes it clear that payments made under the Deed of Covenant should be made at least 7 days before the end of each accounting period. That is the trading company's accounting period and not the charity's. The payment must be made physically by transferring money (by inter account transfer) or by cheque (cleared through the trading company's and the charity's account) by the end of the financial period. A mere ledger adjustment between the two entities will **not** suffice.

Obviously until the trading company has had its year-end accounts prepared and audited and its taxable profits and gains and disallowable expenditure calculated, it cannot be certain how much it should pay under the Deed of Covenant (assuming that states the company will give 100% of taxable profits). Clause 4 of the Sample Deed makes it clear that the trading company can estimate the sum payable under the Deed. That estimated sum will be paid over prior to the financial year end (see above). If it subsequently transpires that there has been an overpayment, the charity can refund the surplus without any problem. This is different from the position with Gift Aid (see *Chapter 10.4*).

If the trading company makes an underestimate of its profits for the year and the taxable profits transpire to be higher than the sum already paid over under the covenant, there can be no retrospective adjustment. Corporation tax will then have to be paid by the trading company on the sum not paid over. This is because a Deed of Covenant is treated for tax purposes as a charge on income. A charge on income **must** be paid within the company's relevant accounting period, and payments made after a year's end will not be treated as a charge on income in the previous financial year. It is therefore wise to *overestimate* the level of profit slightly when making the covenant payment, and make a subsequent adjustment once the actual profits of the trading company are known.

(d) **How much profit?**

The sample Deed of Covenant is drafted on the basis that 100% of the taxable profits (as defined) will be covenanted to the charity. This is the conventional method. But it is not mandatory. A trading company could covenant, say, 60% of its taxable profits (as defined) and retain 40% on which it would pay corporation tax at the appropriate rate. This is not tax-efficient, and it would be an expensive way of building the resources of the trading company (as compared with providing additional share or loan capital). There are circumstances, however, where such an arrangement might be appropriate.

Such an arrangement may be agreed, for example, in the case of a trading company which is jointly owned by a charity and a commercial partner - say in the proportions 60% (to the charity) and 40% (to the commercial partner). In this case, the Articles of Association could stipulate that the charity holds "A" shares with no rights to dividend, and the commercial partner holds "B" shares which could receive dividends of up to 40% of the profits available for distribution. The charity could then strip out its 60% share under a deed of covenant. The Articles of Association of the joint venture company should make it clear that the minority shareholder does not object to such a Deed of Covenant.

10.6. Cash flow

Deeds of Covenant can cause serious cash flow problems for the trading company. The principle reason for this is that, although the trading company makes a profit in its accounts, it may not have cash to hand equal to those profits.

◆◆ *example*

XYZ Trading Limited has £250,000 of debtors just before its year end. It estimates it will make taxable profits based on sales made but it is strapped for cash due to the failure of its debtors to pay.

XYZ Trading Limited needs to make its payment of 100% of its taxable profits before its financial year end under a Deed of Covenant. But it lacks the necessary cash.

The dilemma

If the trading company does not make the payment under the Deed it will be in breach of its covenant. This will put those trustees of the charity who are also directors of the trading company in a conflict of interest.

If the trading company fails to make the payment in the financial period it will lose the tax relief on the profits which could in time expose the trustees to criticism from the Charity Commission for failing to arrange the charity's and its trading company's affairs in the most tax-efficient manner.

So what does the trading company do?

Answer: It borrows the necessary cash either from the charity or from the trading company's bankers. It then pays the cash over to the charity under the Deed of Covenant. Hence, it will have honoured its obligation under the Deed of Covenant, but it will still owe either the bank or the charity the borrowed cash! If the loan is made by the charity the points concerning loans made in *Chapter 7* should be followed. If the loan is made by a bank the trading company will no doubt seek to repay that as soon as its cash flow permits, but that may be difficult!

◆◆ *example*

On 20/12/93 XYZ Trading Limited estimates its taxable profits due to be paid under the Deed of Covenant at £100,000, but it only has £20,000 in its bank account from which to make the payment.

On 21/12/93 XYZ Trading borrows £80,000 from ABC Bankers.

On 22/12/93 XYZ Trading pays £75,000 cash to XYZ Charity and £25,000 tax to the Inland Revenue.

On 1/1/94 XYZ Charity lends £80,000 to XYZ Trading Limited. XYZ Charity has received the net covenant payment of £75,000 but is also able to recover the tax paid to the Inland Revenue which it will normally receive within 10 working days of making a claim.

On 2/1/94 XYZ Trading Limited repays £80,000 plus interest to ABC Bankers.

Hence most of the money has gone around the houses and lands back in XYZ Trading Limited.

The payment under the Deed of Covenant has ensured that no Corporation Tax will be paid by XYZ Trading Limited, but XYZ Trading is kept solvent only because most of the moneys paid under the Deed have been lent back. If this had not been done, XYZ would have been unable to pay its debts as they fall due. It would be out of cash and insolvent (see *Chapter 13*).

This recycling of cash (which is now common practice) makes many advisers and finance officers nervous. Some people fear that the Inland Revenue may attack such loanback arrangements as a form of tax evasion - the revenue has the means in the controls on qualifying loans discussed in *Chapter 7.8*. To the author's knowledge, this has not happened to date.

Even if the cash is not lent back in circumstances such as those illustrated in the example (to fund the repayment of the bank loan), moneys paid under a Deed of Covenant (or Gift Aid) are frequently lent back by charities so as to give their trading companies sufficient working capital - as they do not have any retained profits to apply for this purpose, given that all the profit is paid away under the Deed of Covenant or Gift Aid.

Such practice can go on year by year with the loan account between the charity and the trading company building up each year. Such arrangements need to be carefully monitored and managed by charity trustees as proper and appropriate. The granting of a loan of the amount required *may* be justified, because the trading company is making consistent profits and of an appropriate amount - such that the granting of the loan helps assure a future stream of profits from the trading company and income for the charity. But if this is not the case, the trustees should consider carefully as to whether or not they should perpetuate the arrangement. In any case any such loan account should be set up in accordance with the Charity Commissioners' guidelines (see *Chapter 7.8*).

Repayment of the loan

Where a charity grants a loan to its trading company, another problem arises. How can a trading company repay a loan account when it covenants 100% of its taxable profits to its patent charity? One way is to **retain** profits in the trading company, if and when the terms of the Deed of Covenant permit this.

◆◆ *example*

XYZ Trading Limited has been lent £250,000 by its parent charity, XYZ Charity.

XYZ Trading Limited covenants 100% of its taxable profits to XYZ Charity, but the existing covenant lapses in 1995.

XYZ Trading Limited makes taxable profits as follows:

Year to 31.12.1994 :	£100,000
Year to 31.12.1995 :	£200,000
Year to 31.12.1996 :	£200,000

XYZ Trading is an expanding business, but as such it needs more cash. In January 1995 it borrows back from the charity a further £75,000 (having paid this and the appropriate tax over prior to 31st December 1994) swelling the loan account to £325,000.

The repayment of a loan (as opposed to interest on it) is not tax deductible. Hence if XYZ Trading Limited does not renew the covenant and retains its profit the position will be:

Year to 31.12.95 Taxable profits		£200,000
less Corporation Tax at 25%	£ 50,000	£150,000

It could then use that cash (when received) to repay the charity some of the loan - provided of course that XYZ Trading can survive by paying away all its cash to its parent charity (an unlikely occurrence!). This could be repeated in the year to 31st December 1996 (if feasible). As a result the loan account would be reduced to £25,000, but £100,000 of corporation tax would have been paid to the Inland Revenue.

If retaining profits in the trading company is tax-inefficient, it is worth trying to find an alternative. One possible alternative is for the trustees of the charity to consider converting the loan account into paid-up shares in XYZ Trading (see *Chapter 7.9*). This could only be done if it was a reasonable and proper investment by the trustees of XYZ Charity to have made at the time. Each case must be taken on its own facts and the advantages and disadvantages weighed up by the trustees.

Because of the problems presented by both these methods, many charities ignore the issue and simply let loan accounts mount up. **This is not a sensible strategy.** The trustees could find themselves being investigated by the Charity Commission - such loans will appear on the charity's accounts, and as the Commission improves its monitoring and surveillance (aided by new computers, accountancy staff and a bigger budget for monitoring and supervision), the number of questions raised about such loan accounts with trading companies will increase. Some professional advisers are now recommending that trading companies keep back some of their profits (and pay corporation tax) so as to reduce the trading company's dependency on loans back from the parent charity. Some commentators are also concerned that loanback arrangements, which allow trading profits to be "filtered" tax-free through a charity may be attacked by the European Commission in its pursuit of the "level playing field". The loanback of tax-free profits is undoubtedly a competitive advantage for such trading companies which may also come under increasing criticisms from commercial competitors (who could also raise the question with the European Commission) - although such a criticism can be met at least in part if the charity is charging a proper rate of interest on the loan (see *Chapter 7.8*).

10.7. Repayment of Taxes on Covenanted Income

The Inland Revenue's Statement of Practice SP3/87 sets out the Revenue's practice on the payment and recovery of tax in paragraphs 3 and 8 as follows:

Profit-shedding covenants

3. "Many charities set up subsidiary companies to carry on fund-raising activities. The profits of such a subsidiary are usually covenanted to the charity, relieving the subsidiary of its corporation tax liabilities. Prior to Finance Act 1986 many of those companies were, under the Group Relief Rules, able to make such covenant payments gross, so that it was unnecessary for the charity to claim repayment.

4. Under Taxes Act 1988 Section 505(2) however, such payments are

now required to be made under the deduction of tax at source. The charity will thus have received income under deduction of tax and will qualify for repayment of tax if it is otherwise eligible for tax exemption under the normal rules.

5. In examining claims for repayment, it is the Revenue's practice in appropriate cases to verify, by reference to the tax records of the person making payment, that the amount claimed is correct and that the tax deducted from the payment has, where necessary, been accounted for. This can take some time.

6. In order to minimise any cash flow disadvantage for charities while awaiting repayment, the Revenue is prepared to repay provisionally the tax apparently suffered without awaiting the results of the verification process described above, provided that:

    (a) the identity of the charity and subsidiary and their relationship to each other, are well known in advance of the claim; and

    (b) the Revenue is satisfied that the affairs of the charity are otherwise in order; and

    (c) the repayment claim is not otherwise likely materially to exceed the amount ultimately due.

7. In order to obtain corporation tax relief, the subsidiary must make its payment during the accounting period in which the profits arise, even though the true profits for corporation tax purposes may not be known for some months after the end of that period. Most companies therefore make a payment which to some extent exceeds the likely profit, accounting for tax on the full amount and adjusting the payments later.

8. It follows that, when the verification referred to above is complete, the tax paid over by the subsidiary, and the tax repayment made to the charity, may prove to be excessive. The Revenue will in such cases have power, under the provisions of Taxes Management Act 1970 Section 30 (as amended by Finance Act 1982 Section 149) to recover the over-repayment from the charity by assessment. In practice, however, unless the amount over-repaid is significant in relation to the sum claimed, it will normally be collected from subsequent repayment claims. Similarly the excess paid over by the subsidiary will be repaid to it by the Inspector or set against any other tax liabilities."

The trading company must deduct basic rate tax from the sum covenanted and pay the net amount to the charity. Thereafter it should within 14 days after the normal quarter-end fill in a form CT61 and pay the tax over to the Inland Revenue. Where a charity's year end differs from the normal calendar quarter-ends, the period between the previous quarter and the year end becomes a fifth CT61 period. In a recent case, the Revenue claimed that the form CT61 must be submitted on time for the charity to get the tax benefit. The Revenue claimed that if the company delivered a late return, the entire payment was disqualified from being a charge on income, and the company had not accounted for the payment in accordance with Schedule 16 to the Taxes Act 1988. The charity appealed to the Special Commissioners and won. Nonetheless the Revenue still see the late submission of CT61 forms as a potential means of abusing the system. Accordingly the message is clear. Submit your CT61 form on time and if payment is made in the earlier part of the CT61 quarter, there can be a cash flow advantage to the charity and its subsidiary taken as a whole as the charity can obtain the tax refund before the subsidiary pays over the tax deducted!

10.7. Example

The trading Company needs to account for the income tax withheld by remitting it together with form CT621 to the Inland Revenue within 14 days of the end of the usual quarter days (31st March, 30th June, 30th September, 31st December) or if this date arises earlier, within 14 days of the company's accounting date.

◆◆ *example*

XYZ Trading Limited covenants all its taxable profits to XYZ Charity.

Financial year end of XYZ Trading Limited is 31st December.

XYZ Trading Limited estimates its taxable profits for the year ended 31st December will be £100,000.

On 1st October XYZ Trading Limited pays £75,000 to XYZ Charity.

XYZ Charity can then immediately submit form R185 (duly filled in by XYZ Trading Limited) along with a claim to recover the tax to the Inland Revenue.

The Inland Revenue expects to pay the tax on non-problem cases within 7-10 days.

Hence XYZ Charity should receive the £25,000 (tax due on £100,000) by 10th October.

XYZ Trading Limited will only have to pay the £25,000 it is due to pay to the Inland Revenue on 14th January (i.e. within 14 days of the end of the CT61 quarter).

10.8. Accounting requirements

Mention has frequently been made in this book of the need to maintain a rigid distinction between the operations and the funds of a charity and its trading company. However, when it comes to accounting requirements, the position is much more blurred, which is unfortunate as this can only cause confusion in the minds of those involved in the charity sector. The Charity Commission, quite correctly, emphasises the need to keep the charity distinct from its trading company, but other regulators give less clear messages!

Statement of Recommended Practice

The Statement of Recommended Practice for charity accounts, known as SORP 2, was originally published in May 1988 by the Accounting Standards Committee. It is currently being revised by the Charity Accounting Review Committee under the auspices of the Charity Commission. The Charity Commission would like the recommendations to apply to all charities and to sit alongside the regulations for Charity Accounts to be issued under the Charities Act 1993. The Charity Commission announced in February 1994 that it would publish the revised Charity SORP together with the draft Regulations on charity accounting, reporting and auditing, as required by the Charities Act 1993.

SORP 2, which will continue in use until the new Charity SORP is produced, is not part of the law, and therefore adherence to its provisions is not mandatory. However, the Charity Commission, in its announcement of February 1994 stated:

"Our view is that compliance with the provisions of SORP is not an end itself, and we will not criticise any charity just because it has not followed one or more recommendations of SORP. We may however, criticise failure to follow SORP if it leads to a distorted misleading or unclear view of some aspects of the charity's affairs. As the revised SORP itself will make clear, the principal aim of trustees should be to present as clear and accurate a picture as possible of the charity's affairs so that the reader can easily understand what the financial position of the charity is. In general, we believe that this will be best achieved by following the recommendations of SORP and that charities should begin with a presumption in favour of SORP, departing from it only where this can clearly be justified in a positive way."

The Charity Commissioners are anxious that even small and medium-sized charities should find it practicable to follow the principles of SORP which apply to them.

SORP 2 states:
"A charity may have one or more subsidiary companies:
The activities of a subsidiary may not be fundamentally different from

those of the charity. For example, the subsidiary may be an investment holding company; it might be concerned solely or largely with fund-raising; or it might be the vehicle used to undertake the charitable activities of the charity. If a charity has such a subsidiary or subsidiaries, it should prepare consolidated accounts for itself and its subsidiary or subsidiaries. Separate accounts for the charity itself should still be prepared.

If a subsidiary undertakes activities which are fundamentally different from those of the charity, for example if it is a trading company, it will not be appropriate to consolidate its accounts with those of the charity. Instead, the investment in the subsidiary should be treated in the same way as other investments are treated. A summary of the transactions, assets and liabilities of the subsidiary, together with an explanation of its activities and their relevance to the charity, should be disclosed in the notes to the accounts. As an alternative to providing a summary of its subsidiary transactions, assets and liabilities, the charity may if it wishes include the accounts of the subsidiary within its annual report."

The current draft for the new Charity SORP (issued in March 1993) states that charities must prepare consolidated accounts when they exceed the following size criteria which are also laid down by the Companies Act for groups of companies. If a charity and its trading company meets **two** of the following requirements, then it is obliged to consolidate:

(a) Turnover (income derived from the provision of goods and services) more than £11.2 million;

(b) Balance sheet total (assets) more than £5.6 million

(c) Number of employees more than 250

The revised SORP draft 2 states at paragraphs 51 and 53:

Method of consolidation

51. "If a charity has one or more subsidiary undertakings which undertake aspects of the parent charity's activities, be they other charities, trading companies or other entities, the normal rules will apply regarding consolidation which should be carried out on a line by line basis as set out in the financial reporting statement number 2.

It is however recognised that often such a method of consolidation may be inappropriate because of the different nature of the activities of subsidiaries. For example, a trading subsidiary may have a very large turnover but if the charity's only interest is in the amount of profit that is transferred to it by way of dividend or covenant, it may be preferable in order to show a true and fair view to bring in only that profit or loss together with other transfers of income made by covenant, gift aid or other method, as a single entry to the credit of the consolidated statement of financial activities as 'net income of trading subsidiaries', leaving the notes to give the gross trading statistics. This is amplified in paragraph 75. The assets and liabilities, however, will be consolidated on a line by line basis in the normal way, as they form an integral part of the group capital structure.

53. In deciding whether or not a charity may be exempted from the need to consolidate its Statement of Financial Activities on a line by line basis and opt instead for a single line net entry, trustees must have regard to the circumstances. The overriding requirement is to give a true and fair view not only of the charity but also of the group. Sometimes the very essence of the charity's activities are carried out by the subsidiary in which case a line by line consolidation will be required. In other cases the subsidiary is merely carrying on an incidental activity of support, in which case the single line treatment would be appropriate."

Companies Act 1989

Quite apart from SORP 2, charities which are incorporated under the Companies Acts also need to think about the impact of company law. The Companies Act 1989 has made a number of significant changes to the circumstances in which a subsidiary company can be excluded from consolidated accounts. Section 229(2) of the Companies Act 1989 permits the exclusion of subsidiaries from consolidation if the inclusion of all excluded subsidiaries taken together is not material to giving a true and fair view of the group's financial position.

Moreover, Section 229(4) provides that where the activities of a subsidiary undertaking are so different from those of other undertakings included in the consolidation, so that its inclusion will be incompatible with the obligation to give a true and fair view, the subsidiary undertaking should be *excluded* from the consolidated accounts. From the point of view of charity law, the activities of a trading company are normally very different from the activities of the charity itself. This will not be the case where a trading company is carrying out the primary purposes or one of the primary purposes of a charity (for reasons of limiting risk, etc.), but this is not often the case. Usually the trading company is set up to carry out trading activities which the charity itself cannot undertake. In such circumstances, it seems entirely appropriate to make use of the exemptions set out in Section 229(4), so that a charity which is itself a company does not have to consolidate its accounts for the purposes of the Companies Acts with those of its trading company.

Financial reporting standards

To make life even more complex, as if SORP and the Companies Act was not enough, the Accounting Standards Board (ASB) has produced Financial Reporting Standard 2 (FRS2) on consolidation which gives further interpretation and guidance on the meaning of the Companies Act 1989.

FRS2 applies to *all parent undertakings*. That includes not merely limited companies but also organisations incorporated by Royal Charter and unincorporated associations, provided they are carrying on a trade or business with or without a view to profit. FRS2 does not include trusts so that a charity which is established as an unincorporated trust will not fall within its parameters. Equally only undertakings which are carrying on a trade or business will be caught. Hence, a grant-giving body which has a trading company attached will probably not be an undertaking for the purpose of FRS2. But the expression "trade or business" has been interpreted very widely in other areas of the law, so that for example, a charity will be regarded as undertaking a trade or business, even if funded by voluntary income, for the purposes of the Landlord and Tenant Act 1954.

FRS2 states that:-

(a) The consolidated financial statements should be prepared by consolidating financial information for the parent and all its subsidiary undertakings, except for any subsidiary undertakings that are to be excluded from consolidation by virtue of the requirements of the Act (i.e. the Companies Act 1989) and the FRS2.

(b) A subsidiary undertaking is to be excluded from consolidation if:

    (i) severe long term restrictions substantially hinder the exercise of the parent undertaking's rights over the subsidiary undertakings, assets or management; or

    (ii) the group's interest in the subsidiary undertakings is held exclusively with a view to subsequent resale and the subsidiary undertaking has not previously been consolidated; or

    (iii) the subsidiary undertaking's activities are so different from those of other undertakings to be included in the consolidation that its inclusion would be incompatible with the obligation to give a true and fair view."

As will be noted, FRS2 uses similar wording to Section 229(4) of the Companies Act 1989. It is understood that the Accounting Standards Board believes that it is exceptional that the activities of a subsidiary undertaking should so differ from those of other undertakings in the group that the inclusion of the subsidiary will be incompatible with the obligation to give a true and fair view. The ASB stated that:

"Unless exceptionally, there are conclusive grounds for believing that the inclusion of a subsidiary undertaking in consolidated accounts is incompatible with showing a true and fair view of the group, all subsidiary undertakings, whatever their activities, should be consolidated with the group."

With respect to the ASB, this flies in the face of the strict requirements of charity law. Indeed in some cases where charities have filed consolidated accounts with the Charity Commission, the Commission has asked them to de-consolidate the accounts!

But it is also worth emphasising that some charities do set up trading companies to carry out similar activities (e.g. fund-raising), which might traditionally have been carried out by the charity itself, especially innovative fund-raising schemes which involve sponsorship (see *Chapter 6*). Equally, the arrangements that have been reached with the Inland Revenue and Customs & Excise concerning affinity cards, will mean that an element of the income is deemed to be trading and will have to be channelled through the trading company whilst the remainder is paid to the charity. In this case, the activities of such a trading company would appear to be required to be consolidated under FRS2! It is difficult to argue that in these circumstances that such activities are "so different" from those of the charity itself as to avoid the requirement to consolidate.

To consolidate or not

The final decision whether to consolidate the results of the trading company with the parent charity rests with the charity's trustees. The charity's auditors then have to make a separate decision as to whether or not the accounts represent a true and fair view and comply with the Companies Acts, FRS2, the charity SORP and SORP2. If a subsidiary is not consolidated on the grounds that the inclusion of the subsidiary would be incompatible with a true and fair view, that should be explained in a note to the accounts. The view apparently favoured by many charities is that whether or not to consolidate depends on the nature of the trading company's activities. Under this view, trading companies which buy and sell goods should be excluded from the consolidation, whereas those whose activities are more akin to the activities of the charity should be included. It is unfortunate that charities face such a complex and contradictory set of regulations on this important subject!

10.9. Conclusions

Treat management charges with caution. They should be based on actual costs and a fair apportionment and not include a profit element. Overstating the charges can cause tax problems. Avoid paying the profits of the trading company back to the charity by way of dividends.

Gift Aid may seem a flexible friend but is not nearly as flexible as a **Deed of Covenant**. Deeds of Covenant are the best mechanism for paying over the profits of the trading company. But the covenant needs to be drawn up properly if tax and cash flow problems are to avoided. Cash flow and working capital problems can arise if all profits are paid back.

The best answer *may* be to retain some profit (if this permitted under the covenant arrangement) but this is *tax-inefficient. Beware* of the *circularity* of loanbacks which could create problems and *beware* the building up of large and increasing loans from the charity. There is no easy answer, but converting outstanding loans into share capital, if this can be a justifiable investment decision, may be sensible.(See *Chapter 7.9.*)

To consolidate the accounts of the trading company or not? Check with your auditors whether or not this is required!

Chapter 11
TERMS OF TRADE

This chapter explores the terms on which a charity or its trading company may conduct its business and includes the following topics: how a contract is made; buying and selling goods; supplying and obtaining services; and liabilities to third parties - under the Consumer Protection Act 1987.

11.1. General principles of contract law

Contract law is the backdrop to commercial life. Charities and their trading companies enter into contracts all the time, whether for the supply of electricity, the hire of a photocopier or the supply of a service.

Many people think that a contract has to be written. That is wrong. It does not. Only contracts for the sale of land, hire purchase agreements, guarantees and some insurance contracts have to be written if they are to be enforceable. Otherwise, an oral or verbal agreement is quite sufficient. Moreover, a contract may be part written, part oral. So just because there is a written contract does *not* mean that statements made at the time of the contract are not part of the contract. They may be, depending on the nature of the statements and the terms of the contract.

Existence of a Contract

When is a contract made? For a contract to exist there must be an **offer** to enter into a contract (e.g. "I would like to buy your car"), an **acceptance** ("OK") and **consideration** has to pass, that is, some value must be given or contemplated ("So we agree, I'll buy your car for £500". "Yes, it's a deal.").

Note that a contract is only complete when all these elements come together. There must be:

(a) An offer: and

(b) An acceptance of the offer (not a counter offer e.g. "£500 is not enough, but I'll take £550.").

Price

Usually the parties will agree the price before the offer is accepted. Once the offer is accepted, the contract is made. With mail order the contract commences when the supplier posts an acceptance letter, a confirmation or the goods (whichever comes first) to the customer.

Terms of the contract

Certain minimum standards have to be met for the supply of goods or services (see below). In addition to these minimum standards, businesses draw up their own terms and conditions of varying degrees of complexity. They are frequently compressed in small print on the back of invoices, order forms or even writing paper. They may appear on notice boards. Some typical points to be included in such standard terms and conditions are considered later in this chapter.

But what is the status of such terms and conditions? Is the contract governed by them?

The answer is that such conditions will usually govern the contract but subject to a few basic points.

(a) **The conditions must be brought to the other party's attention before he or she makes the contract.** Hence. it is no use a charity's trading company relying on a statement limiting its responsibility for supplying defective goods which is sent out *after* a customer has ordered goods from a catalogue. However, if the customer had seen the terms having previously purchased goods through the catalogue, he or she would almost certainly be considered to be aware of the statement by virtue of having seen it previously.

(b) **The last terms and conditions specified before acceptance of an offer apply to the contract. In the legal world this is known as the *"battle of the forms"*.** What happens if XYZ orders goods from ABC and sends a purchase order to ABC? On the back of XYZ's purchase order are its standard terms and conditions and they state that XYZ's terms are to apply. On receipt of the order ABC sends a confirmation notice, including ABC's standard terms and conditions! ABC produces the goods and sends them off with a delivery note, again including ABC's terms. XYZ accepts the goods. ABC despatches an invoice, also incorporating ABC's terms and conditions.

If there is a dispute over the contract (e.g. over the quality of ABC's goods), *whose* terms and conditions apply?

This is a very real problem. It is what lawyers call a "grey area". The law is uncertain. There are conflicting views as to whose conditions would apply but the general view is that the applicable terms are the last ones despatched before conclusion of the contract. Hence, in this illustration, ABC's terms would apply.

(c) **If there is any ambiguity or uncertainty in the contract terms, these will be interpreted against the person who inserted them and now seeks to rely on them.**

(d) **Some terms may be unreasonable, unfair and/or unenforceable due to being in breach of various Acts of Parliament** (see below).

Not every charity or its associated trading company will need to draw up terms and conditions of business. It will depend on the nature and complexity of the business in which a charity or its trading company is involved.

11.2. Buying and selling goods

Types of contract

It is important for charities or their associated trading companies to distinguish between two types of contract for the sale of goods:

(a) **Consumer contracts**; the contract is made with the consumer (e.g., a charity shop in a museum sells a book to a customer).

(b) **Non consumer contracts** (e.g., a charitable consultancy undertakes work for a government department).

Consumer contracts - implied terms

The Sale of Goods Act 1979 and the Supply of Goods and Services Act 1982 lay down certain fundamental terms about the sale of goods and contracts for the supply of goods and services which all *consumer* contracts must comply with. These are:

(a) **That the seller has the right to sell the goods** (i.e., if the goods turn out to be stolen, the purchaser can claim his money back).

(b) **That the goods are of satisfactory quality** (i.e., fit for their normal expected use).

(c) **That if the purchaser makes known to the seller a particular purpose for which the purchaser wishes to use the goods, the goods must be fit to fulfil that particular purpose rather than being of general satisfactory quality.**

(d) **That the goods are as described.**

The term "satisfactory quality" has replaced the old term "merchantable quality" but seems much the same! For example, in one court case a delivery of "Coalite" bought by a consumer exploded when put in the grate owing to the fact that a high explosive charge was lying in it! The court ruled the coal merchant had broken the contract by selling the Coalite irretrievably mixed up with the unmerchantable explosive.

But the obligation to sell goods of satisfactory quality is not an obligation to sell perfect goods. Minor blemishes, scratches etc are not usually considered to be a breach of the obligations.

Misrepresentation

A representation is a ***statement of fact*** made by one party to a contract to another which does not form part of the contract but is one of the reasons that makes the buyer enter into the contract. A misrepresentation is a representation that is ***untrue***. It is covered both by the general law and by the Misrepresentation Act 1967.

The law of misrepresentation is unfortunately extraordinarily complex for what should be a straightforward matter. A brief summary is:

(a) **Not all statements made by salesmen are representations.** The law accepts that they use exaggerated language to sell their wares (e.g. "great value", "unbeatable"). These are known as "puffs"; just because the item is not "unbeatable" does not mean the customer can claim misrepresentation.

(b) **A statement of opinion is not a representation** (i.e., "That is a fantastically interesting book"). So if a consumer purchased a book on such recommendation in a charity shop and found it to be deeply boring, he could not claim that there had been a misrepresentation.

(c) **Misrepresentation must relate to a fact** (e.g., "These bookshelves will last indefinitely"). If the bookshelves collapse after 3 months, this would be a misrepresentation, even if the seller honestly believed the statement to be true. It is still a misrepresentation.

(d) **The misrepresentation must have been relied on to the buyer's detriment.**

(e) **Misrepresentation can be written or oral.**

Proving a misrepresentation has been made is often very difficult as it will frequently be a case of the purchaser's word against the salesperson's. If the purchaser has an independent witness he will find it easier to prove his case.

Business contracts - implied terms

The same obligations are implied in business contracts as in consumer contracts, namely that:

(a) The seller must have title;

(b) Goods must be of a satisfactory quality;

(c) Goods must be fit for a particular purpose;

(d) Goods must be as described;

(e) There must be no misrepresentations.

However, there are exceptions.

11.3. Contracting out

It is possible, to some extent, to contract out of the terms set out in the Sale of Goods Act 1979, the Supply of Goods and Services Act 1982, the Misrepresentation Act 1967 and the European Directive on Unfair Standard Term Contracts with Consumers 1994 in business and consumer contracts. This is governed by the Unfair Contract Terms Act 1977. The rules for consumer and business contracts are given below.

For consumer contracts

(a) The seller cannot avoid liability for death or personal injury arising from his negligence by any contract term or notice. For example, the Youth Hostels Association cannot avoid liability should a youth hosteller be injured or killed at a youth hostel because of its negligence.

(b) The seller cannot exclude his obligations under the Sale of Goods Act 1979 and the Supply of Goods and Services Act 1982 to sell only goods for which he has title. Hence, a charity shop cannot sell stolen goods without being in breach of the Acts.

(c) The seller cannot exclude his liability under the Sale of Goods Act 1979 and the Supply of Goods and Services Act 1982 to sell goods that are of satisfactory quality, fit for a particular purpose or as described. In the case of the sale of secondhand goods (see *Chapter 3*), the standard of care will be lower than for new goods.

(d) The seller can exclude liability for misrepresentation, if this is *"reasonable"*, as laid down in the Unfair Contract Terms Act 1977 (see the "reasonableness" test on the following page).

(e) European Directive on Unfair Standard Term Contracts with Consumers 1994; any term which the consumer can show to be *"unfair"* will not be legally binding on the consumer.

For business contracts

(a) The seller cannot avoid liability for death or personal injury by any contract term or notice.

(b) The seller cannot exclude the obligation under the Sale of Goods Act 1979 to sell goods for which he has title.

(c) The seller can exclude his obligation under Sections 13, 14 or 15 of the Sale of Goods Act 1979 to sell goods that are as described or sampled or of satisfactory quality or fit for a particular purpose provided that it is "reasonable" to do so. This limitation only applies if the contract is made on standard written terms of business. If a charity or its trading company negotiates an individual contract with its business customer (or vice versa) then the Act does not apply and the parties can contract out of these various obligations even if that appears to be "unreasonable".

(d) The seller can exclude liability for misrepresentation, again if this is "reasonable".

(e) The seller can exclude any other liabilities arising from a breach of the contract e.g. for delay, distress or economic loss, if this is "reasonable".

The reasonableness test

Clearly it is crucial to determine whether or not an exclusion of liability clause is *"reasonable"* under UK legislation or *"fair"* under the European Directive. If it is *"reasonable"* or *"fair"* the trader can exclude or limit liability under the contract to a very considerable degree. If it is not *"reasonable"* or *"fair"* to exclude his liability then the trader will have much great contractual obligations.

The test of what is or is not *reasonable* depends on the court's interpretation of Section 11 of the Unfair Contract Terms Act 1977 which provides that the exclusion of liability clause shall be "fair and reasonable.... having regard to the circumstances which were, or ought reasonably to have been, known or in the contemplation of the parties when the contract was made". The Section gives a Judge some guidelines to apply when considering whether or not a clause is *"reasonable"*. These include the following:

(a) The relative bargaining strength of the parties, (e.g. can XYZ charity with annual turnover £1 million really negotiate a contract with the Overseas Development Administration?).

(b) Did one party receive an inducement to accept the terms (e.g. "accept my terms, and I shall reduce the price by 10%")?

(c) Were the terms widespread in the trade, and were they therefore well known or have there been any previous dealings?

(d) Were the goods manufactured, processed or adapted to the special order of the purchaser?

(e) Where liability is limited to a specific limit (e.g. "maximum liability accepted £500"), could the supplier have covered the risk by insurance and, if so, at what cost?

As an illustration of how the reasonableness test works, in one case the defendants supplied £130 worth of cabbage seeds. The seeds were useless - they were not cabbage seeds. No cabbages grew. The plaintiff farmer sued for his loss of profit on the crop (£61,000). The defendants tried to rely on an exclusion clause which limited their liability to the cost of the seeds (£130), but it was held by the court that the exclusion clause was unreasonable, and damages were awarded to the farmer for the loss of his profit (£61,000).

The fairness test

The European Directive is very new. There have been no cases to interpret its meaning. It specifies that a term in a contract may be unfair if, contrary to the requirements of "good faith", the term causes a significant imbalance in the parties' rights and obligations under the contract to the detriment of the consumer.

11.4. Breach of contract

A breach of contract occurs when one of the parties to the contract breaks one of the terms of the contract. What happens if there is a breach of contract?

Breach by the seller

Assuming there are no valid exclusion clauses in a consumer contract, a buyer has a right to *reject* goods until such time as he has *accepted* them. This is a little known or used area of the law, but is very valuable.

Acceptance is *not* the same as payment. The buyer is not treated as having accepted the goods until he has had a reasonable opportunity to inspect them to see whether they conform to the contract.

As ever, the word *"reasonable"* crops up! What is a *"reasonable"* opportunity to inspect the goods? Again the law is by no means clear. There have only been a few cases concerning this section of the Sale of Goods Act 1979. In one case in 1986 involving a family Nissan car, the High Court said that keeping a brand new car for three weeks, despite many complaints, constituted "acceptance". So, if a buyer wishes to reject goods he needs to act quickly. It is sensible not to have faulty goods repaired by the supplier because acceptance of the repair can be deemed to be acceptance of the goods. It goes without saying that if a buyer rejects goods, he is entitled to have his money back.

If it is too late to reject the goods and thus cancel the contract, the buyer can still claim damages for all losses "naturally and directly" flowing, in the ordinary course of events, from the breach of contract. The precise amount of damages to be claimed will depend on the circumstances.

Non-delivery by the seller

The buyer should buy similar goods (if available) at the normal market price and claim the difference (if any) from the seller. If the buyer cannot buy alternative goods, then he can sue for the loss of profit he would have made on resale of the goods, but is unable to make because the goods were not available.

Delay in delivery

If a seller makes a late delivery of a profit-earning item (e.g. machinery), the buyer can recover damages for loss of use based on normal use made of that item.

Defective quality

The measure of damages for a breach of contract will be that the seller should pay the buyer the sum necessary to put him in the position in which he would have been had the contract been performed. Any loss must have been reasonably within the contemplation of the parties. For example:

(a) The difference between the actual value of the delivered goods and the value they would have had if they complied with the original contract;

(b) Any fine the buyer has to pay (e.g. caused by food being unfit for human consumption);

(c) Buyer's loss of profit under a subsale (e.g. where the seller knows the buyer intends to re-sell the goods and it is "reasonable" to expect that the seller knew the buyer would lose profits if the goods were defective);

(d) Compensation for physical injury to the buyer;

(e) Compensation for injury to other property of the buyer (e.g., in one case dairy farmers bought meal for feeding to their pheasants. Many chicks died and others grew up stunted, as the meal contained a toxic substance. It was held that the farmer could recover damages for the loss of the birds and the reduced value of the survivors).

Obligation to mitigate

The buyer's right to claim damages for breach is subject to a very important obligation. He must take reasonable steps to reduce or mitigate his loss. He cannot sit back, do nothing and let the damages mount up. He must, so far as is reasonable, try to limit the damage to his business. If he succeeds in avoiding his loss, then he can make *no* claim for damages. Any expenses or losses he incurs in carrying out his duty to mitigate his loss are recoverable from the seller even if his attempts to mitigate fail.

Seller's remedies for buyer's breach of contract

The normal way in which a contract is broken by a buyer is by his failure to pay. Direct remedies include:

(a) If the seller has control of the goods he can exercise a lien. A lien is the right to hold goods until they are paid for.

(b) If the buyer becomes insolvent whilst the goods are in transit, the seller can tell the carrier to stop the goods and, if the seller wishes, to bring them back.

(c) The seller can retain ownership or title of the goods even after they have been delivered and accepted by the buyer. This requires a special clause in the seller's terms and conditions of business, known by lawyers as a Romalpa or Reservation of Title clause. If the seller's terms and conditions apply to the contract and contain such a clause, the seller can go into the buyer's premises and seize back his goods which have not been paid for.

It is essential to ensure that any reservation of title clause is well drafted and legal advice should be taken on this. Such clauses can be very useful. Charities or their trading companies which sell goods wholesale, raw materials or on payments by instalments should seriously consider including such a clause in their terms and conditions of business.

(d) Sue for the price. If the seller cannot exercise any direct remedies he can sue for the price of the goods delivered plus interest.

11.5. The supply and purchase of services

The Supply of Goods and Services Act 1982 obliges suppliers of services (e.g. charities giving consultancy advice; advising on legal matters;

repairing houses, in the case of a housing association), to have a duty to exercise reasonable care and skill in carrying out their jobs. This applies only where the services are provided as part of a business. It does not apply to services given by a charity free of charge.

But what is "reasonable care and skill"? As with the old "merchantable quality" test there is much room for dispute and it is not a standard of perfection. For example, it has been held that a solicitor is not bound to have a perfect knowledge of the law but he should have a sound knowledge. The distinction between a "perfect" and a "sound" level of knowledge is a subtle matter to be decided on the facts of each individual case!

As under the Sale of Goods Act this implied term (i.e. that the supplier will carry out the service with reasonable care and skill), can be excluded from a *non-consumer* contract if the exclusion clause is *"reasonable"*.

Suitable materials

The 1982 Act implies that the supplier will use suitable materials of proper quality. Again this term can be excluded from a non-consumer contract if it is *"reasonable"*.

Reasonable period

If the time for carrying out the service is not fixed by the contract, the 1982 Act implies that it will be carried out within a reasonable time. The implied term that a service will be completed in a reasonable period can be excluded from a non-consumer contract if this is *"reasonable"*.

Reasonable price

If the price for a service is not fixed by the contract there is an implied term that the charge made will be *"reasonable"*. This applies to all contracts, not just ones where the supplier is in business. Note too this implied term applies only if the parties have not agreed a price. If they have, that price is binding, however unreasonable it may be. This implied term can also be excluded from non-consumer contracts if it is *reasonable* to do so.

11.6. Standard terms of business

Does a charity or its trading company need to draw up standard terms of business to apply to its trading contracts? Or should the charity or its trading company rely on oral contracts with the implied terms set out above? The answer will vary depending on the type of the business involved, but as a general rule it is sensible to have written terms and conditions and to seek to impose these. It may be possible to use a standard set of terms and conditions which apply to a charity's particular area of activity (e.g. the supply of services to run a residential care home). It is wise to instruct a solicitor to draw up your terms and conditions. Too many charities think they can cobble together a set of business conditions by taking what they regard as the choicest morsels from various documents and merge them together in what can be a frightful legal hotchpotch. Be warned. By all means take along examples of similar terms and conditions to your solicitor for her to be aware of the particular problems associated with your industry. She will know that slavishly copying them will be a breach of copyright.

Once you have settled on the standard form, you should have it printed. Many commercial organisations do this in tiny print in faint grey on flimsy paper so that the terms are barely readable. This is not a good idea. If the conditions are too difficult to read then a judge might rule that they do not apply. By all means *print* standard terms and conditions of business on the back of quotations or order forms or invoices, but do print them legibly!

Checklist of standard terms and conditions

Set out below is a short checklist to be included in a general set of terms and conditions of trading. They are not exhaustive. They merely highlight certain important issues. They are made on the basis of the sale of goods but suitable adapted could apply to a supply of services. Clearly, each individual case will demand its own particular type of terms and conditions.

(a) **Parties**

Who are the parties? Do make sure, for example, that if the contract is with the charity's trading company and not the charity itself, this is clearly stipulated. This is vital.

(b) **Date**

What is the date of the agreement? It is amazing how many contracts are entered into without the date being specified.

(c) **Scope of contract**

What does the contract cover? What are the seller's obligations? Does the seller seek to limit his obligations as to satisfactory quality, fitness for purpose or correspondence with samples under the Sale of Goods Act or the equivalent obligations in respect of services?

(d) **Limitation of liability**

Does the seller seek to limit his liability for any losses arising out of the contract so that his liability for negligence, delay, consequential loss, etc. is limited (e.g. to the value of goods sold)?

(e) **Price**

Can the seller increase the price, if so, how? Is the price exclusive of VAT? Does it include carriage, insurance or freight?

(f) **Terms of payment**

What time is given to pay? If it is an export contract, in what currency is payment to be made?

(g) **Interest**

Is interest due on unpaid invoices? If so, at what rate? From when will interest be charged?

(h) **Delivery**

Who delivers? Are delivery dates estimates only?

(i) **Risk and property**

When does the buyer take on the risk of damage to or loss of the goods (i.e. the need to insure), as opposed to taking physical delivery of the goods?

(j) **Reservation of title**

Does the contract contain a reservation of title clause? If there is a reservation of title clause, is the buyer obliged to store the seller's goods separately and mark them as being the property of the seller?

(k) **Force Majeure**

Is there a force majeure clause which allows the seller to avoid liability for any loss caused by his failure to fulfil his obligations under the contract for reasons beyond his control (e.g. fire, bad weather, strikes or destruction of premises)?

(l) **Arbitration**

Should disputes be referred to an expert arbitrator rather than being left to the courts? This only applies to business contracts. Arbitration clauses in consumer contracts which automatically refer disputes to arbitration rather than to the courts are banned by the Consumer Arbitration Agreements Act 1988.

If arbitration is necessary, who is to appoint the arbitrator?

(m) **Termination**

How is the contract to be ended if it is more than a one-off agreement? What notice should be given? What happens if there is a breach of contract by one party? Does that automatically give the other party the right to terminate?

(n) **Governing law**

Does the contract stipulate which legal system is to regulate any disputes? This is very important as otherwise legal costs may be incurred in deciding which legal system applies to the contract. This is relevant even for trading within the United Kingdom as English and Scottish law can differ. It is another example of why it can be very important to ensure that your trading conditions apply to the contract.

11.7. Liabilities to third parties

So far in this chapter we have considered contracts. But it is also necessary to look at the obligations owed to persons who are *not* parties to a contract. For convenience, such persons are refered to as "third parties". Consider the following example:

A charity's trading company runs a restaurant open to the general public. It sells salmonella-infected chicken nuggets to Danny. Danny gives some to Smithy, Smithy falls ill. Danny has a contract with the trading company. Danny can sue the trading company for breach of the obligations to supply satisfactory chicken nuggets. But Smithy has no contract. For the purposes of contract law he is a **third party**. But he too has legal rights against the trading company. He can sue, not in contract, but in a completely separate area of the law called **tort** and claim damages on the grounds that the trading company has been *negligent* in selling salmonella infected chicken nuggets. "Tort" is the legal word for the law concerning wrongs done to a person for which compensation can be obtained, but where there may be no contract.

In contract, Danny would merely have to prove that the chicken nuggets were infected with salmonella (which should be quite straightforward), and therefore were not of satisfactory quality. However, as Smithy is suing in tort he would have to prove:

(a) That the trading company had been negligent in allowing salmonella to get into the chicken (which might be much harder to prove than just establishing that the chicken contained the salmonella);

(b) That he was owed a duty of care by the trading company not to be negligent;

(c) That it was reasonably foreseeable that he would suffer loss or injury as a result of the negligence;

If he can establish that the company had been negligent and that it did owe him a duty of care and that it was reasonably foreseeable that he would suffer loss, then he will be able to recover damages in negligence.

Third parties also have rights under the Consumer Protection Act 1987 (see below).

11.8. The Consumer Protection Act 1987 and the supply of goods

It is often very difficult for third parties to prove that manufacturers or suppliers have been negligent. To combat this, the European Commission proposed that what is called "strict liability" be imposed on producers or importers of defective products. Strict liability means that the producer of a product is liable for *any* damage which is caused by a defect in that product. All the plaintiff has to do is to prove to the court that:

(a) There was a defect;

(b) The defect caused damage.

The plaintiff no longer has to prove the producer was negligent. If he can prove there was a defect and this caused the damage, the producer is automatically (or strictly) liable for that damage.

This is now set out in the Consumer Protection Act 1987. It must be emphasised that that Act applies not only to third parties. The purchaser of the defective goods who has rights in contract (for breach of satisfactory quality) also has rights under the Consumer Protection Act. In summary, the Act makes the producer of a product (and certain others) liable in damages for personal injury and some property damage caused by a defect in the product, without the plaintiff having to show fault, although certain defences may be used by the producer.

What is defective? A product is defective if the safety of the product is not such as persons are generally entitled to expect. The persons who may be liable for supplying defective products are:

(a) **The producer;**

(b) **Any person who puts his name on the product;**

(c) **Any person who imports the item from outside the European Community.**

The Act does not apply to unprocessed agricultural or game produce, so a fresh apple is not be covered by the Act, but an apple tart is.

The Act only applies to defective products which are ordinarily intended for private use, occupation or consumption and which were intended by the person suffering the loss or damage for his own private use, occupation or consumption. Hence, where business property is damaged, the Act does not apply. Its title is absolutely correct - it is all about consumer protection.

Damages

Damages which can be recovered under the Consumer Protection Act are only in respect of death, personal injury or any loss of or damage to property. This does not cover economic loss, i.e. loss of profits or consequential loss. Thus, if an engine component in a car exploded damaging the engine, the damages which could be claimed would be the costs of repairing the damage to the engine. No claim can be made for any loss of sales caused by the owner not having his car, i.e. consequential loss, as the Act is concerned with consumers only. There is also no liability for the loss of or damage to the defective product itself. Hence if a component merely self-destructed, there could be no claim.

Defences

Certain defences are available to a claim made under the Act:

(a) The defect did not exist at the time of supply.

(b) The stage of scientific and technical knowledge at the relevant time was not such that a producer of such products might be expected to have discovered the defect. This is called the "development risk" defence. Reasonable though it may sound, it is highly controversial, as many consumer groups consider that it puts back on the victim the job of proving the producer was negligent, which is what the Consumer Protection Act was designed to stop.

A producer or supplier cannot "contract out" of its obligations under the 1987 Act. Accordingly, the best protection a producer or supplier or importer of non-EC goods can provide is to make sure it has adequate insurance cover for product liability.

Negligence

English law had already developed considerable rights for third parties to sue for damages in respect of losses caused by defective products before the Consumer Protection Act was passed. Although the Consumer Protection Act now makes it no longer necessary to use the law of negligence so far as consumer products are concerned, it is still relevant:

(a) For cases of defective non-consumer products;

(b) If a consumer wishes to sue for consequential loss caused by a defective product, as this cannot be recovered under the Consumer Protection Act.

11.9. Negligence and the supply of services

A charity or its trading company may prepare a report which is then used not by its client (with whom it has a contract) but by a third party. In this case, the law of negligence applies, as in the case of *Smith v. Eric Bush (1989) 2WLR 790.* A surveyor prepared a report on a house for a building society. The report was negligently prepared. The report was passed on by the building society to the purchaser who bought the house on the strength of it, only to find defects later. The purchaser sued the surveyor and received damages despite the fact that the survey had included a disclaimer of liability clause. The House of Lords held that the disclaimer was unreasonable under the Unfair Contract Terms Act 1977, and hence could not be relied upon by the surveyor.

Equally, a charity could prepare a report for a client which was then used by a third party. If that report had been negligently prepared, but it was held that the charity owed a duty of care to the third party and it was reasonably foreseeable that the third party would suffer loss, the charity could be made liable for these losses.

Getting out of liability for negligence

Can a supplier get out of liabilities for negligence by a suitably worded notice?

Back to the Unfair Contract Terms Act - it does not apply just to contracts despite its name! **The supplier cannot limit liability for death or personal injury.** It can limit liability for other forms of damage if it is **reasonable** to do so - the question of reasonableness is determined by whether it is "fair and reasonable" to allow reliance on it having regard to all the circumstances when the liability arose.

Many suppliers of services use the expression "E and O E" (errors and omissions excepted) rather like a mantra hoping it will ward off the perils of liability, but it may well not do so if challenged. If suppliers wish to exclude liability they should do so clearly.

11.10. Insurance

Any charity or its trading company which is engaged in trading activities needs to be aware of what risks it should be covering by insurance. Business carries many risks and insurance is designed to cover some of those risks. Law is crucial to insurance; be it the legal complexities of the relationship between insurer and insured, the meaning of the risks or perils insured against or the legal liabilities which insurance is designed to cover.

Employer's liability insurance

The Employer's Liability (Compulsory Insurance) Act 1969 requires that every employer carrying on a business, trade or profession in Great Britain (separate legislation applies for Northern Ireland) takes out and maintains insurance with an authorised insurer against liability for bodily injury or disease sustained by his employees arising out of their employment.

(a) The indemnity is usually unlimited.

(b) A certificate of insurance has to be displayed at the employer's premises.

(c) The premium is based on the estimated amount of annual wages and salaries.

(d) The insurance only applies to employees but not to independent contractors.

Just because employers' liability insurance is compulsory does not mean that the employer is automatically liable for any injury that an employee sustains as a result of his employment. The employee still has to prove that the injury was a result of:

(a) Negligence by his employer; or

(b) Breach of statutory duty (e.g., breach of the Health & Safety at Work Act); or

(c) Personal negligence of fellow employees.

A charity is considered to carry on a business or trade for these purposes.

So far as volunteers are concerned, it is best to treat them as employees and include them on any declaration to the Employer's Liability insurer.

Motor insurance

Section 143(1) of the Road Traffic Act 1988 requires every person who uses or causes or permits another person to use a motor vehicle on a road to have a policy of insurance to cover any liability which may be incurred as a result of the death of, or bodily injury to, any person or damage to property caused by, or arising out of, the use of the vehicle on a road in Great Britain.

Note that insurance is *not required* by law against the following risks which arise from using a motor vehicle on a road in Great Britain:

(a) Liability for death or bodily injury or property damage arising out of and in the course of *employment* of an employee of the person insured. The reason for this exception is that employers have to insure against their liability for death or bodily injury of employees under the Employer's Liability (Compulsory Insurance) Act (see above). Strangely enough, employers are not compelled to insure against their liability for damage to their employees' property either under the 1969 or 1988 Acts, but it might be worth considering extending insurances to cover this risk.

(b) Damage to the owner's vehicle - in other words only third party insurance is compulsory.

(c) Liability for damage to goods carried for hire by the vehicle or any trader (such goods would normally be insured separately).

(d) For more than a quarter of a million pounds in respect of liability for damage to property (but not death or bodily injury) arising out of any one accident.

A policy is of no effect under the 1988 Act unless and until the insurer delivers to the insured "a certificate in the prescribed form". The certificate is different from the policy.

Damage to buildings insurance

This is optional. It is not normal for the tenant of a building to have to arrange insurance for damage to the building. It is normal for the landlord to insure. However, this is not always the case (e.g. British Rail puts the obligation to insure any property it leases onto the tenant). The normal risks or perils to insure against are destruction or damage by fire, lightning, explosion, storm, tempest and flood. If a charity or its trading company owns a building freehold it should insure it - if it is mortgaged the mortgagee will require that it is insured.

When insuring a building or just checking that a landlord's insurance cover is sufficient under a lease, it is wise to check that:-

(a) The sum insured to cover the cost of rebuilding is adequate, bearing in mind the length of time it can take to get planning permission and rebuild, and the nasty habit of building costs to escalate;

(b) The perils insured against are wide enough to cover all possible risks - many policies, for example, do not cover subsidence which has become much more widespread following dry summers;

(c) The policy covers not merely building costs, but also professional fees (e.g. architects, surveyors, etc).

If you are letting out your building or are a tenant, make sure that:

(a) The policy covers a reasonable period, e.g. two years' loss of rent;

(b) Your tenant's interest is noted on the policy;

(c) The proceeds of the insurances are divided between the landlord and the tenant in accordance with their respective interests in the premises - this means that if the tenant has carried out extensive improvements and these are destroyed, he will be reimbursed for the value of those improvements from the landlord's insurance policy. If the landlord's insurance policy does not cover this, the tenant should insure his own improvements separately - this can be very important in retail outlets where considerable sums can be spent in refitting.

Insurance against loss and damage to contents

It is wise to insure the contents of business premises against loss or damage. This covers stocks, machinery, computers, office equipment, furnishings and employees' personal belongings. Insurance should be taken out against:

(a) Physical damage (e.g. fire, explosion, flood, etc.);

(b) Theft;

(c) Possibly "all risks" in respect of valuable machinery or equipment. "All risks" is a misnomer. Such a policy covers most forms of physical loss or damage, but excludes loss or damage caused by war, nuclear contamination, wear and tear and riot and civil commotion.

Business interruption insurance

If business premises are destroyed, be it partially or totally, the business will suffer. Not only will it have to replace its damaged premises but trading revenues will be lost too. So as to cover this potential loss, most businesses take out consequential loss or business interruption insurance (they mean the same thing). To add to the confusion, some insurers call such policies "loss of profits" insurance.

Such policies generally cover not only loss of revenue, but also additional expenditure which a business may have to incur in consequence of loss, damage or destruction of premises. It will include the cost of fitting out replacement premises, increased rent, charges, rates, lighting, heating, moving costs, etc.

The premiums for this type of insurance vary according to the risks insured against, the level of indemnity and the length of cover. It would be normal to insure against the same risks as are covered by the buildings insurance policy. The length of cover after the loss is known as the indemnity period and is a matter of individual choice. It should not be less than 12 months.

Public liability insurance

The purpose of taking out public liability insurance is to cover the business against its liabilities to third parties for causing death, personal injury or damage to their property. The policy excludes risks covered by other types of policy (e.g. employer's liability and road traffic insurance). The two broad areas covered by public liability are:

(a) Risks arising from the ownership, occupation or management of premises.

(b) Risks arising from the activities of employees to third parties.

Briefly, these are as follows:

Premises risks

(a) Escape of dangerous things from your land/buildings (e.g. a tile falling from a roof).

(b) Dangerous premises. Under the Occupiers Liability Act 1957 the occupier of any premises owes a duty of care to his visitor(s) to see that the visitor is reasonably safe when on the premises for the purpose for which he is invited. By taking on a lease or buying a freehold, a business person is under a duty to ensure that the premises are reasonably safe. If they are not and someone is injured or the property damaged, the occupier can be sued.

Under the Health & Safety at Work, etc. Act 1974, duties are owed to visitors (as well as to employees) who visit premises.

Employees' activities

The risks arising from the activities of employees and agents arise from what lawyers call "vicarious liabilities".

An employer is liable for the negligent acts or omissions of his employees causing death, bodily injury or damage to property during the course of employment. Beware, as for these purposes "an employee" has a very wide meaning. For the purpose of vicarious liability a person is treated as an employee if the insured has the right to control the way in which the negligent deed was done. Hence, for example, a volunteer will be covered by the doctrine of vicarious liability.

The public liability policy is not all-embracing. It excludes many forms of liability which are covered by other insurance policies, such as:

(a) Employer's liability;

(b) Motor vehicles;

(c) Liability arising under contract;

(d) Product liability.

It is best to select a decent level of indemnity for your public liability policy. This type of insurance is quite cheap, so £1 million of cover should not cost too much and is well worth effecting. Many organisations which undertake contractual work (e.g. under contracts for the delivery of care in the community services), are obligated under contract to effect public liability insurance.

Product liability insurance

Mention was made earlier in this Chapter of the obligations imposed on producers or importers of certain types of goods under the Consumer Protection Act 1987, the Sale of Goods Act 1979, or under the common law rules of negligence. Claims under these Acts for negligence could render a business insolvent.

◆◆ *example*

A trading company owned by a charity produces or imports a defective product. A consumer sustains serious long-term injuries from using the product and sues the trading company. The costs of defending the action and of meeting any court award or out-of-court settlement could run into hundreds of thousands of pounds. Such costs could well force the trading company into insolvency, and would also mean that the trustees of the charity which owns the trading company would be forced to write-off the charity's investment in it. The position is even worse if the item concerned had been sold by an unincorporated charity, in which case the action will be brought against the trustees of the charity personally, and the claim could result in their personal bankruptcy. If a claim were to be brought in the United States where juries have a tendency to award enormous damages for the most trifling injury, the potential liabilities could be huge.

To cover this risk, a business can take out product liability insurance. Such insurance is not cheap. Premiums depend on such obvious factors as amount of turnover; the nature of the business; where goods are exported; the manufacturing process, etc. If you are manufacturing goods, the insurers will almost certainly want to inspect the premises.

The policy will contain certain exclusions (e.g. the cost of actually replacing a defective product). This insurance will cover product liability, that is liability for loss, damage or bodily injury arising from defective products. It will not cover any costs of replacing a defective product. Such insurance can be obtained (at a price) - it is called product guarantee insurance.

Professional indemnity insurance

By the Supply of Goods and Services Act 1982 and common law, suppliers of services are under an obligation to use reasonable skill and care in carrying out their duties. Professionals are under a higher duty (see earlier in this chapter). A professional indemnity insurance policy will cover the supplier's liability for breach of his professional duties.

The title "professional indemnity" insurance is a misnomer. This type of cover is not only available for what are usually termed "professionals". Insurance can be obtained for those who provide a whole range of services as well as for professionals (e.g. plumbers, carpenters, etc.).

Other insurances you might consider taking out

(a) **Legal expenses insurance**

Taking legal proceedings is expensive. Even if at the end of the day the plaintiff wins and recovers some of its costs, it will still have a major financial commitment whilst fighting the case and until the judge or arbitrator gives his decision, the plaintiff will not know for certain if it will win. The fear of legal costs puts many people off fighting genuine claims. To plug this particular hole you can take out legal expenses insurance. As charities become more and more involved in the contract culture, either through primary purposes trading or through trading companies, it is wise for them to consider whether or not they need to take out legal expenses insurance so as to give them the backing of an insurance policy to fight legal battles.

There are various types of legal expenses insurance. Some are very specialised. Others are more general, and give an indemnity for a wide range of legal costs. There is a limit to the amount of expenses that can be claimed in any year. It is worth considering the policy documentation in detail to ensure that it covers the particular risks that you require covering.

(b) **Defamation insurance**

If a charity or its trading company is involved in printing or publishing books, magazines or journals, it should certainly consider effecting defamation insurance.

(c) **Fidelity insurance**

This insures a business against employees stealing the firm's money. There have been some spectacular cases of such thefts (involving charities), and charities should consider taking out such insurance. Charities involved in trading may be exposed to a greater risk in this area than a conventional grant making trust.

Insurance policies and others

A number of different people may be interested in the insurance policies entered into by a business:

(a) The landlord - you may have to insure leased premises.

(b) Mortgagees - if a charity or its trading company mortgages property (e.g. to a bank), the mortgagee will wish to make sure it is adequately insured Depending on what property is mortgaged, this can cover buildings, stock, plant and machinery, goods in transit and consequential loss.

(c) Finance companies - if you hire purchase, hire or lease equipment, in the small print of the contract there is invariably an obligation on the hiree or lessee (not the owner) to insure the equipment against "all risks" and to note the interest of the owner on the policy.

(d) Employees - they may demand pensions or medical expenses insurance or permanent health insurance.

When is it worthwhile taking out insurance?

It is easy to imagine that all types of disaster may strike a charity or its trading company and that therefore it should take out extensive insurance against the widest range of risks for the maximum sum insured. If this is done, the charity/trading company will probably have spent most of its working capital! So before deciding whether to take out insurance and the amount of such cover that is appropriate, try to answer the following questions first:

(a) Is this insurance obligatory?

(b) Is this insurance necessary?

(c) Is it prudent to take it out?

(d) Does the person recommending it understand the particular business?

(e) What is the premium?

(f) Is there an alternative quotation? Remember there are lots of insurance companies all, in theory, competing.

(g) Has the proposal form been completed in full? Remember that insurance policies are contracts of utmost good faith which obliges the insured to disclose all material facts to the insurer.

(h) What risks are covered by the policy?

(i) What risks are excluded?

(j)   What are the conditions of the policy (e.g. about storage of stock, etc.)?

Each year, about two months before the insurance policies are due for renewal, you should review them with your insurer or insurance broker to make sure that the business is adequately insured both as regards:

(a)   Level of cover; and

(b)   Risks covered.

During the year remember to:

(a)   Promptly notify insurers of all claims under any insurance policy

   and

(b)   Promptly advise them of any significant change in the risk (e.g., have you started to store high explosives?).

11.11   Trading and people with disabilities

Chapter 4 dealt with primary purposes trading. One classic example is the sale by a charity for people with disabilities of products created by people with disabilities in a workshop. It is worth mentioning the Trading Representations (Disabled Persons) Act 1958. That Act makes it a criminal offence to sell any goods or solicit orders for goods of any description in the course of a business carried on by any person coupled with a representation that "blind or otherwise disabled persons":

(a)   are employed in the production, preparation or packing of the goods, article or thing; or

(b)   benefit from the sale of the goods or the carrying out of the business;

in the course of visits from house to house, or by post (e.g. catalogue sales) or by telephone. The maximum penalty is two years imprisonment or a £2,000 fine or both. The Act applies in England, Scotland and Wales. The Act does not apply to businesses carried on:

(a)   By a local authority; or

(b)   By a company, association or body providing facilities under Section 15 of the Disabled Persons (Employment) Act 1944; or

There used to be an exemption for charities registered under the War Charities Act 1940, but that exemption was repealed in September 1992 by Schedule 7 of the Charities Act 1992. Hence by this Act a charity established to help people with disabilities and which seeks to sell products or solicit orders (e.g. for a printing business run by people with disabilities) by house-to-house visits or mail order cannot imply that "blind or otherwise disabled persons" are employed in the business! At one blow the charity's unique selling point has been removed!

The 1958 Act does *not* apply to sales or representations made in a retail outlet but only a representation made by house-to-house visits, by post or by telephone.

The exemption for companies providing facilities under the 1944 Act may well not apply to many charities as the facilities have to be approved by the Secretary of State.

If a charity or its trading company is concerned about its position under this Act it should seek appropriate professional advice.

Chapter 12
COMPETITION LAW & ANTI-COMPETITIVE AGREEMENTS

This chapter covers: the Restrictive Trade Practices Act 1976; Articles 85 and 86 of the Treaty of Rome; the European Commission rules on Exclusive Distribution Agreement; and Compulsory Competitive Tendering.

12.1. Introduction

The laws relating to the control of restrictive trade practices, monopolies and mergers may seem a far cry from the activities of charities and their associated trading companies. Of course, that is true for the great bulk of charities which carry on trade at modest levels. Nonetheless, these laws have a far wider scope than many people realise and charities (and/or their trading companies) could find that they have unwittingly broken the law. This risk will increase as charities' trading activities increase and competition law is more vigorously enforced. One should not overplay this risk but nor should one blithely ignore it. The tide of law coming in from Europe is impressive and it has made itself particularly felt in the field of competition law, where the European Commission seeks to establish a fair and open market. The recent spectacular fines on British Steel illustrate this. Charities may wish to reach agreements about not competing with each other and then find that they have acted in breach of these laws. This chapter is not a detailed study of competition law. Instead, it offers some fairly simple guidelines about how various UK and European laws, which seek to regulate anti-competitive practices, could affect charities which carry on primary purposes trading and/or their trading companies. It does not deal with monopolies and mergers legislation, which seems unlikely to be significant to charities and/or their trading companies.

12.2. The Restrictive Trade Practices Act 1976

The Restrictive Trade Practices Act 1976 (RTPA) applies to agreements between two or more persons carrying on business within the United Kingdom, where two or more parties accept restrictions in respect of:-

(a) The prices to be charged or quoted (e.g. competitors, agreeing not to undercut each other's prices - the classic price-fixing cartel);

(b) The prices to be recommended or suggested for the resale of goods (i.e., agreements between competitors to recommend agreed minimum prices to their distributors);

(c) The terms or conditions on which goods are to be supplied (e.g., competitors agreeing to the same very restricted terms of contract - this can cause problems with a trade association's standard terms of business);

(d) Quantities of goods to be supplied (e.g., competitors agree to restrict output);

(e) The process of manufacture to be applied to any goods;

(f) The persons to, for or from whom or where goods are to be supplied or acquired (e.g., where competitors agree to divide a market up between them).

Hence, two charities running competitive shops both selling donated goods might think it a good idea if they agree not to undercut each other's prices and agree a tariff - a minimum price per item. Technically, such an agreement would be in breach of the RTPA and would need to be registered (see below).

Services - Section 11 RTPA

Section 11 applies (in conjunction with the Restrictive Trade Practices (Services) Order 1976) to all agreements made between two or more persons carrying on business in the UK in the supply of services (save as listed below), if the agreement deals with:

(a) The charges to be made, quoted, or paid for services (e.g., a price-fixing cartel);

(b) The terms and conditions or subject to which services are to be supplied or obtained - this can cause problems for trade associations' standard terms of business;

(c) The extent (if any) to which services are to be made available, supplied or obtained (e.g., in one case a charity's trading company entered into an agreement with a commercial partner to promote a joint activity. Both parties agreed not to compete with the joint activity. This would be a breach of the RTPA);

(d) The form or manner in which services are to be supplied or obtained. (Hence a recommendation, for example, by the Institute of Charity Fund-raising Managers as to how members should supply their services could be caught by this, such as a recommendation that they only work on a flat rate and not on a commission);

(e) The class of persons for whom or from whom or the areas or places from which services are to be made available or supplied (e.g., environmental charities agreeing not to compete with each other in different areas - Charity A gets Hertfordshire, Charity B gets Essex).

For the purposes of both goods and services, an "agreement" has a very wide meaning and includes any agreement or arrangement, whether or not it is intended to be enforceable. Hence 'nudge, nudge, wink, wink' verbal collusions between two parties will be caught.

Exclusions

Certain types of service are excluded. The liberal professions do well out of this! The exceptions are legal, medical, dental and veterinary services, architects, nurses, midwives, physiotherapists, chiropodists, accounting and audit services, insolvency services, patent agents, surveyors, engineers, the provision of primary, secondary, further or higher education and the services of ministers of religion. Insurance services, international sea transport, carriage by air and unit trust schemes are also excluded.

Clearly, some of these exceptions may be important to charities which carry on primary purpose trading (e.g., charitable schools).

Excepted Agreements

Section 28 to the RTPA provides that the agreements listed in Schedule 3 are not covered by the Act. Broadly speaking these agreements are:-

(a) Know-how licences for goods or services;

(b) Trade mark licences (see Chapter 8);

(c) Patent licences (see Chapter 8);

(d) Copyright licences (see Chapter 8);

(e) Exclusive supply agreements (e.g., where a charity specialising in child care might agree only to provide its services to one health authority and not to another).

12.3. What happens if RTPA applies to an agreement?

Any agreement to which the RTPA applies must be registered with the Director General of Fair Trading (DGFT). He keeps a register which is open to public inspection (except for a special section in which sensitive or secret information is kept). If an agreement which should be registered is not registered within the appropriate time limit (or within such further period as the DGFT may allow) then:

(a) All the restrictions in the agreement are void;

(b) It is unlawful to give effect to those restrictions;

(c) The DGFT can bring proceedings in the Restrictive Practices Court to obtain an order to restrain a breach of the RTPA;

(d) Although no criminal proceedings can be brought against any person in respect of a breach of the RTPA a competitor who has been "locked out" and who is affected by the restrictions can bring a *civil* action and claim damages for breach of statutory duty.

Because a failure to register has such consequences it is vital for organisations which are considering entering into restrictions to take advice as to whether or not the RTPA applies. Because it is by no means clear whether the RTPA does apply to a particular agreement, many agreements are submitted for registration to the Director General of Fair Trading on a "fail-safe" basis. It is obviously prudent to furnish particulars if there is any doubt as to whether or not an agreement is registerable. Clearly in many cases, particulars are supplied on this basis. The DGFT's 1991 Annual Report showed:

Year	Number of agreements submitted	Number registered
1990	1,230	715
1991	1,327	619

Once an agreement has been registered, the DGFT has to decide whether the restriction should be referred to the Restrictive Practices Court for a decision whether the restrictions in question operate against the public interest.

Under Section 21, the DGFT is entitled to refrain from taking proceedings if he believes that the restrictions are insignificant. Whether or not a restriction is insignificant is essentially an economic question - does the restriction cause detriment to consumers or traders? Large numbers of agreements are dealt with in this way. By the end of 1988, out of 6653 agreements on the register, 1,496 (over 25%) were regarded as *insignificant*.

Section 27A of the RTP inserted by the Deregulation and Contracting Out Act 1994 takes this process further. The government has chosen to reform the RTPA by introducing a new category of agreements, called "non-notifiable agreements" which will be defined by orders to be made by the Secretary of State from time to time. Particulars of such non-notifiable agreements will not need to be furnished to the Office of Fair Trading (OFT). Such agreements may be defined, for example, by reference to the turnover or market share (which implies that a de minimus exemption will be introduced) or to European Union exemptions (e.g. block exemptions) so that if an agreement is covered by an exemption issued by the European Commission it will be automatically lifted out of the controls of the RTPA. (see *Chapter 12.4*). However, price-fixing agreements will remain notifiable.

As this is *another* area of change in the law the concerned reader should check on the current position with an appropriate expert.

The RTPA could effect certain mutual restrictions accepted by charities and/or their trading companies. If in doubt consider registering the agreement with the DGFT. It is highly likely that even if registered it will be deemed to be insignificant - and the new provisions introduced by the Deregulation Act should make even this unnecessary.

12.4. Article 85 of the Treaty of Rome

The Treaty of Rome is part of United Kingdom law by virtue of the European Communities Act 1972. Article 85 prohibits all agreements between undertakings which may affect trade between Member States which have the effect of preventing, restricting or distorting competition within the European Union. In particular it covers price-fixing, market rigging, market-sharing or other forms of collusion. As can be seen, in common with European practice, Article 85 is drafted in very sweeping terms!

Undertakings

Article 85 applies to "undertakings". This term is not defined. Given the policy of Article 85, it seems that any natural or legal person of whatever legal nature capable of carrying on some commercial or economic activity should qualify as an undertaking. Hence a charity which undertakes a trade (however that charity is established) could be treated as an undertaking for the purposes of Article 85, as could a charity's trading company.

Agreements, decisions and concerted practices

Just as with the RTPA, Article 85 is not concerned just with legal agreements. It covers forms of collaboration through trade associations and informed understandings, such as "gentlemen's" agreements. There have been many decisions by the European Court of Justice (ECJ) on the meaning of a "concerted practice", but this is not the place to deal with that in detail. Readers who want more information should refer to one of the specialist legal textbooks such as Butterworth's "Competition Law".

Exceptions to Article 85

1. **Notices**: The European Commission has published several notices in which it has indicated types of agreement which may not infringe Article 85(1). These are known in an ugly phrase, as "block negative clearances". They cover such matters as:

   (a) An agreement within a single economic unit. Hence an agreement which contained restrictions between a parent charity and its trading company would be outside Article 85.

   (b) Co-operation agreements (e.g. joint market research; preparation of statistics and exchanges of information).

2. **The effect on inter-state trade**: Article 85(1) only applies to agreements, decisions or concerted practices which "may affect trade between Member States." It might be thought that this meant that Article 85 would only apply if an agreement effected the actual flow of trade between states. But that would be too simple! The ECJ has given the phrase an incredibly wide meaning. "Trade" has been interpreted as covering services including those of opera singers! Thus, the effects of an agreement on any commercial activity may be taken into account. An agreement may breach Article 85 and be deemed to have an effect on inter-state trade even though it operates only within one Member State.

◆◆ *example*

CUTSFORTH v. MANSFIELD INNS (1986) 1A11ER 77 - A DECISION OF THE ENGLISH HIGH COURT.

The plaintiff complained that the defendant brewer had removed his name from a list of persons authorised to supply games machines to public houses in the East Midlands. This did not have an effect on inter-state trade. But the brewer had also entered into exclusive purchasing deals for the sale of beer with various publicans, and those agreements also dealt with the supply of games machines. The exclusive purchase agreements were held to have an effect on inter-state trade because other brewers were locked out. Hence, the agreement was prohibited under Article 85, and the supplier of games machines was able to resume his business.

Very few cases under Article 85 have been successfully resisted on the grounds that they did *not* affect inter-state trade. The European Commission and the ECJ interpret the phrase very widely. It is possible that the development of the "subsidiarity" principle following the Maastricht Treaty may cause the ECJ to retreat from its very liberal (one could say, loose) interpretation of the effect on "inter-state trade".

3. **De minimis exemption**: What is taken with one hand is given back with the other. Having stretched the meaning of "affecting trade between Member States", so that many agreements fell within the ambit of Article 85, the ECJ then developed another doctrine to draw the sting from its own invention! The ECJ has ruled that some agreements which may affect competition within Article 85 (because of its own wide definition) may nevertheless not be caught, because they do not have an appreciable impact on competition or inter-state trade. As the reader will appreciate, this *de minimis* doctrine, is very significant in practical terms. Many agreements will escape EC Competition Law (with all its consequences - see below) because it is of minor importance. The Commission issued a Notice in 1986 (C231/2) to clarify the *de minimis* doctrine. It states that a restrictive agreement will be ignored as *de minimis* if:

    (a) The relevant goods and services of the undertakings concerned do not represent more than 5% of the total market for such goods or services; *and*

    (b) The aggregate annual turnover of the participating undertakings do not exceed 200 million ECU (approximately £140 million in 1994).

Clearly, both tests have to be satisfied. So if the undertakings concerned have a combined annual turnover of less than 200 million ECU *but* control more than 5% of the relevant market the agreement is *not* de minimis. Hence, calculating what is the relevant market is crucial. There are two factors:

(a) **Geography**: the area in the European Union in which the agreement produces its effect. This could be one part of one Member State;

(b) **The product (or services) market**: this means the products which are subject to the agreement and any other products which are identical or equivalent. Although the Notice is helpful it still raises problems. In each case one must ask, what is the *relevant* market and bear in mind that this is *not* the total EU market. Some charities operate catchment area agreements, whereby they agree not to compete against each other for customers. Could such agreements be a breach of Article 85? On the face of it they are. But would they fall within the de minimis exemption? That all depends on how wide the geographical market is drawn, and then within it how one assesses the size of the particular market. Each case will turn on its own facts.

Some trading companies of national networks of charities also operate non-competition arrangements (e.g., they agree to grant each other a geographical exclusion zone). These too might in theory be in breach of Article 85, although they may well be de minimis.

What happens if an agreement breaches Article 85?

The following are the consequences of breaching Article 85

(a) An agreement which breaches Article 85(1) is void;

(b) Third parties who claim to have suffered damage from the operation of such an agreement may seek damages or an injunction;

(c) The European Commission can impose heavy fines of up to 10% of the annual turnover of each of the undertakings involved;

But:

(d) Fines and the risk of legal proceedings can be avoided by submitting the agreement to the Commission for notification and negative clearance.

12.5.   Article 86 of the Treaty of Rome

Article 86 prohibits the abuse by one or more undertakings of a dominant position within the common market of the European Union or a substantial part of it, insofar as it may affect trade between member states.

Such abuse may, in particular, consist in:-

(a) Directly or indirectly imposing unfair purchase or selling prices or unfair trading conditions;

(b) Limiting production, markets or technical development to the prejudice of consumers;

(c) Applying dissimilar conditions to equivalent transactions with other trading parties, thereby placing them at a competitive disadvantage;

(d) Making the conclusion of contracts subject to acceptance of supplementary obligations, which, by their nature or according to commercial usage, have no connection with the subject of such contracts.

Hence, for Article 86 to come into effect there must be:

(a) One or more undertakings (see definition in *Chapter 12.4*).

(b) In a dominant position-viz "a position of economic strength being enjoyed by an undertaking which enables it to prevent effective competition being maintained...by affording it the power to behave to an appreciable extent independently of its competitors, customers and ultimately of its consumers" [Case 27/76 *United Brands -v- EC Commission* (1978) ECR 207].

(c) Within the Common Market or a substantial part of it. This is a question of fact in each case. Part of a Member State may be a substantial part (e.g., Southern Germany and South-East England). Where very special markets exist, it is possible for a specific place to be a substantial part of the Common Market - see *SeaLink/B&I Holyhead : Interim Measures* (1992) 5 CMLR 255, a case concerning ferry schedules in which the European Commission held that the port of Holyhead constituted "a substantial part", because it was one of the main links between two member states!

(d) Abusing the dominant position. The term "abuse" is not defined. Broadly, it means using market power to improve prices or conditions or to obtain benefits which could not be obtained under normal conditions.

(e) In such a way as effects trade between Member States (see the discussion under Article 85, *Chapter 12.4*).

A number of not-for-profit organisations in the United Kingdom might be deemed to have a dominant position. Could such organisations be found to have breached Article 86 when carrying out primary purpose trading through operating differential pricing to conferences depending on whether attenders were charities, for-profit organisations or individuals? Could a refusal to supply education or services by a charitable religious school to someone from a different faith be seen as abuse of dominant position? Clearly, as under Article 85 each case will depend on its facts. It may seem far-fetched to think that charities or their trading companies could be subject to EC Competition law, but its ambit is theoretically wide and its tentacles long. If the Commission investigates an alleged breach of Article 86, it can give a negative clearance, or order that the infringement cease and can impose heavy fines (as under Article 85). There is *no de minimis exemption* for Article 86.

12.6. Exclusive distribution agreements

The European Commission has issued a number of block exemptions pursuant to its powers under Article 85(3), exempting certain types of agreement from the impact of Article 85. The most important for charities' trading companies is likely to be the one on *exclusive distribution agreements*, but it is also worth noting that there are block exemptions for patent licences, research and development licences, and know-how licensing, all of which could be relevant to research charities and/or associated trading companies. The Block Exemption for exclusive distribution agreements provides that such agreements will not be treated as a breach of Article 85, provided they contain the so called "white" or approved clauses and do not include the so-called "black" or unapproved items.

An exclusive distribution agreement must:

(a) Be between only two undertakings;

(b) Only deal with distribution of goods and not provision of services, but the exemption still applies if the seller provides customer or after-sales services incidental to re-sale of goods;

(c) Appoint the distributor as exclusive distributor for the whole or part of the EU - hence an agreement will usually appoint the distributor for a named state or states;

(d) Limit the supplier to supplying goods for re-sale to the other party in the licensed territory;

(e) Not limit the distributor from selling competing products for a period which is longer than the exclusive distribution agreement.

In addition, the agreement may oblige the distributor to:

(a) Not seek customers, establish a branch or maintain a distribution depot outside the territory;

(b) Purchase a range and minimum quantity of goods;

(c) Promote the reputation of the supplier's products and not to apply its trade-mark to the product.

The block exemption will *not* apply if:

(a) The parties are competing manufacturers;

(b) There is no alternative source of supply for consumers apart from the exclusive distributor;

(c) Either party makes it difficult for users to obtain the products in the contract territory from other dealers.

Note that the Block Exemption is due to expire on 31st December 1997, but will almost certainly be renewed.

If a charity or its trading company is considering entering into a distribution agreement or granting one within the European Union, it must consider the impact of Article 85 and whether or not the Block Exemption applies. Failure to deal with this could result in costly investigations, the non-enforceability of the agreement and (possibly) fines. If a trading company has invested heavily in promoting a product which it believed it had the exclusive right to distribute, only to find that parts of the agreement were not enforceable because of a breach of Article 85, it may be faced with the unhappy necessity of being forced to write off its investment and scrap the distribution agreement. Hence it is *vital* that proper legal advice is taken before entering into such agreements.

12.7. Conflicts between EC and UK law

What happens if an agreement falls foul of Article 85 or constitutes a breach of Article 86 but is not a breach of the RTPA? Answer: European Community law takes precedence - the wrongdoer cannot shelter behind the RTPA. A much more likely occurrence is that an agreement might fall within one of the block exemptions under Article 85, but still fall foul of the RTPA. Should the more stringent provisions of the RTPA apply? The likelihood of this happening will be far less once the amendments to the RTPA set out in the Deregulation Act have come into effect. There is no clear judicial ruling on this point - but a respectable argument is that an EU exemption constitutes positive action by the EU and national laws should not thwart this. Hence the *exemption* (EU law) should prevail. That is certainly the Commission's view - but whether an English court would abide by that appears not to have been resolved.

Finally it might happen that an agreement was valid under Article 85 or 86, but could still be in breach of RTPA. Can the parties claim that as the agreement is permissible under EU law, this overrides the harsher provisions of domestic law? It seems they cannot. In a case in the ECJ (*Procureur de la Republique -v- Biry & Guerlain* (1980) ECR 2327), it was made clear that it is permissible for stricter *national* laws provisions to be applied.

Accordingly, one cannot ignore the RTPA and only concentrate on EU law. *Both* must be considered in connection with agreements which may have an anti-competitive effect.

12.8 Compulsive Competitive Tendering

Under various European Union Directives certain types of contracts to be awarded by public bodies have to be publicly advertised. This may be of advantage to charities (or their trading companies) if they have the appropriate skills. These rules do not apply if the contract falls below certain thresholds; for example, in the case of a contract for services, the threshold for all contracting authorities (as at 1st January

1994) is £149,728.

There are complex rules to stop the Directive being avoided by splitting one large contract which is over the threshold into a number of smaller contracts which are under the threshold. If the Directives apply, then the public body concerned has to advertise the prospective contract and abide by criteria for awarding the contract. This is not the place to go into detail on these Regulations but charities which are tendering for major contracts with, for example, local authorities should be aware of them. Equally, an exempt charity such as a higher education corporation will be *bound* by the Directives when granting contracts eg for the supply of computer equipment. If one of the Directives is broken, an aggrieved would-be contractor must lodge a complaint within three months with the contracting authority. The aggrieved would-be contractor can apply to the High Court which has the power to grant an injunction, suspending the contract award procedures and awarding damages to the plaintiff.

Conclusion

The laws controlling anti-competitive practices are unlikely to affect most charities and/or their associated trading companies, but nonetheless may be of significance to some. In those cases where they are of relevance they should not be ignored. The price of disregarding them can be very high.

Chapter 13
INSOLVENCY

Charities which engage in trading, whether such trading is in fulfilment of a primary purpose or through a trading company may well need to consider questions of solvency or insolvency. This chapter covers the definition of insolvency; the insolvency of limited companies and unincorporated organisations; the liquidation of limited companies; the administration of limited companies; the bankruptcy of unincorporated organisations; the consequences of insolvency; how to limit liability; and the relationship between charities and their trading companies with regard to payment of debts.

13.1. Introduction

Charities which engage in trading inevitably take greater risks than a grant giving trust. Some of the risks which charities face when involved in trading are beyond their control; e.g., a number of charities involved in the provision of training programmes to government departments have experienced very sudden reductions in fee income as a result of a change in government policy. A charitable, fee-paying school may decided to invest in building expensive new facilities but then fail to attract additional pupils; a charity running workshops for people with disabilities may take on extra staff in order to manufacture and build up additional stocks which do not sell; a charitable consultancy might experience a drop in orders for one reason or other and, of course, there can be a simple downturn in the economy which affects all businesses, including charities carrying on primary purpose trading or charities' trading companies. Such events can affect a charity or a trading company's *solvency*.

13.2. What is Insolvency?

Charities operate under a number of varying constitutional forms: ***companies limited by guarantee or by shares, societies incorporated by Royal Charter, industrial and provident societies, unincorporated associations or trusts.*** As will be seen, the law relating to insolvency has a different impact depending on how a charity is constituted. Emphasis is placed in this chapter on company law, for the good reason that company law relating to insolvency is much more sophisticated and complex than the bankruptcy laws (which apply to individuals) and that most charities carrying on primary purpose trading will be incorporated and their trading companies are always so established. But, it must be remembered that only approximately 20,000 of the 170,000 or so registered charities are set up as limited companies. The Insolvency Act also applies, with modifications, to Friendly Societies, including its provisions on fraudulent and wrongful trading (see *Chapter 13.9*), but the Act does not apply to Industrial and Provident Societies.

In company law (which applies to all companies whether limited by guarantee or shares), "insolvency" and "insolvent" have no uniform or comprehensive meaning. Broadly speaking there are two separate tests to determine if a company is insolvent. These two tests are also used in relation to individual insolvency and it is therefore important to understand them.

The going concern test

The basis of the going concern test is whether a company can pay its debts as they fall due. This is also known as the *cash flow test*. This test is applied in various cases:

(a) For the purposes of a declaration of solvency (a pre-requisite for the solvent winding up of a company), the directors have to state whether the company will be able to pay its debts in full plus interest over a twelve month period.

(b) Section 122(1)(f) of the Insolvency Act 1986 provides that a company may be wound up by order of the court as insolvent if it is unable to pay its debts as they fall due.

Obviously this test may be used by the directors of a company or of an unincorporated trust who are concerned about its solvency, in order to check on its financial health.

The balance sheet test

Under the balance sheet test, insolvency denotes the actual or anticipated deficiency of assets to meet a company's liabilities. This is reflected in Section 122(1)(f) Insolvency Act 1986, which provides a second ground for winding up a company as unable to pay its debts if the value of its assets is less than the amount of its liabilities, taking into account its contingent and prospective liabilities. Again, the directors may use this test to check on the company's financial health.

By Section 41(2)(b) of the Charities Act 1993, the accounting records of a registered charity must contain:

"A record of the assets and liabilities of the charity".

This does not apply to charities which are companies. They are excluded by Section 41(5), but they must maintain identical accounting records by virtue of Section 221 Companies Act 1985, the wording of which is mirrored in Section 41. Nor does Section 41 apply to exempt charities. They are excluded by Section 46(1), which makes it clear that they must continue to comply with the general obligation to keep accounts laid down by Section 36 of the 1993 Act.

The liabilities which a company must record are stated at paragraph 89, Schedule 4 Companies Act 1985:

"Any liability or loss which is either likely to be incurred or certain to be incurred but uncertain as to amount or as to the date on which it will arise".

Interrelationship of the cashflow and balance sheet tests

The inter-relationship between the *balance sheet test* and its requirement that full account be taken of contingent and prospective liabilities, and the *going concern* test of calculating liabilities causes difficulties. Under the going concern test it is assumed that a company will continue to trade and therefore that liabilities which would crystallise should the company cease to trade are not taken into account in assessing the company's actual or contingent liabilities. The going concern test is rather like a bicycle. So long as the cyclist maintains forward momentum, all is well. But if the rider loses impetus, the bicycle wobbles and falls over. Crash. So too with a company.

If a calculation of the value of assets and liabilities is made on the basis of the company ceasing to trade, as compared with the going concern test, the effect on the company's balance sheet may well be enormous. This is called the "break up basis of valuation". Firstly, the value of the assets may be written down greatly - secondhand goods will almost certainly command a much lower price on the open market than their book value as stated in the company's accounts. Secondly, stopping trading will cause a number of major liabilities to crystallise and thus increase the company's indebtedness.

For example:

(a) **Staff will be made redundant, thus triggering compensation payments for notice periods and redundancy;**

(b) **Leasing companies who have hired out photocopiers or computers or cars (etc) will terminate the contracts and**

demand all the future instalments due under the terms of the lease less a small discount to reflect early repayment;

(c) **The landlord of leasehold premises will demand any unpaid rent and may slap in a claim for damages for breach of a covenant in the lease (e.g., to repair);**

(d) **Claims may arise for breach of a contract to deliver services.**

(e) **Bank borrowings which were used to fund the ongoing operation will have to be repaid.**

If the balance sheet test is not calculated on a going concern but on a break up basis, the results will almost inevitably be much worse, and the prospects of insolvency much greater. It is thus very important for directors to know whether a valuation is to be done on the going concern or the break up basis as the results will be very different. Directors may have a valuation prepared on the going concern basis, provided that they have *reasonable grounds* to consider that the company will be able to continue to trade. If on the other hand, they conclude that it is not reasonable to assume that the company will be able to continue to trade, they *must* have the valuation prepared on a break up basis.

The cash flow and balance sheet tests cannot be seen as a strictly either/or test. The two may well impact on each other. Hence, a deficiency of assets may eventually result in a cash flow crisis. Equally, an adverse cash flow may force a company to sell off assets cheaply, thereby causing it to *fail* the balance sheet test.

The consequences of insolvency will depend on the form of the organisation. Different rules apply to limited companies and industrial and provident societies. For trusts, the claims will be pursued against the trustees and for associations against the management committee and possibly also the membership.

13.3. The insolvency of trusts

The debts of a **limited company** are its and its alone. If a company is insolvent, it may be forced into insolvent liquidation. The directors of that company will *not* incur any personal liability for the debts of the company, *except* in limited circumstances (see below).

The position is very different for an **unincorporated association** or a **trust**. In either case there is no separate entity with limited liability. The debts of a charitable organisation without limited liability are ultimately the responsibility of the **charity trustees**.

If a charitable trust is sued for a debt, then it is the charity trustees' names which will appear on the writ. If a trust incurs an obligation, for example, enters into a lease or contract, it is the charity trustees' names which appear on the lease or contract. A trust or an unincorporated association has no legal personality of its own. This is subject to the provisions of Sections 50 to 62 of the Charities Act 1993 which allow charity trustees to incorporate their trust. But incorporation under these sections does *not* affect the charity trustees' personal liabilities.

Many trust deeds contain an indemnity from the trust to the charity trustees for any liability properly incurred by them in the course of fulfilling their duties as trustees, such that the charity's funds can be used to pay these liabilities. However, this indemnity is useless if the trust lacks the financial resources to honour it.

◆◆ *example*

A charitable school, which had been carrying on primary purpose trading, closed down. The school was run by an unincorporated trust. The trust had insufficient reserves to meet its redundancy liabilities to the staff. The charity trustees were sued personally by the staff and each trustee had to pay £5,000 to meet the redundancy costs. The indemnity in the trust deed was useless.

If the trustees are held personally liable, the liability of the trustees is 'joint and several'. This means that all the trustees could be held equally liable or that the whole or a large part of the claim could be pursued against any one of the trustees.

If the liabilities of the trust exceed the trustees' personal wealth the charity trustees could themselves be forced into personal bankruptcy.

A creditor may petition for the bankruptcy of an individual if the debtor owes a debt above a minimum of £750 and the debtor appears to be unable to pay, or appears to have no reasonable prospect of being able to pay that debt. A debtor appears to be unable to pay a debt if he has been served with a statutory demand and more than three weeks have elapsed since the demand was served upon him and he has neither complied with the demand nor applied to have it set aside. A creditor can sue only one of a group of trustees if he wishes. He can "pick off" the one most likely to pay. The charity trustee who is forced to pay up has a right to petition the court for a contribution from each of the other trustees for a proportionate part of the debt due. Under the Civil Liability (Contribution) Act 1978, the court has the power to award in favour of one trustee against another a contribution of such amount as the court considers to be just and equitable, having regard to the extent of the responsibility of that other trustee for loss. The court may exempt any person from liability to make a contribution.

◆◆ *example*

A Trust incurs trading debts to a third party and has insufficient resources to meet the debt. Trustee A is sued and pays £10,000 damages. The plaintiff does not sue the other trustees.

There are four other trustees. A may seek an order from the court to force the other trustees to contribute to A.

If one of the trustees is unable to meet any contributions ordered by the court (e.g., because he is insolvent) the other trustees will have to meet the liability of the bankrupt trustee equally amongst themselves.

13.4. The insolvency of unincorporated associations

The members of the management committee of an unincorporated association are in the same position as the charity trustees of a trust - they too are charity trustees - except for one difference. Under the rules of an unincorporated association, the members of the association, who elect the management committee, may agree to indemnify the management committee members for liabilities properly incurred by them in serving on the management committee. It must be emphasised that the committee can only make the general members of the association personally liable if the association's constitution clearly provides for this or if the members sanction the liability within the constitution.

In such circumstances if an unincorporated association is unable to pay its debts as they fall due or if its liabilities exceed its assets, ultimately the members of the association may be liable equally for the association's debts. However, a creditor will be entitled to sue the members of the management committee who will have been responsible for running the association. The members of the management committee will then have to seek indemnity from the members, if this is appropriate.

13.5. The insolvency of incorporated organisations

If a company is insolvent, it will usually be forced into insolvent liquidation by a dissatisfied creditor who will petition the court to have the company wound up on the grounds that it cannot pay its debts. This is established if the creditor has served a statutory demand for a minimum sum of £750 and the company has neglected to pay the sum or to secure it to the reasonable satisfaction of the creditor within three weeks. Equally, a company is deemed to be unable to pay its debts if it fails the balance sheet test (i.e. its liabilities outstrip its assets).

Alternatively, to pre-empt the creditors, the members can pass *a special resolution* (i.e. one passed by 75% of the members present and voting at a duly convened meeting on 21 days notice) and put the company into voluntary liquidation.

Whichever path is chosen, a petition is presented to either the High Court or the appropriate county court for the company to be wound up. The court will, if it thinks fit, appoint a liquidator. He will either be the Official Receiver - who is a civil servant - or if there is a prospect of the liquidation being able to sustain the payment of professional fees - a private insolvency practitioner.

The liquidator's task is to gather in the assets of the insolvent company for the benefit of its creditors and pay them off in the order of priority shown below. If there are insufficient assets to pay off, for example, the unsecured creditors in full, they are each paid a "dividend" (a rather confusing word in this context) of, say, 10p for each £1 owed to them. The same would apply to preferential creditors, if there are insufficient funds to pay them in full.

There are four types of creditor who rank in order of payment as follows:

1. **Pre-preferential** (i.e. the liquidator's fees), which take priority over all other claims.

2. **Secured** (e.g., a bank with a mortgage ("security") over an asset of the company), which are paid insofar as the security given covers the liability. Any shortfall is treated as an unsecured debt.

3. **Preferential**; which consist of PAYE, VAT, social security contributions, occupational pension scheme contributions, and amounts due to employees for wages for the four months prior to the making of the winding up order or resolution to wind up, for each employee but not exceeding £800 per employee, together with all arrears of holiday pay.

4. **Unsecured**; which are the ordinary debts neither secured nor preferential.

Administration of limited companies

British company law has long been criticised for being too simplistic in its treatment of insolvent companies. For many years it offered no means of nursing an insolvent company back to financial health, unlike in the United States of America where Chapter ll of the Bankruptcy Code enables a company facing financial difficulties to obtain the protection of the court from its creditors.

To remedy this deficiency and building on the US experience, the Insolvency Act 1986 introduced the Administration Order. An Administration Order can be made:

(a) To ensure the survival of the company in whole or in part as a going concern; or

(b) To ensure a more advantageous realisation of the company's assets than would be the case in a winding up.

How to obtain an Administration Order

An Administration Order is made on a petition to either the relevant county court or the High Court, backed up (usually) by the proposed administrator's report.

If the court makes an Administration order, no steps can be taken against the company or its property (e.g., suing for a debt) except with leave of the court. No security (e.g., a mortgage) can be enforced against the company. In other words, the company is in a court-protected safe haven, immune from its creditors, whilst it is nursed back to health by the administrator, who has similar powers to a receiver (i.e. to buy and sell property and to manage the company's affairs), so long as the creditors agree to the administration. The powers of the company directors are effectively suspended for the duration of the administration order.

13.6. Bankruptcy of unincorporated association and trusts

Although an unincorporated organisation can become insolvent, the consequences are very different from the insolvency of a limited company. If an unincorporated charity cannot pays its debts, the creditor will be entitled to sue the charity trustees. There is no legal mechanism for the organisation itself to be put into liquidation or administration.

If the unincorporated organisation lacks the resources to meet its liabilities, the burden will fall on the trustees or members of the management committee *personally*. If they fail to meet those obligations, the creditor can sue them (or any of them) and petition to have them made bankrupt. If the petition is successful, the trustee's assets become vested in an individual appointed by the court, bearing the somewhat confusing title of "Trustee in Bankruptcy".

The Trustee in Bankruptcy can be either a government official (the Official Receiver) or a private insolvency practitioner. The Trustee in Bankruptcy, just like the liquidator of a limited company, is responsible for gathering in the bankrupt's assets and paying off the creditors. The order of priority for paying off the debts of a limited company applies equally to an individual. There is no legal provision for administration in the case of an individual, so he cannot trade his way back to solvency with the aid of the court.

If an individual is made bankrupt, he loses all his assets; he cannot obtain credit or serve as a director of a company. If he is a professional (e.g. a solicitor or a Member of Parliament), he will lose that status. He is automatically discharged from the bankruptcy after three years, in normal circumstances.

On the other hand, so as to avoid bankruptcy an individual debtor can try to strike a voluntary arrangement with his creditors. This can be achieved by getting 75% of the creditors (calculated by value) to vote to accept a compromise plan whereby the debtor agrees to pay a limited amount (e.g., 50p in the £) to each creditor over an agreed period in return for the creditors not making him bankrupt. This compromise binds all creditors (even if they voted against the plan), so that they cannot seek to bankrupt him in respect of the debts which are subject to the voluntary arrangement.

13.7. The consequences of ignoring potential insolvency

The consequences of a charity becoming insolvent depend on its constitutional structure. If the charity is unincorporated, the liabilities of the charity will be borne by the charity trustees (which could ultimately result in personal bankruptcy for some or all of them). If the charity is a limited company or an industrial and provident society, its debts are the debts of the organisation and not of the directors or the members personally. In the case of a company limited by guarantee, the members will be liable to pay the guarantee they have given as members - this is usually only £1 but it may be more. The level of guarantee is stated in the charity's Memorandum and Articles of Association. This guarantee is only given by the members. It is not given by the directors (unless they are also members).

13.8. Loss of limited liability protection

The protections of limited liability are *not absolute*. The directors of a limited company may *lose* the protections of limited liability and be made to contribute from their own personal assets towards the debts of an insolvent company in certain circumstances.

Fraudulent Trading

By Section 213 Insolvency Act 1986, on the application of the liquidator of a company, the court may order that any persons who were knowingly party to carrying on the business of the company with intent to defraud creditors must make a contribution to the company's assets.

Intent to defraud creditors must be proved and the onus of proof is on the liquidator. There must be evidence of *actual* dishonesty.

◆◆ *example*

R v. Grantham (1984) 3 A11ER 166: It was held that an intent to defraud might be inferred if the person concerned obtained credit when he knew there was no good reason for thinking that funds would be available to pay the debt when it became due or shortly afterwards.

and

Re a Company (No. 001418 of 1988): A company went into insolvent liquidation owing £212,681. The Court held on the facts that there had been fraudulent trading. It ruled that a person was knowingly party to the business of the company having been carried on with intent to defraud creditors if:

(a) At the time when debts were incurred by the company, he had no good reason for thinking that funds would be available to pay those debts when they became due or shortly afterwards; and

(b) There was dishonesty involving real moral blame according to current notions of fair trading.

The Chairman, managing director and major shareholders had to pay £156,000 to the creditors.

It should be noted that it is not only directors who can be made liable for fraudulent trading. In the case of a charity or trading company, in addition to the charity trustees or directors of the trading company, the employees of an insolvent charitable company or trading company could be liable for fraudulent trading (if proven).

Wrongful trading

This is a new form of civil liability, introduced by the Insolvency Act 1986 to counter criticisms that fraudulent trading was too difficult to prove and creditors were suffering due to the negligence of directors. Its covers cases where the persons concerned have failed to exercise sufficient diligence in monitoring the company's affairs and in taking corrective action when insolvency loomed, but have not acted in bad faith or fraudulently.

Wrongful trading applies to directors and to shadow directors. For the purposes of the Companies Acts a director is anyone who occupies the *position* of a director, by whatever name called. It is not necessary, in order to be treated as a director, for the director to have been registered as such at Companies House. This could include, for example, a Chief Executive. A "shadow director" is a person in accordance with whose directions or instructions the directors of the company have been accustomed to act. This does not apply where the directors act on advice given to them by that person in a professional capacity. In the case of a charitable company or a trading company it is possible that a charismatic and powerful chief executive (who almost invariably will not be a trustee and may not be a director of the trading company) could be *treated* as a shadow director.

Wrongful trading is established if the court concludes that at some time before the company went into insolvent liquidation the director(s) or shadow director(s) *knew* or *ought to have concluded* that there was no reasonable prospect that the company would avoid going into insolvent liquidation, unless the court is satisfied that the director(s) took every step with a view to minimising the potential loss to the company's creditors as he (they) ought to have taken.

The test is an *objective one*. The director must act as a reasonably diligent person having both the director's own knowledge, skill and experience and the general knowledge, skill and experience that may *reasonably* be expected of a person carrying out the same functions as the director. The standard expected will vary from one case to another. In *Re Produce Marketing Consortium Limited (1989) 3 A11ER 1,* the court held that the expertise expected of a director is much less extensive in a small company in a modest way of business with simple accounting procedures and equipment than in a large company with sophisticated procedures.

This is of particular relevance to charity trustees. Charity trustees are almost invariably non-executive directors of charitable companies. They meet rarely (say 4 or 6 times a year) and are very dependent on the professional full time staff. They have to trust their staff. This is entirely fair, and a recent case has shown that a director is entitled to trust persons in a position of responsibility until there is reason to distrust them - *(Norman v. Theodore Goddard (1991) BCLC 1028)*. What standard of duty will the court expect of charity trustees in a wrongful trading case? Will it be a lower standard than that of a full time employee who is also a director (which is almost invariably the case in the private sector)? So far (to the writer's knowledge) no case of wrongful trading has been bought against the volunteer directors of a charitable company or a trading company, but it would be reasonable to argue for a lower standard than for a full time employee/director. It should be emphasised that a person with financial or legal skills or a financial function (for example, the Treasurer) would not be judged on this basis (i.e. of a lower standard of duty) and thus will be at *greater* risk.

Section 727 Companies Act 1985 provides that in any proceedings for "negligence, default, breach of duty or breach of trust" against any officer of a company, the court may wholly or partly relieve him of responsibility as it thinks fit if the director has acted honestly and reasonably and if having regard to all the circumstances he ought fairly to be excused of responsibility. It has been held that Section 727 does *not* apply to wrongful trading. In other words, if a director is found to be guilty of wrongful trading, he cannot look to Section 727 to exonerate him from liability.

There is a similar provision in relation to unincorporated organisations in Section 61 of the Trustees Act 1925. This gives the Court the power to relieve a trustee wholly or partly from personal liability if it appears that the trustee has acted honestly and reasonably and ought fairly to be excused for a breach of trust. This provision will be of no use in excusing a charity trustee of an unincorporated trust from liability to creditors of that charity. Section 61 only applies to a breach of trust. The personal liability of a charity trustee for the debts of the charity to third parties does not arise from a breach of trust by the trustee.

13.9. Looming Insolvency - the practical implications

If insolvency looms for a charity or its trading company the advice to give the charity trustees will vary according to the form of the charity's constitutional structure.

The implications for unincorporated organisations

As the debts and obligations of an unincorporated organisation are the personal liability and responsibility of the charity trustees (if the charity has insufficient assets to meet the debts and obligations), the primary aim of the trustees will be to minimise the build-up of debts and liabilities and to increase the assets by raising cash. But if attempts to generate income or cash fail, then in view of their personal risk, charity trustees may be keen to run down the organisation so as to minimise the chance of incurring personal debts or even bankruptcy or being accused of breach of trust. On the other hand, by closing down, new liabilities will crystallise. Moreover, closing down is easier said than done. Many charities will have long term liabilities (e.g., a lease of a building or obligations under a contract), which it may prove impossible to assign. Hence, the trustees may find themselves obliged to continue to pay rent and service charge even after the charity has ceased to operate. If the charity lacks the means to pay these costs, the trustees will have to meet them personally. The advice about monitoring the charity's financial position and meeting regularly given for companies (see below) applies equally to unincorporated organisations.

The implication for companies

In the case of a limited company, the charity trustees or the directors of a trading company will be anxious to ensure that the protections of limited liability are not lost. That means avoiding any allegation that the charity trustees or the directors have been guilty of wrongful trading or breach of trust.

Charity trustees and directors must be able to show that they took all *reasonable steps* to minimise the loss to the company's creditors. This means in practical terms that if they know or ought to know that there is no reasonable prospect of avoiding insolvent liquidation the charity trustees/directors must:

1. **Recognise that their primary duty is no longer to fulfil the objects of the charity or the trading company, but to act in the best interests of the creditors.** Hence, they should not incur further liabilities (in the case of a charity) on charitable purposes, but rather should endeavour to pay off the creditors;

   The dilemma which the charity trustees/directors face in such circumstances is difficult. They must be neither cowardly nor rash. They must **not** rush into liquidation (which might damage the interests of the creditors), nor must they plough on with insouciant disregard for the potential damage to creditors. They must not be carried away by the idea that because the charity fulfils a noble cause, and the trading company helps it, that this allows them to ignore their legal obligations to creditors. Nor should trustees or directors succumb to the inherent optimism of many that, in the words of Mr Micawber, "something will turn up". To protect the charity trustees and directors from a claim of wrongful trading, their actions must have been reasonable as viewed from the standpoint of the reasonable director. Belief in a possibility or trust in providence (cynical though this may sound) is not regarded by sceptical British judges as being reasonable.

2. **Hold regular meetings to show that they took matters seriously and acted with the interests of the creditors in mind.** This may mean - if time is short - that charity trustees and directors have to meet on a weekend!

3. **Ensure that they have appropriate written legal advice, again, so that they can show that they have acted responsibly.** Such advice should be given to all the trustees and directors. It is not sufficient for it to be given to the chairman or chief executive - they should ensure that it is passed on, so that all the trustees and directors can make an informed decision. Equally, the organisation's legal advisor should seek to ensure that this is done.

4. **Ensure that proper and detailed minutes are kept of all meetings so that there is an adequate "paper trail" to show how decisions were reached.** Provided decisions are made carefully and with the benefit of professional advice (assuming of course that the charity or trading company has the financial resources to pay for such advice), a court will be reluctant to substitute with the benefit of hindsight its own commercial judgement for that of the charity trustees and directors, unless it considers that no reasonable director could have concluded that the action taken was in the interest of the creditors.

The concerns of the Charity Commission

If a charity or its trading company becomes insolvent and creditors are unpaid there is a good chance of adverse press publicity or a complaint being made to a Member of Parliament or to the Charity Commission. In either case, this could trigger an investigation by the Charity Commissioners into the conduct of the charity's affairs. The Charity Commissioners act to protect the interests of the beneficiaries and potential beneficiaries of the charity. If the inquiry concludes that the charity trustees have been negligent in their conduct of the charity's affairs, the Charity Commissioners have the power to petition the court for an order that the trustees make a contribution from their own assets to the charity to compensate the charity for loss suffered as a result of the breach of trust by the trustees. Negligence can constitute a breach of trust. This can apply to any charity howsoever constituted, whether incorporated or unincorporated. Limited liability gives the charity trustees no protection in this context.

◆◆ *example*

A charity lends £250,000 to its trading company. The trading company becomes insolvent. The charity is forced to write off the loan. As a result it fails the balance sheet test and the loss of the cash means it also fails the cash flow test.

The charity ceases its activities as it is insolvent. The Charity Commission concludes that the investment by the charity in the company was negligent and seeks to recover the moneys lost from the charity trustees personally.

Although this train of events has not yet happened (to the writer's knowledge) such a scenario is perfectly possible.

This example illustrates again the need for the charity trustees to have proper minutes of all meetings and decisions so that, if investigated, they can show that, for example, the decision to invest charity moneys in a trading company was fair and reasonable.

Personal Guarantees

A director of a limited company may agree to give a personal guarantee for the obligations of the company (e.g., under a lease). In such a case, that director will be personally liable under the guarantee.

13.10. Personal liabilities of charity trustees - what can be done?

Limiting liability by insurance

Some of the risks faced by charities which carry on trade or by their trading companies and which may force them into insolvency can be reduced by effecting appropriate insurance cover. (See *Chapter 11*). All charities (but especially unincorporated charters, in view of the potential personal liability of the trustees) should consider the relevance of:

(a) **Public liability insurance;**

(b) **Product liability insurance** (if selling/manufacturing products);

(c) **Professional indemnity insurance** (if supplying services);

(d) **Defamation insurance** (if publishing material);

(e) **Fidelity insurance** (to protect the charity/trading company if an employee or trustee runs off with the charity's money);

(f) **Contents insurance** (to protect the charity/trading company from loss or damage to its property, bearing in mind that if it leases equipment the lease will almost certainly oblige the tenant to insure the property).

Failing to have adequate insurance could mean claims being made against the trustees *personally* (in the case of an unincorporated charity), if the charity does not have the assets to meet an uninsured claim. Moreover, *failure to insure might be held to constitute a breach of duty by the trustees*, exposing them (however constituted) to personal liability.

One form of insurance policy - **trustees indemnity insurance** - covers particular risks to which charity trustees are exposed.

Under a trustees indemnity policy, a charity trustee (and this can also be used for employees such as the chief executive) will have cover against personal liability arising from his breach of duty, breach of trust, negligence, error or omission or wrongful trading.

The insurance cover will *not* protect the insured trustee if he has been guilty of a criminal act or has acted deliberately or recklessly. If the charity trustees pay for the insurance *personally*, the Charity Commissioners cannot object. But the Charity Commissioners *are* concerned if the *charity* pays the premium - this is because for many years the payment of such a premium by a charity has been held to *benefit* the charity trustees. Charity trustees are obliged by law, unless the constitution expressly states otherwise, to serve as trustees for no reward and to receive no benefit. In the case of an existing charity without the appropriate constitutional powers, it is necessary to obtain the *consent* of the Charity Commission to amend the charity's constitution in order to expend the charity's moneys on trustees indemnity insurance. In the case of a charitable company, certain amendments need to be made to the company's Memorandum and Articles of Association under company law in order to enable it to effect this insurance.

Trustees indemnity insurance is not a form of financial guarantee. It does not underwrite charity trustees' liabilities for the debts of a charity due to a third party if the charity is insolvent. It does not remove the trading risks to which in particular the charity trustees of an unincorporated charity are exposed.

A similar form of insurance - **directors liability insurance** - can be taken out to protect the directors of a trading company. In this case, the consent of the Charity Commission is not required to any constitutional amendments.

Limiting liability by contract

As has been seen, charity trustees of an unincorporated charity do not enjoy the benefits of limited liability, (although these protections are not absolute). But it is perfectly legitimate and effective for the charity trustees of an unincorporated charity to seek to have written into any contract to which the charity is party that the liability of the charity trustees be limited to the assets of the charity, so that the charity trustees shall incur no personal liability whatsoever. When it is explained that charity trustees are volunteers who perform their task free, it is often possible to negotiate such a clause (e.g., on a contract for the delivery of services). It is more difficult to do this when acquiring something on a standard form contract (e.g., the purchase of goods or the hire of a photocopier). It is simple to do when the charity is issuing its own contracts (e.g., in standard terms and conditions of employment for staff). This is only useful in the case of contracts. It does not limit the charity trustees' liability in relation to third parties not party to a contract (see *Chapter 11*). To cover some or all of these other risks, it is necessary to have proper insurance cover. However, for unincorporated charities which are carrying on a trade, clauses to limit trustees' personal liability written into contracts could be vital.

Limiting liability by incorporation

The trustees of an unincorporated charity labour under greater risks if the charity is insolvent as compared with the trustees of a charity which is a limited company. Hence, it makes good sense for any unincorporated charity which is carrying on any serious trading activities or employing staff, leasing buildings or equipment or engaging in any form of service provision, to consider transforming the charity into a limited company. This will require the consent of the Charity Commissioners.

13.11. The consequences of insolvency

The consequences of insolvency have already been discussed at various points, but the following examples further illustrate the points discussed:

(a) **Uncompleted contracts**

The other party to the contract will have a claim for breach of contract if a charity or a trading company ceases to deliver its contractual obligations due to insolvency. In the case of a limited company this claim will be made against the liquidator. The claimant will be one of the unsecured creditors of the company. Hence, the chance of the claimant recovering much by way of damages is remote. In the case of an unincorporated charity the position is different. If the contract did not contain a clause limiting the trustees' liability, the claimant will be able to sue the trustees personally (or any one or more of them) if the charity has insufficient resources to meet the liability.

(b) **Employment rights of employees**

Certain sums due to employees (up to four months arrears of wages plus accrued holiday pay up to a maximum of £800) are preferential, so that if the charity (being a limited company) or a trading company becomes insolvent, the employees' claim in the liquidation for these sums will rank in priority to the ordinary creditors. If the charity is unincorporated and action is brought against the trustees personally, forcing any of them into personal bankruptcy, the same rules concerning preference apply. However, it should be noted that an employee's entitlement to pay for the notice period and/or to a redundancy payment on termination of his employment is *not* a preferential debt. Employees rank as normal, unsecured creditors insofar as their claims for redundancy payments are concerned.

The Department of Employment covers various liabilities of insolvent employees out of the National Insurance Fund.

The fund will cover the following claims by employees:

(a) Not more than eight weeks' arrears of pay;

(b) The net of tax salary for or in lieu of the minimum statutory notice period;

(c) Holiday pay for periods not exceeding six weeks due during the twelve months preceding the insolvency;

(d) Statutory redundancy payments.

All of these entitlements are restricted to a maximum weekly pay rate of £705 (currently).

13.12. The inter-relationship between an insolvent trading company and its parent charity

As mentioned in *Chapter 7*, the relationship between a charity and its trading company has to be kept at arms length. The two are distinct legal entities and although the same, or many of the same, people may serve on the board of the trading company and as trustees of the charity, those individuals have different duties and responsibilities depending upon which particular role they are fulfilling at any one time. Provided all is well financially, these distinctions should not cause any problems. But if the trading company's financial position weakens and questions arise about its solvency, then the distinctions between the two organisations become more stark, and the differing duties of the directors and trustees become more obvious.

The relationship between a charity and its insolvent trading company will vary as to whether or not the trading company is fulfilling one of the primary purposes of the charity. Some charities, so as to lessen risk, put some of their primary purpose trading activities through a trading company. For example, an educational charity might put its book publishing activities through a separate trading company. In this case, the relationship between the charity and the trading company will be different from that where the charity's trading company is undertaking a pure trading activity which does not fulfil one of the charity's primary purposes.

In the case of the trading company which is fulfilling the charity's primary purpose, the charity could, for example, take the activities of the trading company back into the charity or support it financially more readily than if the trading company is purely undertaking general trading.

Mention has already been made (see *Chapter 13.2*) of the balance sheet and cash flow tests which are used to assess whether or not a limited company is solvent. The trading company might be insolvent on the balance sheet test because its liabilities outstrip its assets. At that point, the directors of the trading company may request the charity (which may have lent monies to the trading company) to convert the loan into share capital in the trading company. This will have the effect of improving the trading company's balance sheet. But this might well damage the charity, because it will forgo its position as a secured creditor, and become instead, as a shareholder, deferred to all other creditors. This may be in the best interests of the trading company so as to allow it to meet the balance sheet test, but it may not be in the best interests of the charity - which will lose its security.

Alternatively, the trading company may fail the cash flow test and need funds in order to meet its obligations as they fall due. It may ask the charity to lend it the necessary working capital. But should the charity agree?

These questions raise the issues of *conflict of interest* which can arise for persons who are both directors of the trading company and trustees of the charity when the trading company faces issues of insolvency.

The trustees have to act *in the best interests of the charity* in order to preserve its reputation and assets and to be able to continue its activities, but as *directors of the trading company*, those same individuals will need to take all necessary steps to act *in the best interests* of the *creditors*. Hence directors of a trading company who are also trustees of the parent charity face a conflict of interests in such circumstances. They may also be concerned about their potential personal liabilities in the event of it being held that as directors of the trading company they had engaged in wrongful trading and therefore have a *personal* interest in ensuring that the trading company continues to trade, even if this means relying on the charity's support. This provides an additional dimension for conflict of interest. Trustees who find themselves in such a position of conflict, should *not* vote on any resolution of the charity which considers giving financial support to the trading company and should *declare their interest* at all meetings considering such matters.

But leaving aside questions of conflict of interest, can a charity give financial support to its trading company when the trading company is facing insolvency? Inevitably, such a decision will depend on the facts of each individual case. No generalised answer can be given. However, a number of issues should be taken into account:

(a) Does the trading company share the same name as the charity? If so, will the charity's reputation be damaged if the trading company is allowed to go into insolvent liquidation? It is highly likely that the trading company will share the charity's name, and that if the trading company goes into insolvent liquidation leaving creditors unpaid, this will damage the charity's reputation. However, just because this is the likely outcome of the trading company's insolvency, this should not in itself permit the charity trustees to expend the charity's monies in supporting the trading company. It is just one factor that can be taken into account, but should not be an overwhelming one.

(b) In their 1980 report, the Charity Commission stated that charity trustees should not use charity monies to prop up insolvent trading companies. Any decision to lend further funds to a trading company must be done on the basis that this is a wise and prudent investment, taking into account the various factors set out in *Chapter 7.8*. Just because the trading company is facing an emergency should not allow the trustees of the charity to suspend their normal obligations to weigh up any proposed investment so as to ensure that it is in the best interests of the charity (see *Chapter 7*).

(c) The trustees should also remember that, although claims may be made by aggrieved creditors of the trading company that the charity is a de facto guarantor of the trading company's debts, this will not, in fact, be the case. The charity does not have the legal capacity to enter into gratuitous guarantees in respect of the debts of its trading company unless, of course, the trading company is fulfilling a primary purpose of the charity.

13.13. Conclusion

If a charity or its trading company appears to be potentially insolvent, the trustees of the charity or the directors of the trading company should assess as quickly as possible the organisation's true financial picture. Such an assessment should be based upon sober realism and not optimism. Any evaluation of the charity's or trading company's liabilities should at least consider the break up basis of valuation (i.e. should take into account those liabilities which will arise if the organisation goes into insolvent liquidation or ceases to trade, such as redundancy payments; termination payments under lease agreements and any financial penalties for breach of contract). It is wise to take professional advice, so as to have an objective assessment of the figures presented, bearing in mind that in some cases the very financial crisis may be the result of ill-considered actions by the self-same people who are now producing the financial information for the trustees/directors to evaluate! Clearly, when an organisation is considering questions of solvency it may be very strapped for cash and time, but nonetheless it is worthwhile taking professional advice in such circumstances if it possibly can. The trustees and directors should ensure that such advice is confirmed in writing and circulated to all members of the governing body or board of directors, so that all the relevant persons are informed.

It is also worth emphasising that there can be considerable personal tensions when questions of insolvency arise. The trustees may feel very nervous about their own personal position (especially if the charity is unincorporated) and their resulting potential personal liabilities. The staff, whom the trustees may feel are responsible for having put the charity or the trading company into the insolvent position that it is in, are unlikely to risk personal liabilities in the same way as the trustees, but may face a loss of employment. Such tensions should, so far as possible, be confronted and understood early on in the process of evaluating the financial position of the insolvent company, so that all parties involved understand the various concerns, and matters can be discussed in an open and thorough manner.

INDEX

D

E

TABLE OF CASES